Magento 2 Beginners Guide

Discover what you need to know to build your own
profitable online stores using the power of Magento 2!

Gabriel Guarino

BIRMINGHAM - MUMBAI

Magento 2 Beginners Guide

First published: March 2017

Production reference: 1060317

Published by Packt Publishing Ltd.
Livery Place
35 Livery Street
Birmingham
B3 2PB, UK.
ISBN 978-1-78588-076-6

www.packtpub.com

Credits

Author
Gabriel Guarino

Reviewer
Eugene Ivashin

Commissioning Editor

Ashwin Nair

Acquisition Editor
Larissa Pinto

Content Development Editor
Nikhil Borkar

Technical Editor
Jijo Maliyekal

Copy Editor
Muktikant Garimella

Project Coordinator
Sheejal Shah

Proofreader

Safis Editing

Indexer
Mariammal Chettiyar

Graphics
Abhinash Sahu

Production Coordinator
Shantanu Zagade

About the Author

Gabriel Guarino has been working with Magento since 2009.

As a Magento specialist he has achieved all the Magento certifications. He is an active member of the community and has been recognized as a Magento Master for 2017.

He is the Chief Operating Officer of Wagento, a full-service Magento Solution Partner with offices in USA, Mexico, Bolivia, India, and Argentina.

He is also a moderator in Magento forums, and he is a frequent speaker at Magento events.

About the Reviewer

Eugene Ivashin is a professional Ukrainian web developer who currently lives and works in Sweden.

He graduated at Dnepr State Academy of Building and Architecture in Dnepropetrovsk, Ukraine, and got a Building Industry Automation Engineer diploma with a distinction in 1997. Programming became his hobby and future profession since then.

Eugene walked a long path in application and web development. Finally, for 4 years, Eugene worked as a software engineer, developer's trainer, and training manager at Varien (later rebranded as Magento Inc. and acquired by eBay). Currently, he works as a principal backend developer at Vaimo Sweden, Enterprise Magento Solutions Partner.

Eugene is involved in active development of Magento-based solutions for Vaimo's clients since 2015. He got certified as a Magento Developer Plus in September 2016.

Eugene reviewed other books at Packt Publishing:

- *Magento Beginners Guide*
- *Magento Site Performance Optimization*

www.PacktPub.com

For support files and downloads related to your book, please visit www.PacktPub.com.

Did you know that Packt offers eBook versions of every book published, with PDF and ePub files available? You can upgrade to the eBook version at www.PacktPub.com and as a print book customer, you are entitled to a discount on the eBook copy. Get in touch with us at service@packtpub.com for more details.

At www.PacktPub.com, you can also read a collection of free technical articles, sign up for a range of free newsletters and receive exclusive discounts and offers on Packt books and eBooks.

https://www.packtpub.com/mapt

Get the most in-demand software skills with Mapt. Mapt gives you full access to all Packt books and video courses, as well as industry-leading tools to help you plan your personal development and advance your career.

Why subscribe?

- Fully searchable across every book published by Packt
- Copy and paste, print, and bookmark content
- On demand and accessible via a web browser

Customer Feedback

Thanks for purchasing this Packt book. At Packt, quality is at the heart of our editorial process. To help us improve, please leave us an honest review on this book's Amazon page at `https://www.amazon.com/dp/1785880764`.

If you'd like to join our team of regular reviewers, you can e-mail us at `customerreviews@packtpub.com`. We award our regular reviewers with free eBooks and videos in exchange for their valuable feedback. Help us be relentless in improving our products!

Table of Contents

Preface	1
Chapter 1: Introduction to Magento 2	7
Magento as a lifestyle	7
Types of e-commerce solutions	8
Self–hosted e-commerce solutions	8
WooCommerce	8
PrestaShop	9
OpenCart	10
Hosted e-commerce solutions	10
Shopify	11
BigCommerce	11
New features in Magento 2	12
New technologies	12
New tools	13
Admin panel changes	13
Frontend changes	14
What do you need to get started?	14
Summary	15
Chapter 2: Installation	17
System requirements for Magento 2	17
Local installation in your computer	19
Getting the Magento code base	20
Setup Wizard installation	22
Command-line installation	30
How to choose the right hosting provider	34
Managed servers	34
Self-managed servers	35
Installing Magento in Amazon EC2	35
Setting up the Amazon AWS account	35
Creating the Amazon EC2 instance	38
Preparing the Amazon instance for Magento 2	44
Summary	49
Chapter 3: Migration	51
Reviewing the current store and preparing a migration plan	51

Code audit 52
Modified Magento core 52
Business logic in templates 52
Third-party extensions 53
Custom extensions 53
Unused extensions 54
Custom JavaScript 54
Migration requirements 54
Using the Data Migration Tool 55
Compatible versions 56
Migration process 56
Summary 75

Chapter 4: Creating Your First Product, Images, Inventory, and Prices 77
Adding your first product 77
Working with images 88
Working with Magento's pricing possibilities 90
Summary 98

Chapter 5: Attribute Sets and Custom Attributes 99
Product attributes 99
Creating a product attribute 102
Attribute sets 110
Associating attribute sets with products 116
Summary 124

Chapter 6: Product Types 125
Introduction to the different product types in Magento 125
Simple products 127
Configurable products 130
Grouped Product 142
Bundle Product 149
Virtual Product 158
Downloadable Product 160
Summary 167

Chapter 7: Categories 169
Categories 169
Hierarchy 181
Top navigation 185
Summary 187

Chapter 8: CMS Pages, Blocks, and Widgets — 189

   CMS Pages — 189
   Static blocks — 196
   Widgets — 199
   Summary — 205

Chapter 9: Managing Scope and Locale Settings — 207

   Magento scopes – websites, stores, and store views — 207
      Websites — 209
      Stores/store groups — 210
      Store views — 210
      Default/global scope — 214
   Summary — 215

Chapter 10: System Configuration — 217

   System configuration sections and fields — 217
      GENERAL | General — 220
      GENERAL | Web — 222
      GENERAL | Currency Setup — 223
      GENERAL | Store Email Addresses — 224
      GENERAL | Contacts — 224
      GENERAL | Contact Management — 224
      CATALOG | Catalog — 224
      CATALOG | Inventory — 226
      CATALOG | Email to a Friend — 227
      CUSTOMERS | Newsletter — 227
      CUSTOMERS | Customer Configuration — 228
      CUSTOMERS | Persistent Shopping Cart — 229
      SALES | Sales — 230
      Sales – Tax — 230
      Sales – Checkout — 231
      Sales – Shipping Settings — 231
      Sales – Multishipping Settings — 232
      Sales – Shipping Methods — 232
      Sales – Google API — 232
      Sales – Payment Methods — 232
      Advanced – Admin — 233
      Advanced – System — 233
      Advanced – Advanced — 234
   Summary — 238

Chapter 11: Working with Customers	239
Working with customer accounts	239
Adding a new customer	246
Summary	248
Chapter 12: Admin Users and Roles	249
Managing admin users	249
Managing roles	252
Summary	257
Chapter 13: Taxes	259
Tax classes and rules	259
Tax zones and rates	266
Summary	268
Chapter 14: Catalog and Shopping Cart Price Rules	269
Catalog price rules	269
Shopping cart price rules	276
Summary	285
Chapter 15: Processing Payments	287
Default Magento payment methods	287
Setting up PayPal	289
PCI compliance	298
Summary	300
Chapter 16: Configuring Shipping	301
Overview of the default Magento shipping methods	301
Flat Rate	303
Free Shipping	305
Table Rates	306
UPS/USPS/FedEx/DHL	309
How to set up shipping with UPS	309
Other carriers	313
Summary	314
Chapter 17: Fulfilling Orders	315
Order management	315
State and status	334
Invoices, shipping, and credit memos	337
Summary	343
Chapter 18: Transactional E-mails and Newsletter	345

Modifying transactional e-mail templates	345
Modifying newsletter templates	351
Handling newsletters and their subscribers	354
Summary	358

Chapter 19: Reports 359

Magento reports	359
Summary	366

Chapter 20: Customizing Your Magento Store 367

How to manage Magento themes	367
How inline translation works	379
Magento Marketplace	383
Summary	386

Chapter 21: Store Maintenance 387

Backup, restore, and database management	387
Performance tuning	394
Search engine optimization	405
Cache and Index Management	411
Upgrading Magento to a new version	414
Summary	422

Index 423

Preface

This is more than a book, it's a reference guide. The reality is that you have to have the right information exactly when you need it; for that reason, the goal of this book is to cover everything you need to know to manage your store. The first time you read the book, you will be able to understand all the concepts related to managing a Magento store, and then you can use the book as a reference and quickly take a look at its pages every time you need. This book consists of four parts. We'll get started with the general understanding of what Magento is, why and how we should use it, and whether it is possible and feasible to migrate an old web store to Magento 2. The migration part will only be interesting for those who wish to give their old websites a new life by migrating them to the new platform. We'll introduce you to the main e-commerce concepts and basic features, and we'll let you play with them so that you can get a taste of how the catalog and content management works. We'll show you how to tune your store for proper use. Finally, we will get serious and try to turn your sample store into a real web store, and teach you how to run it for real.

What this book covers

Chapter 1, *Introduction to Magento 2*, covers what Magento is and what you can do with it, a comparison with the most popular competitors, and a walk-through of the new features of Magento 2.

Chapter 2, *Installation*, describes the system requirements for Magento, installing Magento on your local computer, selecting a hosting provider, and installing Magento there.

Chapter 3, *Migration*, explores how the existing Magento users can migrate their web store from Magento 1 to Magento 2, and contains a detailed guide and recommendations.

Chapter 4, *Creating Your First Product, Images, Inventory, and Prices*, teaches you how to add products to your store and include detailed descriptions, images, price, and inventory information.

Chapter 5, *Attribute Sets and Custom Attributes*, explains how to work with product attribute sets and product attributes.

Chapter 6, *Product Types*, describes all the supported default product types and working with configurable, grouped, and downloadable products.

Chapter 7, *Categories*, covers the management of categories in your Magento store.

Chapter 8, *CMS Pages, Blocks, and Widgets,* covers using pages, blocks, and widgets to add content to your Magento store.

Chapter 9, *Managing Scope and Locale Settings*, explains scope--one of the most fundamental concepts of Magento--and how to set it up.

Chapter 10, *System Configuration*, reviews the most important system configuration sections and fields in Magento.

Chapter 11, *Working with Customers*, teaches you to manage customer accounts in your Magento store.

Chapter 12, *Admin Users and Roles*, covers managing admin users, granting permissions to specific roles, and basic security.

Chapter 13, *Taxes*, explains how having taxes calculated properly is what makes you secure when you offer different types of products for different regions and different delivery points.

Chapter 14, *Catalog and Shopping Cart Price Rules*, teaches price rules, an essential marketing tool that brings your Magento store to a professional level; you can manage discounts and coupons based on various conditions.

Chapter 15, *Processing Payments*, gives an overview of the default Magento payment methods, setting up PayPal for your Magento store, and PCI compliance.

Chapter 16, *Configuring Shipping*, gives an overview of the default Magento shipping methods and explains how to set up shipping with UPS.

Chapter 17, *Fulfilling Orders*, walks you through order fulfillment; discover your options for handling order fulfillment by observing the life cycle of an order in Magento.

Chapter 18, *Transactional E-mails and Newsletter*, explains the setup of a newsletter and transactional e-mails so that the communication from your website corresponds to the website's look and feel.

Chapter 19, *Reports*, teaches you how to generate reports to track the activity and conversion rates of your Magento store.

Chapter 20, *Customizing Your Magento Store*, explains how to manage the Magento themes, use the inline translation tool, and review the Magento Marketplace to find new extensions, themes, and language packs.

Chapter 21, *Store Maintenance*, teaches you how to position the website within search engines, Cache and Index management, tuning up performance and Magento backups and how to upgrade Magento to a new version.

What you need for this book

You don't need any technical skills in order to read the book and follow each of the guides from the chapters.

Who this book is for

This book is for merchants, e-commerce managers, and store administrators. Even more than that, this book is for everyone who has a good product to sell but needs a guide.

Conventions

In this book, you will find a number of text styles that distinguish between different kinds of information. Here are some examples of these styles and an explanation of their meaning.

Code words in text, database table names, folder names, filenames, file extensions, pathnames, dummy URLs, user input, and Twitter handles are shown as follows: "The next lines of code read the link and assign it to the to the BeautifulSoup function." Any command-line input or output is written as follows:

```
php bin/magento indexer:reindex
```

New terms and **important words** are shown in bold. Words that you see on the screen, for example, in menus or dialog boxes, appear in the text like this: "In order to reindex, you can click on the **Indexers are Invalid** link on the popup from the latest screenshot or go to the **System | Tools | Index Management** menu item."

Warnings or important notes appear in a box like this.

 Tips and tricks appear like this.

Reader feedback

Feedback from our readers is always welcome. Let us know what you think about this book-what you liked or disliked. Reader feedback is important for us as it helps us develop titles that you will really get the most out of. To send us general feedback, simply e-mail feedback@packtpub.com, and mention the book's title in the subject of your message. If there is a topic that you have expertise in and you are interested in either writing or contributing to a book, see our author guide at www.packtpub.com/authors.

Customer support

Now that you are the proud owner of a Packt book, we have a number of things to help you to get the most from your purchase.

Downloading the color images of this book

We also provide you with a PDF file that has color images of the screenshots/diagrams used in this book. The color images will help you better understand the changes in the output. You can download this file from https://www.packtpub.com/sites/default/files/downloads/Magento2BeginnersGuide_ColorImages.pdf.

Errata

Although we have taken every care to ensure the accuracy of our content, mistakes do happen. If you find a mistake in one of our books-maybe a mistake in the text or the code-we would be grateful if you could report this to us. By doing so, you can save other readers from frustration and help us improve subsequent versions of this book. If you find any errata, please report them by visiting http://www.packtpub.com/submit-errata, selecting your book, clicking on the **Errata Submission Form** link, and entering the details of your errata. Once your errata are verified, your submission will be accepted and the errata will be uploaded to our website or added to any list of existing errata under the Errata section of that title.

To view the previously submitted errata, go to https://www.packtpub.com/books/content/support and enter the name of the book in the search field. The required information will appear under the **Errata** section.

Piracy

Piracy of copyrighted material on the Internet is an ongoing problem across all media. At Packt, we take the protection of our copyright and licenses very seriously. If you come across any illegal copies of our works in any form on the Internet, please provide us with the location address or website name immediately so that we can pursue a remedy.

Please contact us at copyright@packtpub.com with a link to the suspected pirated material.

We appreciate your help in protecting our authors and our ability to bring you valuable content.

Questions

If you have a problem with any aspect of this book, you can contact us at questions@packtpub.com, and we will do our best to address the problem.

1
Introduction to Magento 2

In this chapter, we will cover the following topics:

- Magento as a life style: Magento as a platform and the Magento community
- Competitors: hosted and self-hosted e-commerce platforms
- New features in Magento 2
- What do you need to get started?

Magento as a lifestyle

Magento is an open source e-commerce platform. That is the short definition, but I would like to define Magento considering the seven years that I have been part of the Magento ecosystem.

In the seven years, Magento has been evolving to where it is today, a complete solution backed up by people with a passion for e-commerce. If you choose Magento as the platform for your e-commerce website, you will receive updates for the platform on a regular basis. Those updates include new features, improvements, and bug fixes to enhance the overall experience in your website.

As a Magento specialist, I can confirm that Magento is a platform that can be customized to fit any requirement. This means that you can add new features, include third-party libraries, and customize the default behavior of Magento. As the saying goes, the only limit is your imagination.

Whenever I have to talk about Magento, I always take some time to talk about its community. Sherrie Rohde is the Magento Community Manager and she has shared some really interesting facts about the Magento community in 2016:

- Delivered over 725 talks on Magento or at Magento-centric events
- Produced over 100 podcast episodes around Magento
- Organized and produced conferences and meetup groups in over 34 countries
- Written over 1,000 blog posts about Magento

Types of e-commerce solutions

There are two types of e-commerce solutions: *hosted* and *self-hosted*.

We will analyze each e-commerce solution type, and we will cover the general information, pros, and cons of each platform from each category.

Self–hosted e-commerce solutions

Self-hosted e-commerce solution is a platform that runs on your server, which means that you can download the code, customize it based on your needs, and then implement it in the server that you prefer. Magento is a self-hosted e-commerce solution, which means that you have absolute control over the customization and implementation of your Magento store.

WooCommerce

WooCommerce is a free shopping cart plugin for WordPress that can be used to create a full-featured e-commerce website. WooCommerce has been created following the architecture and standards of WordPress, which means that you can customize it with themes and plugins. The plugin currently has more than 18,000,000 downloads, which represents over 39% of all online stores.

Now, we will review the pros and cons of WooCommerce:

Pros:

- It can be downloaded for free
- Easy setup and configuration
- A lot of themes available
- Almost 400 extensions in the marketplace
- Support through the WooCommerce help desk

Cons:

- WooCommerce cannot be used without WordPress
- Some essential features are not included out-of-the-box, such us PayPal as a payment method, which means that you need to buy several extensions to add those features
- Adding custom features to WooCommerce through extensions can be expensive

PrestaShop

PrestaShop is a free open source e-commerce platform. The platform is currently used by more than 250,000 online stores and is backed by a community of more than 1,000,000 members. The company behind PrestaShop provides a range of paid services, such us technical support, migration, and training to run, manage, and maintain the store.

Now, let's take a look at the pros and cons of Prestashop:

Pros:

- Free and open source
- 310 integrated features
- 3,500 modules and templates in the marketplace
- Downloaded over 4 million times
- 63 languages

Cons:

- As with WooCommerce, many basic features are not included by default and adding those features through extensions is expensive
- Multiple bugs and complaints from the PrestaShop community

OpenCart

OpenCart is an open source platform for e-commerce, available under the GNU General Public License. OpenCart is a good choice for a basic e-commerce website.

Now, let's take a look at the pros and cons of OpenCart:

Pros:

- Free and open source
- Easy learning curve
- More than 13,000 extensions available
- More than 1,500 themes available

Cons:

- Limited features
- Not ready for SEO
- No cache management page in admin panel
- Hard to customize

Hosted e-commerce solutions

A hosted e-commerce solution is a platform that runs on the server belonging to the company that provides that service, which means that the solution is easier to set up but there are limitations and you don't have the freedom to customize the solution according to your needs. The monthly or annual fees increase when the store attracts more traffic and has more customers and orders placed.

Shopify

Shopify is a cloud-based e-commerce platform for small and medium-sized business. The platform currently powers over 325,000 online stores in approximately 150 countries.

Below, we will mention the pros and cons of Shopify:

Pros:

- No technical skills required to use the platform
- Tool to import products from another platform during the sign up process
- More than 1,500 apps and integrations
- 24/7 support through phone, chat, and e-mail

Cons:

- The source code is not provided
- Recurring fee to use the platform
- Hard to migrate from Shopify to another platform

BigCommerce

BigCommerce is one of the most popular hosted e-commerce platforms, and powers more than 95,000 stores in 150 countries.

Finally, we will review the pros and cons of BigCommerce:

Pros:

- No technical skills required to use the platform
- More than 300 apps and integrations available
- More than 75 themes available

Cons:

- The source code is not provided
- Recurring fee to use the platform
- Hard to migrate from BigCommerce to another platform

New features in Magento 2

Magento 2 is a new generation of the platform, with new features, technologies, and improvements that make Magento one of the most robust and complete e-commerce solutions available at the moment. In this section, we will describe the main differences between Magento 1 and Magento 2.

First, let's review the new technologies that are available in Magento 2:

New technologies

- **Composer**: This is a dependency manager for PHP. Dependencies can be declared and Composer will manage these dependencies by installing and updating them. In Magento 2, Composer simplifies the process of installing and upgrading extensions and upgrading Magento.
- **Varnish 4**: This is an open source HTTP accelerator. Varnish stores pages and other assets in memory to reduce the response time and network bandwidth consumption.
- **Full Page Caching**: In Magento 1, Full Page Caching was only included in the Magento Enterprise Edition. In Magento 2, Full Page Caching is included in all editions, allowing the content from static pages to be cached, increasing the performance and reducing the server load.
- **Elasticsearch**: This is a search engine that improves the search quality in Magento and provides background re-indexing and horizontal scaling.
- **RequireJS**: It is a library to load Javascript files on-the-fly, reducing the number of HTTP requests and improving the speed of the Magento Store.
- **jQuery**: The frontend in Magento 1 was implemented using Prototype as the language for Javascript. In Magento 2, the language for Javascript code is jQuery.
- **Knockout.js**: This is an open source Javascript library that implements the **Model-View-ViewModel** (**MVVM**) pattern, providing a great way of creating interactive frontend components.
- **LESS**: This is an open source CSS preprocessor that allows the developer to write styles for the store in a more maintainable and extendable way.
- **Magento UI Library**: This is a modular frontend library that uses a set of mix-ins for general elements and allows developers to work more efficiently on frontend tasks.

Now, let's review the new tools that are available in Magento 2:

New tools

- **Magento Performance Toolkit**: This is a tool that allows merchants and developers to test the performance of the Magento installation and customizations.
- **Magento 2 Command Line Tool**: This is a tool to run a set of commands in the Magento installation to clear the cache, re-index the store, create database backups, enable maintenance mode, and more.
- **Data Migration Tool**: This tool allows developers to migrate the existing data from Magento 1.x to Magento 2. The tool includes verification, progress tracking, logging, and testing functions.
- **Code Migration Toolkit**: This allows developers to migrate Magento 1.x extensions and customizations to Magento 2. Manual verification and updates are required in order to make the Magento 1.x extensions compatible with Magento 2.
- **Magento 2 Developer Documentation**: One of the complaints by the Magento community was that Magento 1 didn't have enough documentation for developers. In order to resolve this problem, the Magento team created the official Magento 2 Developer Documentation with information for developers, system administrators, designers, and QA specialists.

Admin panel changes

- **Better UI**: The admin panel has a new look-and-feel, which is more intuitive and easier to use. In addition to that, the admin panel is now responsive and can be viewed from any device in any resolution.
- **Inline editing**: The admin panel grids allow inline editing to manage data in a more effective way.
- **Step-by-step product creation**: The product add/edit page is one of the most important pages in the admin panel. The Magento team worked hard to create a different experience when it comes to adding/editing products in the Magento admin panel, and the result is that you can manage products with a step-by-step page that includes the fields and import tools separated in different sections.

Frontend changes

- **Integrated video in product page**: Magento 2 allows you to add a video to the product, introducing a new way of displaying products in the catalog.
- **Simplified checkout**: The steps in the checkout page have been reduced to allow customers to place orders in less time, increasing the conversion rate of the Magento store.
- **Register section removed from checkout page**: In Magento 1, the customer had the opportunity to register from step 1 of the checkout page. This required the customer to think about his account and the password before completing the order. In order to make the checkout simpler, Magento 2 allows the customer to register from the order success page without delaying the checkout process.

What do you need to get started?

Magento is a really powerful platform and there is always something new to learn. Just when you think you know everything about Magento, a new version is released with new features to discover. This makes Magento fun and unique as an e-commerce platform.

That being said, this book will be your guide to discover everything you need to know to implement, manage, and maintain your first Magento store.

In addition to that, I would like to highlight additional resources that will be useful in your journey of mastering Magento:

- **Official Magento Blog** (`https://magento.com/blog`): Get the latest news from the Magento team: best practices, customer stories, information related to events, and general Magento news
- **Magento Resources Library** (`https://magento.com/resources`): Videos, webinars and publications covering useful information organized by categories: order management, marketing and merchandising, international expansion, customer experience, mobile architecture and technology, performance and scalability, security, payments and fraud, retail innovation, and business flexibility

- **Magento Release Information** (`http://devdocs.magento.com/guides/v2.1/release-notes/bk-release-notes.html`): This is the place where you will get all the information about the latest Magento releases, including the highlights of each release, security enhancements, information about known issues, new features, and instructions for upgrade
- **Magento Security Center** (`https://magento.com/security`): Information about each of the Magento security patches as well as best practices and guidelines to keep your Magento store secure
- **Upcoming Events and Webinars** (`https://magento.com/events`): The official list of upcoming Magento events, including live events and webinars
- **Official Magento Forums** (`https://community.magento.com`): Get feedback from the Magento community in the official Magento Forums

Summary

In this chapter, we reviewed Magento 2 and the changes that have been introduced in the new version of the platform. We also analyzed the types of e-commerce solutions and the most important platforms available. In the next chapter, we will review the process of installing Magento 2 to start working with the platform.

2
Installation

In this chapter, we will cover the tasks related to installing Magento 2 in a Linux server, including the following ones:

- Setting up an AWS server
- Installing PHP
- Installing MySQL
- Installing Magento dependencies
- Creating a custom domain for the server
- Setting up GIT for version control
- Setting the right permissions for the server

System requirements for Magento 2

Before moving forward with the installation, we should review the system requirements for Magento 2 to ensure that the environment is correct for Magento to run properly.

The following are the system requirements for Magento 2:

- Operating System:
  - Linux
- Web servers:
  - Apache 2.2 or 2.4
  - nginx 1.8

- Database:
  - MySQL 5.6
    or
  - MySQL 5.7 (Magento 2.1.2 or above)
    or
  - MariaDB
    or
  - Percona
- PHP:
  - PHP 5.6 and later. PHP 7.0.2, 7.0.4, 7.0.6-7.0.x (Magento 2.1.2 and later)
  - PHP 7.0.2, 7.0.6-7.0.x (all Magento 2.1.x versions)
  - PHP 5.6.x (Magento 2.1.0)
- Required PHP extensions:
  - BC Math
  - curl
  - GD, ImageMagick 6.3.7 (or later), or both
  - intl
  - mbstring
  - Mcrypt
  - Mhash
  - OpenSSL
  - PDO/MySQL
  - SimpleXML
  - OPCache
  - SOAP
  - xml
  - XSL
  - Zip
  - JSON (PHP 7 only)
  - iconv (PHP 7 only)

- PHP Dependency Manager:
    - Composer
- SSL:
    - Valid security certificate (required for HTTPS)
    - **Transport Layer Security** (**TLS**) requirement
- Mail Server:
    - **Mail Transfer Agent** (**MTA**) or SMTP server
- Optional:
    - Redis 3.0
    - Varnish 3.5 or latest stable 4.x version
    - Memcached
    - Xdebug
    - PHPUnit

Local installation in your computer

In this section, we will review the general process to set up Magento with sample data in your local computer. In the next two sections, we will review the process of choosing the right hosting provider and set up a server to install Magento from scratch.

Taking that into consideration, we will assume that you have PHP 7 and MySQL running in your local machine and all the dependencies listed in the previous section as well.

Besides that, you should have your virtual host for the local instance already created (that is, `http://magento2-playground.dev`), the hosts file with the new entry for the local Magento instance (`127.0.0.1 magento2-playground.dev`), and an empty database.

Getting the Magento code base

The first step is to get the latest version of the Magento code base. In order to do that, you should visit the Magento download page (`https://magento.com/tech-resources/downlo ad`) and choose the latest version of Magento:

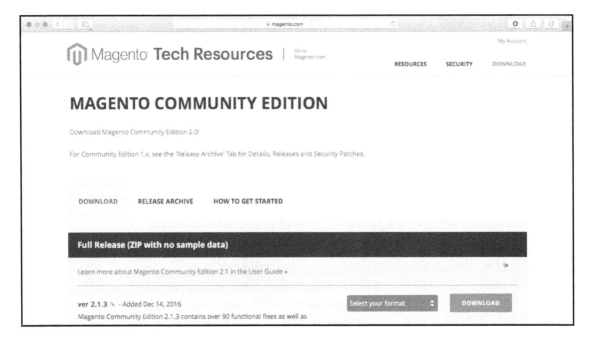

In order to have products, categories, and other useful information for our local Magento installation, we will choose the latest version from the **Full Release with Sample Data (ZIP with sample data)** section:

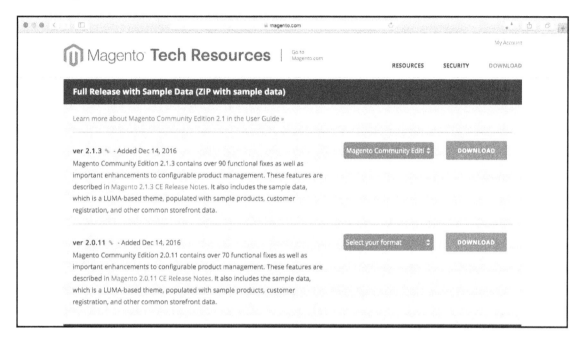

Once you download the file, you should uncompress it in the document root of your local machine.

After uncompressing the file, you should see a similar output to the following screenshot:

Now, we have the code base in place to move ahead with the installation.

There are two ways of installing Magento:

- Setup Wizard installation
- Command-line installation

Setup Wizard installation

The Setup Wizard is a simple installation process that is performed from the browser.

In order to install Magento using the Setup Wizard, you should follow these steps:

1. Open your favorite web browser.
2. Go to the `http://<host name>/setup` Setup Wizard URL. The host name is the one that you assigned in your virtual host configuration for the local Magento 2 installation. For example, in this section we declared `magento2-playground.dev` as the host name, so the URL for the Setup Wizard will be `http://magento2-playground.dev/setup`.
3. Click on **Agree and Setup Magento** to proceed to the first step of the installation:

4. **Readiness Check**: In this step, the Setup Wizard will check whether your local machine is ready for Magento 2, reviewing the following things:
   - PHP version
   - PHP settings
   - Enabled PHP extensions
   - File permissions

When the check is performed, you will receive confirmation to move to the next step:

5. **Add a Database**:
   In this step, you will specify the connection details for the empty database that you created for the Magento 2 installation:

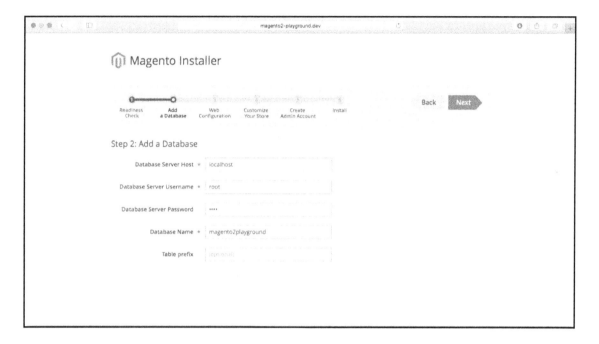

6. **Web Configuration**:

   In this step, you should specify the virtual host that you created for the Magento 2 website (autocompleted by default), and you can define a custom URL for the admin as well as **Advanced Options**, such as **HTTPS Options**, **Apache Rewrites**, **Encryption Key**, and the **Session Save** configuration.

7. **Customize Your Store**:

This step includes the time zone, currency, and language configuration, as well as the list of modules from Magento to enable/disable for the instance:

8. **Create Admin Account**:
   In this step, you can create the first user for the Magento Admin panel:

9. **Install**:

This is the final step and you will find an **Install Now** button to proceed with the installation.

When you click on that button, Magento will proceed with the installation. You will be able to keep track of the installation by looking at the progress bar.

In addition to that, you can open the console log using the link below the progress bar to see the full report of the progress for the installation.

Since we are installing Magento with sample data, the Setup Wizard will take time to install all the products, categories, attributes, and so on.

When the installation is finished, you should see the following success page in the Setup Wizard:

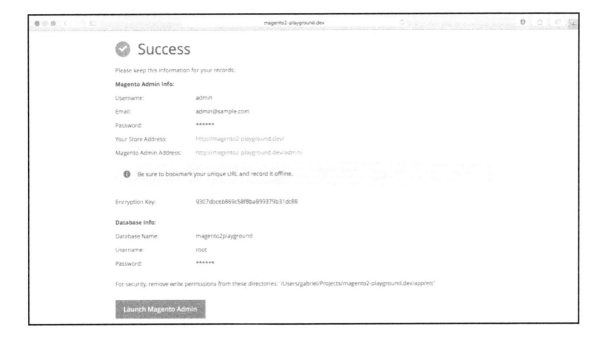

Command-line installation

The command-line installation is the alternative method that Magento provides to install Magento 2 from the Terminal.

These are the steps to proceed with the installation:

1. Open the Terminal and go to the directory of your local Magento installation.
2. The command-line installation is done using the Magento 2 command-line tool. You can confirm that you are in the right directory by running php bin/magento. You will see the output with a list of all the commands from the Magento 2 command-line tool:

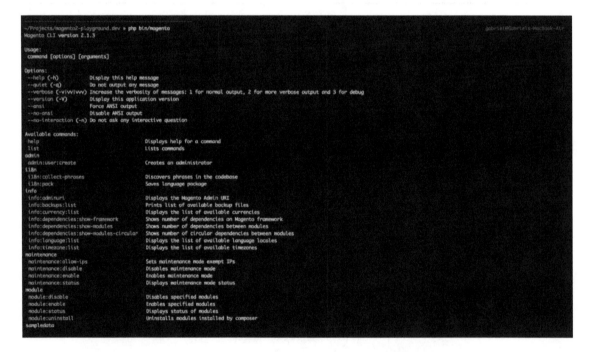

3. The next step is running Composer in the project directory. If you don't have Composer installed in your local machine, you can follow the instructions on the official Composer website: https://getcomposer.org/.
   Then, you should run the following command in the Terminal:

```
composer install
```

If everything goes well, you should see an output similar to the following:

```
~/Projects/magento2-playground.dev » composer install                                    gabriel@Gabriels-MacBook-Air
Loading composer repositories with package information
Installing dependencies (including require-dev) from lock file
Nothing to install or update
Generating autoload files
```

4. Finally, you should run `setup:install` to install Magento with your local configuration.That said, this is a long command and you can customize it to match your local configuration. We will review each of the parameters in the command:

```
php bin/magento setup:install
--db-host=localhost
--db-name=magento2playground
--db-user=root
--db-password=root
--backend-frontname=admin
--admin-user=admin
--admin-password=ABC123xyz
--admin-email=email@sample.com
--admin-firstname=Gabriel
--admin-lastname=Guarino
--base-url=http://magento2-playground.dev/
--language=en_US
--currency=USD
--use-rewrites=1
--use-secure=0
--use-secure-admin=0
```

- `db-host`: Host for your local database (localhost or 127.0.0.1)
- `db-name`: Name of the empty database for the Magento installation
- `db-user`: MySQL username
- `db-password`: MySQL password
- `backend-frontname`: URL (frontname) for the Magento Admin panel
- `admin-user`: Username for your first admin user
- `admin-password`: Password for your first admin user
- `admin-email`: E-mail for your first admin user
- `admin-firstname`: First name for your first admin user
- `admin-lastname`: Last name for your first admin user
- `base-url`: Base URL for the local Magento installation
- `language`: Language for the Magento installation

- `currency`: Currency for the Magento installation
- `use-rewrites`: Enable/disable URL rewrites
- `use-secure`: Enable/disable HTTPS on the frontend
- `use-secure-admin`: Enable/disable HTTPS in the admin panel

After running the `setup` command, you will see the following output confirming that the installation has been successfully completed:

Now that you have installed Magento on your local machine, you can access Magento using the URL that you declared before.

The URL to access the frontend will be `http://magento2-playground.dev/`:

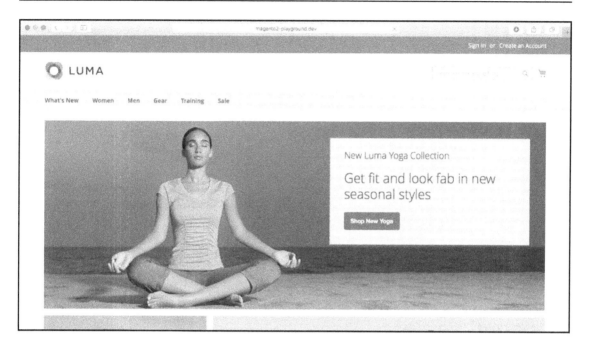

The URL to access the Admin Panel will be `http://magento2-playground.dev/admin/`:

How to choose the right hosting provider

Magento is a big platform with a huge community that provides all the services that you need, from design and development to hosting for the store.

The advantage when there is a big community behind a product is that you get specialized professionals who can help resolve your problems.

It is an advantage that you can use to ensure that your Magento store is always in good shape and that you are ready to resolve emergencies, if necessary.

That being said, it's really important to choose the right server for the Magento store. There are two types of servers that hosting providers offer:

- Managed servers
- Self-managed server

Managed servers

Managed servers are managed by the hosting provider. This means that the hosting provider is in charge of keeping the server up and running.

If there is any problem related to the server, you can create a ticket on the helpdesk of the hosting provider.

When you choose this type of server, you should find a good hosting provider with extensive knowledge and experience of Magento. This is essential to ensure that the hosting provider will be able to investigate and review the Magento instance when an emergency occurs.

Here is a list of recommended managed servers for Magento:

- **Nexcess:** https://www.nexcess.net/magento/hosting
- **MageMojo:** https://magemojo.com/
- **Rackspace:** https://www.rackspace.com/digital/magento

Self-managed servers

We have the self-managed servers; when you choose this type of server, the configuration, upgrades, and monitoring are the responsibilities of the user.

This is the best option for advanced users or merchants who have their own system administrator. You have total control of the server, which is really important when it comes to managing a Magento store. At the same time, you are in charge of resolving emergencies if the server is down or if there are other kinds of problems related to the server.

When you choose this type of server, you should have knowledge of server administration or find a really good system administrator who can handle emergencies and configure the server properly.

Here is a list of recommended self-managed servers for Magento:

- Amazon EC2: `https://aws.amazon.com/ec2/`
- DigitalOcean: `https://www.digitalocean.com/`
- Linode: `https://www.linode.com/`

Installing Magento in Amazon EC2

In this section, we will set up a server in Amazon from scratch. The server will be ready for Magento with all the requirements and dependencies installed, so you can manage your first Magento development server.

Setting up the Amazon AWS account

The first step is setting up your Amazon AWS account to create the server instance in Amazon EC2.

In order to do this, you should follow these steps:

1. Go to the Amazon AWS homepage at `https://aws.amazon.com/`. It will look something like this:

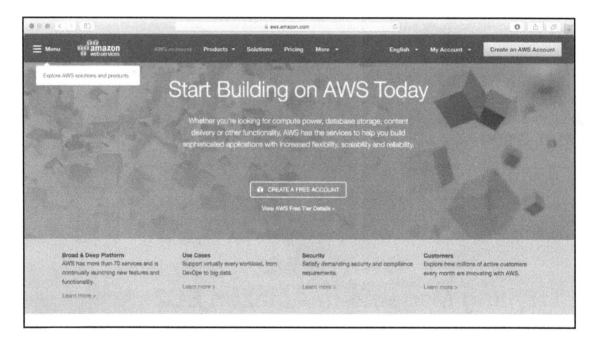

2. Click on **Create an AWS Account**.

3. Add your e-mail or phone number and select **I am a new user.**:

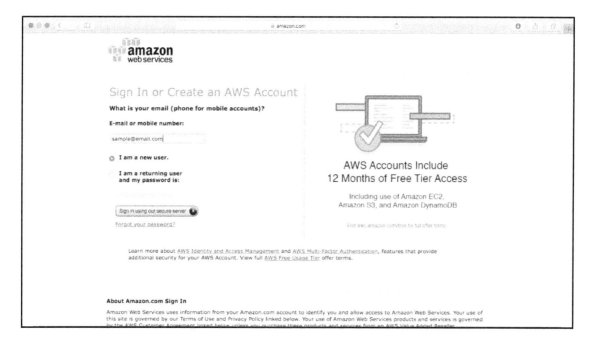

4. Click on **Sign in using our secure server**.

5. Complete the form with your personal information and click on **Create account**:

Creating the Amazon EC2 instance

After verifying the Amazon AWS account, you can create your first Amazon EC2 instance. Instances are virtual servers that can run web applications. Let's go through the steps to create the Amazon EC2 instance:

1. Go to the Amazon EC2 landing page, that is, `https://aws.amazon.com/ec2/`, which will look something like this:

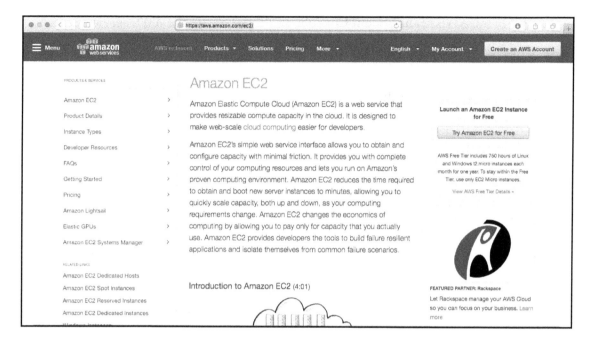

2. Click on **My Account** in the top-right of the screen, then click on **AWS Management Console** and, finally, sign in using your Amazon account.

3. On the **AWS Management Console**, search for ec2 in the **AWS** services search box:

4. You will be redirected to the EC2 dashboard. This will be the place to control and monitor your Amazon instances. Next, you click on **Launch Instance** in the middle of the page:

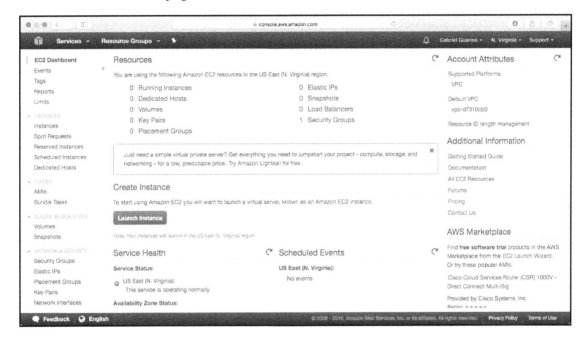

Choose an Instance Type: On this page, you can see the different instance types that you can choose depending on the size of the Magento store. For now, we will choose the **t2.micro Free tier eligible** instance type:

5. Instance Setup Wizard:
    1. **Choose an Amazon Machine Image (AMI)**: In this step, you can choose the software configuration for the Amazon instance. For this guide, we will choose Ubuntu Server:

2. **Choose an Instance Type**: On this page, you can see the different instance types that you can choose depending on the size of the Magento store. For now, we will choose the **t2.micro Free tier eligible** instance type:

3. **Configure Instance**: You can set advanced options for your instance in this step. We will keep the configuration by default in this step to proceed to step 4 of the Setup Wizard.

4. **Add Storage**: In this step, you can specify the storage for your instance. Since the size of the Magento 2 code base with sample data is 530 MB, we will keep the default size for the volume (8 GB).

5. **Add Tags**: This step is helpful when you have multiple Amazon instances since you can add tags to categorize the resources in your Amazon account.

6. **Configure Security Group**: The security group is a set of rules that controls the traffic of the Amazon instance. The default rule port is SSH, which allows the user to access the instance from the terminal. In order to allow Internet traffic for the Magento store, you should enable the HTTP and HTTPS ports. You can add these ports by clicking on **Add Rule** and then selecting **HTTP** and **HTTPS** from the **Custom TCP Rule** dropdown.

7. **Review**: In this step, you can review the configuration for your Amazon instance. Click on **Launch** at the bottom-right of the screen:

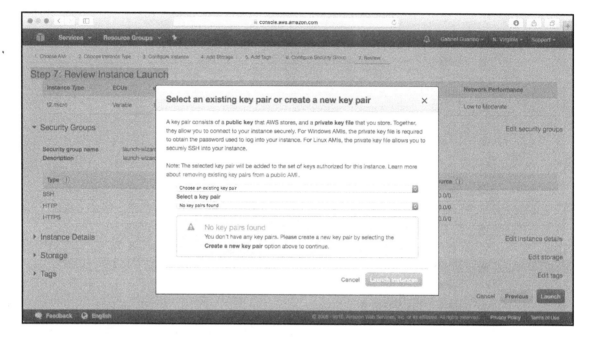

This is a really important part of the process. You can access the Amazon instance by using a private key file.

The only way to access the new instance is using the key pair, which is a combination of the public key that AWS stores and your private key file.

Choose **Create a new key pair** and then set the key pair name and click on **Download Key Pair**. Never lose the private key file since that is the **master key** to access your Amazon instance.

Finally, click on **Launch Instance** to finish the Setup Wizard.

Preparing the Amazon instance for Magento 2

Now that you created the Amazon instance, we are ready to install all the packages and dependencies to prepare the instance for Magento 2.

The first step is to log in to the server using the private key file that you downloaded from the Setup Wizard.

To log in, you need to know the public DNS or the public IP for the instance. You can get those values from the AWS EC2 Management Console:

1. Go to the `https://console.aws.amazon.com/ec2/` AWS EC2 Management Console.
2. You will see the instance that we just created in the list. Scroll to the right in the table to find the **Public DNS** and the **Public IP** for the instance:

3. Before logging in to the server, we should give the right permissions to the private key file. Locate the file in the Terminal and run the following command:

```
chmod 400 ~/Key Pairs/sample.pem
```

Now we are ready to log in to the AWS instance using the following command:

```
ssh -i ~/sample.pem ubuntu@107.20.106.201
```

We can alternatively use this command:

```
ssh -i ~/sample.pem ubuntu@ec2-107-20-106-201.compute-1.amazonaws.com
```

Once you log in to the development server, you should get sudo privileges to proceed with the installation of all the dependencies without problems:

```
sudo su
```

Now, it is time to set up all the dependencies for Magento 2:

1. Update all the existing packages in the server:

   ```
   apt-get update
   ```

2. We will install Apache, PHP, and the required PHP modules and composer using the following commands:

   ```
   apt-get install
   sudo apt-get install apache2
   sudo apt-get install php7.0
   sudo apt-get install libapache2-mod-php
   sudo apt-get install php7.0-simplexml
   sudo apt-get install php7.0-curl
   sudo apt-get install php7.0-intl
   sudo apt-get install php7.0-xsl
   sudo apt-get install php7.0-zip
   sudo apt-get install php7.0-xml
   sudo apt-get install php7.0-curl
   sudo apt-get install php7.0-gd
   sudo apt-get install php7.0-mcrypt
   sudo apt-get install php7.0-dom
   sudo apt-get install php7.0-mbstring
   sudo apt-get install composer
   ```

   You can run the installation for all the dependencies in one command, like this:
   ```
   sudo apt-get install apache2 php7.0 libapache2-mod-php
   php7.0-dom php7.0-simplexml php7.0-curl php7.0-intl
   php7.0-xsl php-mbstring php7.0-zip php7.0-xml php7.0-curl
   php7.0-gd php7.0-mcrypt php7.0-dom php7.0-mbstring
   composer
   ```

3. Next, we will install MySQL. Note that the installer will ask you to set the password for the root user:

```
sudo apt-get install mysql-server
sudo apt-get install php-mysql
```

4. Secure the MySQL installation. To do this, run the following command:

```
mysql_secure_installation
```

It will ask for the MySQL password you configured previously:

- Remove anonymous users: Yes
- Disallow login remotely: Yes
- Remove test database and access to it: Yes
- Reload privilege tables now?: Yes

5. Open the `apache2.conf` file and set `AllowOverride all` to grant the right permissions to the document root.

6. Find the following block of code:

```
<Directory /var/www/>
  Options Indexes FollowSymLinks
  AllowOverride none
  Require all granted
</Directory>
```

Replace it with the following code:

```
<Directory /var/www/>
  Options Indexes FollowSymLinks
  AllowOverride all
  Require all granted
</Directory>
```

7. Restart the Apache server to apply the changes:

```
sudo service apache2 restart
```

8. Create a sample `phpinfo.php` file in the document root:

```
cd /var/www/html
rm index.html
echo "<?php echo phpinfo();" > phpinfo.php
```

9. Then, you can access the document root and see the output for the `phpinfo.php` file in the browser. For example, `<Public IP>/phpinfo.php`.

You should see the following page in the browser:

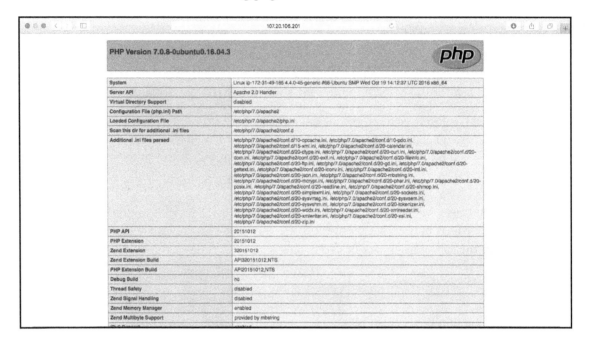

10. If `phpinfo.php` is displayed properly, remove the `phpinfo.php` file and create a custom MySQL user and database to import Magento (create the same username as the old server):

```
mysql -u root -p
CREATE USER '<username>'@'localhost' IDENTIFIED BY 'password';
GRANT ALL PRIVILEGES ON * . * TO '<username>'@'localhost';
FLUSH PRIVILEGES;
CREATE DATABASE <databasename>;
```

The Amazon instance is now ready for Magento 2 and you can proceed with the Setup Wizard or the command-line installation method that we saw in the previous section.

Summary

In this chapter, we reviewed the system requirements for Magento. We installed an instance in our local machine, and we even set up an Amazon server from scratch for Magento 2. In the next chapter, we will review the process of migrating a store from Magento 1 to Magento 2.

3
Migration

Migration from Magento 1.x to Magento 2 is one of the most popular topics in the Magento community. In this chapter, we will cover the following topics:

- Reviewing the current store and preparing a migration plan
- Using the Data Migration Tool

Reviewing the current store and preparing a migration plan

If you have decided to migrate your store from Magento 1.x to Magento 2, then you should follow a process to ensure that the migration is done in the right way, without any issues after the migration.

That said, the first step is reviewing the current store and having a migration plan.

Analysis should be done prior to the migration, and should include:

- Code audit
- Migration requirements

Code audit

A senior software engineer should review the code base of your current Magento 1.x store and take notes about the current state of the code.

This means that the software engineer will ensure that there are no bad practices in the Magento 1.x store because that would lead to missing features in the Magento 2.x store.

Modified Magento core

An example of a bad practice in Magento 1.x is directly modifying the Magento core. Some developers do this instead of creating custom modules, which results in changes in the platform that are not visible in the code base through the custom modules. This will prevent those features from being migrated to Magento 2, since they are not visible to the developers when they review the custom modules.

If their core has been modified, then that will be the first step: moving those changes from the core to custom extensions, and restoring the original core files from Magento.

You can download any version of Magento, 1.0 onwards, from the Magento Tech Resources downloads page at `https://magento.com/tech-resources/download`.

The software engineer will be able to compare the current state of the core of your store with the original Magento core.

Business logic in templates

Another bad programming practice in Magento is placing business logic in templates instead of custom extensions. The right way of adding business logic to templates in Magento is adding that logic in blocks in custom extensions, but some developers include PHP code in frontend templates instead.

The software engineer should review the frontend templates to see if there is any custom business logic that needs to be moved to custom extensions.

Third-party extensions

I don't recommend having a lot of third-party extensions. You should have just the ones that you need and that you consider essential for your store.

That said, you should review whether the third-party extensions from your store are available for Magento 2. This means that you should go to the website from the module vendor and check whether a new extension has been created for Magento 2.

It's very important to mention that some module vendors are creating a version of Magento 2 for their extensions, but those extensions for Magento 2 don't have all the features from the extension for Magento 1.

This means that you should not only check whether the extension is available, but also whether all the features that you use in Magento 1 for that extension are available in the extension for Magento 2.

If an extension is not available for Magento 2, then you should analyze whether you really need that extension. In case you need it, you can contact the module vendor to see if there is a planned release soon. If the module vendor is not planning to release a new version for Magento 2 soon, then you should create that extension from scratch for Magento 2.

Custom extensions

If you were looking for a custom feature in Magento 1 but didn't find any extension in Magento Connect, then you had to implement custom code to support that extension. These are custom extensions that are available in Magento 1 but that are not compatible with Magento 2.

Magento 2 is a new platform with a new data structure and new coding practices. You should create a new version from scratch for those extensions with compatible code for Magento 2.

Unused extensions

Are there unused custom or third-party extensions? If that is the case, you should review the features from those extensions to see if you really need them. By reducing the number of extensions, you reduce the amount of code to migrate and you keep a cleaner Magento 2 instance.

Custom JavaScript

Custom JavaScript is not migrated to Magento 2 and you need to take note of the custom features that you implemented using JavaScript. Those features should be manually migrated by an experienced Magento developer to Magento 2 to use RequireJS.

Migration requirements

Now that you have analyzed the code, it's time to review the migration requirements. Sometimes, the original requirement changes after the code audit. That is reasonable since you will have more information about the current state of your store and you will create a plan of action based on that.

After the code audit process, you will have a list including:

- Changes in the core to move to custom extensions
- Business logic in templates to move to custom extensions
- Third-party extensions ready for Magento 2
- Third-party extensions that should be updated for Magento 2
- Custom extensions that should be updated for Magento 2
- Unused extensions that won't be implemented in Magento 2
- Custom Javascript to implement in Magento 2

There is something else to consider–the theme. The theme is not automatically migrated from Magento 1 to Magento 2. Just as you did for the third-party extensions, you should review whether the theme is available for Magento 2 and contact the theme developer, if necessary, to see if there is a planned release coming soon.

If you want to keep the same look and feel for your store, then you should consider that the theme should be created from scratch for Magento 2 if the theme is not available for the new version of Magento.

Now, the plan to move ahead with the migration should be similar to the following:

- Prepare everything from the list that you created before
- Make sure that there are no issues in the code since those issues will persist when you migrate to Magento 2
- Upgrade Magento 1.x to the latest Magento 1.x version
- If you move ahead with all the preceding items, you will be ready for data migration

Using the Data Migration Tool

The Data Migration Tool has been created by the Magento team to allow store owners to move from Magento 1 to Magento 2.

The tool helps you migrate the database information to Magento 2, such as the products, orders, customers, store configurations, and more.

You can access the code for the Data Migration Tool from the following address in Github: `https://github.com/magento/data-migration-tool`

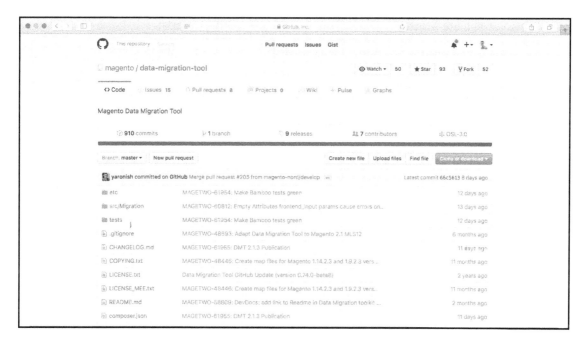

Compatible versions

It's good to mention that the Data Migration Tool is compatible with the following Magento versions:

- Magento Community Edition:
  - Version 1.6.x
  - Version 1.7.x
  - Version 1.8.x
  - Version 1.9.x

- Magento Enterprise Edition:
  - Version 1.11.x
  - Version 1.12.x
  - Version 1.13.x
  - Version 1.14.x

Migration process

Before using the Data Migration Tool, you should follow these steps:

1. **Set up an empty Magento 2 instance**: The instance should meet the requirements described in `Chapter 2`, *Installation* and the cron jobs shouldn't be enabled.

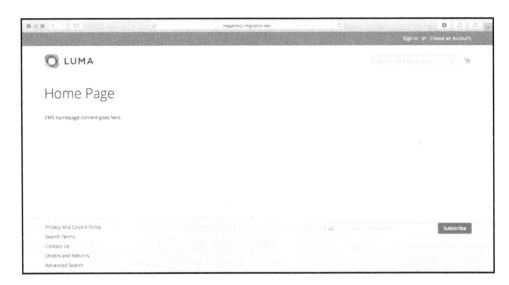

2. **Prepare your Magento 1.x instance**: From this point, make sure you don't modify the catalog, such as Products or Categories, until everything is migrated to Magento 2. Also, disable all the cron jobs and create a database backup before moving forward. It's also required to put the store into maintenance mode during the migration process. In the following image, you can see that we created a database backup using the command line:

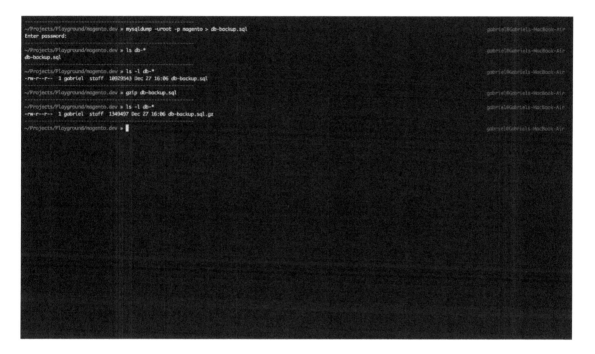

3. **Ensure that you are using PHP 7 to** ensure **the best performance of the Data Migration Tool**:

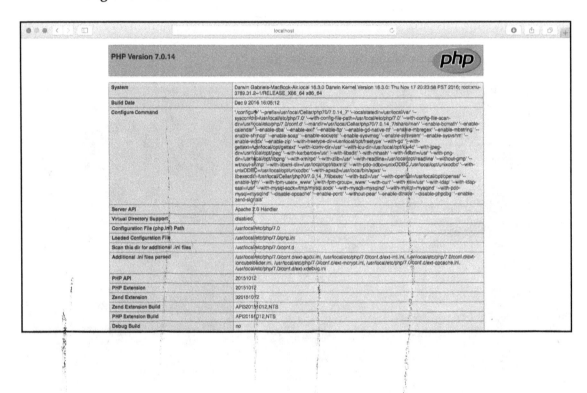

4. **Install the Data Migration Tool in your Magento 2 directory by following these instructions**:

   1. Go to the Magento 2 directory using the Terminal:

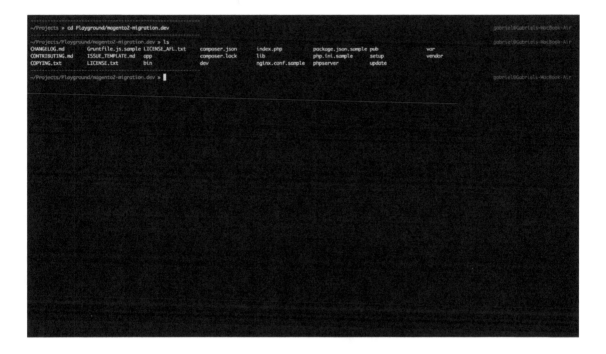

2. Check the latest release version of the Data Migration Tool at `https://git hub.com/magento/data-migration-tool/releases`:

3. Run the following commands in the Terminal:

```
composer config repositories.data-migration-tool git
https://github.com/magento/data-migration-tool
composer require magento/data-migration-tool:2.1.3
```

Please note that the second command includes the latest version of the Data Migration Tool at the end (`2.1.3`). Make sure you update that command to match the latest release version from Github.

The second command will require authentication from `repo.magento.com`. You can get these credentials from your Magento account by following these steps:

1. Go to `http://magento.com` and click on **MY ACCOUNT** at the top-right of the screen:

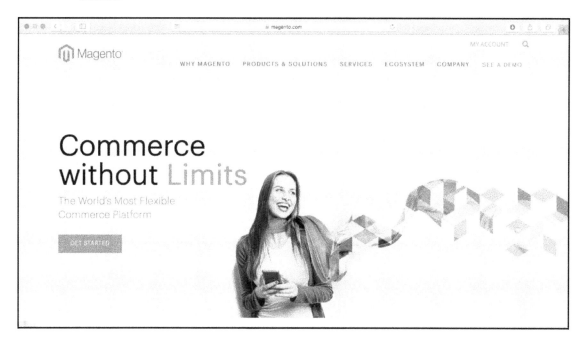

2. If you have a Magento account, log in using your username and password. If not, create your account by clicking on the **Register** button on the right:

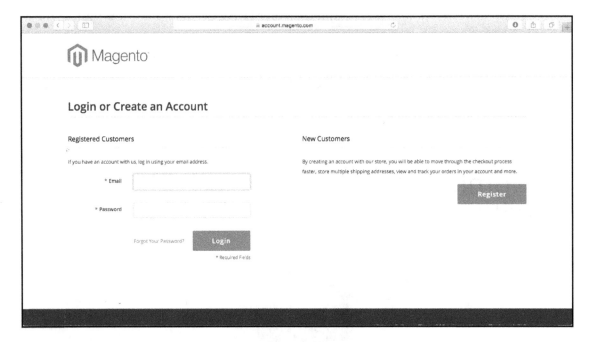

3. Click on the **Marketplace** tab and go to the **My Access Keys** link from the **My Products** section:

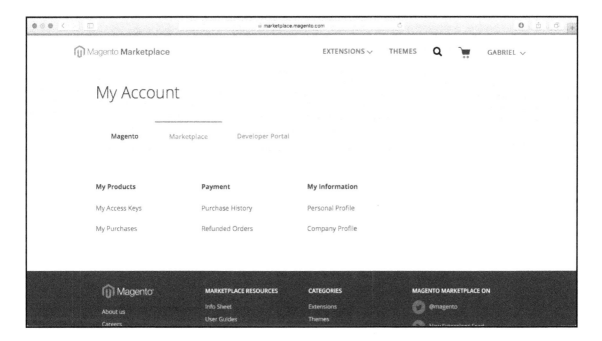

4. Click on the **Magento 2** tab and then **Create A New Access Key**:

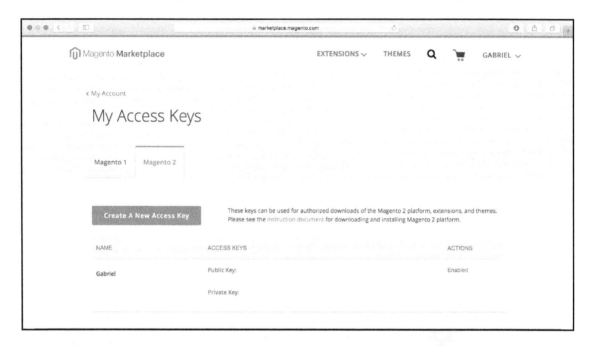

Now that you have your Access Keys, you can finish the Data Migration Tool installation by adding your credentials after running the command:

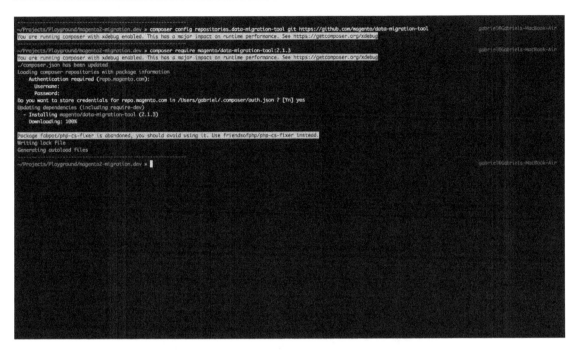

5. **Configure the Data Migration Tool**: After the installation, you will find the directory that contains the mapping and configuration files in the following locations in the Magento 2 directory:

- Migration from Magento 1 Community Edition to Magento 2 Community Edition:

  ```
  vendor/magento/data-migration-tool/etc/ce-to-ce
  ```

- Migration from Magento 1 Community Edition to Magento 2 Enterprise Edition:

  ```
  vendor/magento/data-migration-tool/etc/ce-to-ee
  ```

- Migration from Magento 1 Enterprise Edition to Magento 2 Enterprise Edition:

  ```
  vendor/magento/data-migration-tool/etc/ee-to-ee
  ```

You can see the content of each of those directories in the following screenshot:

```
~/Projects/Playground/magenta2-migration.dev/vendor/magenta/data-migration-tool/etc/ce-to-ce » ls                                    gabriel@Gabriels-MacBook-Air
1.6.0.0              1.8.1.0              1.9.2.2              customer-document-groups.xml.dist    map-eav.xml.dist
1.6.1.0              1.9.0.0              1.9.2.3              deltalog.xml.dist                    map-log.xml.dist
1.6.2.0              1.9.0.1              1.9.2.4              eav-attribute-groups.xml.dist        map-tier-price.xml.dist
1.7.0.0              1.9.1.0              1.9.3.0              eav-document-groups.xml.dist         order-grids-document-groups.xml.dist
1.7.0.1              1.9.1.1              1.9.3.1              log-document-groups.xml.dist         settings.xml.dist
1.7.0.2              1.9.2.0              class-map.xml.dist   map-customer.xml.dist
1.8.0.0              1.9.2.1              customer-attribute-groups.xml.dist  map-document-groups.xml.dist

~/Projects/Playground/magenta2-migration.dev/vendor/magenta/data-migration-tool/etc/ce-to-ce » cd ../ce-to-ee && ls               gabriel@Gabriels-MacBook-Air
1.6.0.0              1.8.1.0              1.9.2.2              customer-document-groups.xml.dist    map-eav.xml.dist
1.6.1.0              1.9.0.0              1.9.2.3              deltalog.xml.dist                    map-log.xml.dist
1.6.2.0              1.9.0.1              1.9.2.4              eav-attribute-groups.xml.dist        map-tier-price.xml.dist
1.7.0.0              1.9.1.0              1.9.3.0              eav-document-groups.xml.dist         order-grids-document-groups.xml.dist
1.7.0.1              1.9.1.1              1.9.3.1              log-document-groups.xml.dist         settings.xml.dist
1.7.0.2              1.9.2.0              class-map.xml.dist   map-customer.xml.dist
1.8.0.0              1.9.2.1              customer-attribute-groups.xml.dist  map-document-groups.xml.dist

~/Projects/Playground/magenta2-migration.dev/vendor/magenta/data-migration-tool/etc/ce-to-ee » cd ../ee-to-ee && ls               gabriel@Gabriels-MacBook-Air
1.11.0.0             1.13.1.0             class-map.xml.dist                    map-eav.xml.dist
1.11.0.1             1.14.0.0             customer-attr-document-groups.xml.dist map-log.xml.dist
1.11.0.2             1.14.0.1             customer-attr-map.xml.dist            map-sales.xml.dist
1.11.1.0             1.14.1.0             customer-attribute-groups.xml.dist    map-tier-price.xml.dist
1.11.2.0             1.14.2.0             customer-document-groups.xml.dist     order-grids-document-groups.xml.dist
1.12.0.0             1.14.2.1             deltalog.xml.dist                     settings.xml.dist
1.12.0.1             1.14.2.2             eav-attribute-groups.xml.dist         visual_merchandiser_attribute_groups.xml.dist
1.12.0.2             1.14.2.3             eav-document-groups.xml.dist          visual_merchandiser_document_groups.xml.dist
1.13.0.0             1.14.2.4             log-document-groups.xml.dist          visual_merchandiser_map.xml.dist
1.13.0.1             1.14.3.0             map-customer.xml.dist
1.13.0.2             1.14.3.1             map-document-groups.xml.dist

~/Projects/Playground/magenta2-migration.dev/vendor/magenta/data-migration-tool/etc/ee-to-ee »                                     gabriel@Gabriels-MacBook-Air
```

Before running the migration process, you should create `config.xml` with all the database connection details for the migration.

Depending on the type of migration (`ce to ce`, `ce to ee`, or `ee to ee`), you should add `config.xml` to the specific location that we previously described.

For this migration, I have prepared a Magento 1 Community Edition with a sample data instance:

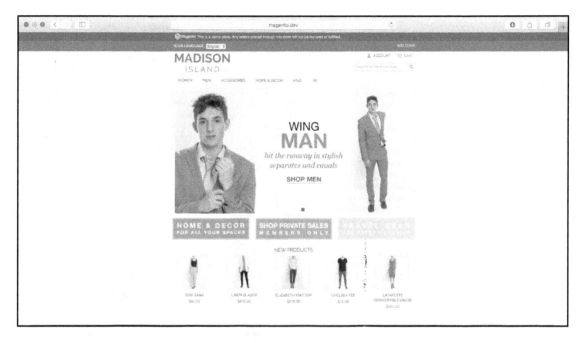

This migration will be from Magento 1 Community Edition to Magento 2 Community Edition, so the location for the configuration file will be `vendor/magento/data-migration-tool/etc/ce-to-ce/<Magento 1 version>/config.xml`.

In the location, the `<Magento 1 version>` is the version number of your Magento 1 store. The installed Magento 1 version in this example is `1.9.2.4`, so the following command should be run to go to the right directory: `cd vendor/magento/data-migration-tool/etc/ce-to-ce/1.9.2.4`

There is a sample configuration file in that directory, so you should go to the directory and run the following command to duplicate it: `cp config.xml.dist config.xml`

Here, you can see all the commands to go to the right directory and duplicate the configuration file, including a preview of that file:

```
~/Projects/Playground/magento2-migration.dev » cd vendor/magento/data-migration-tool/etc/ce-to-ce/1.9.2.4          gabriel@Gabriels-MacBook-Air

~/Projects/Playground/magento2-migration.dev/vendor/magento/data-migration-tool/etc/ce-to-ce/1.9.2.4 » ls          gabriel@Gabriels-MacBook-Air
config.xml.dist map.xml.dist

~/Projects/Playground/magento2-migration.dev/vendor/magento/data-migration-tool/etc/ce-to-ce/1.9.2.4 » ls -lat     gabriel@Gabriels-MacBook-Air
total 144
drwxr-xr-x   4 gabriel  staff     136 Dec 27 16:25 .
drwxr-xr-x  35 gabriel  staff    1190 Dec 27 16:25 ..
-rw-rw-rw-   1 gabriel  staff    7002 Dec 19 11:38 config.xml.dist
-rw-rw-rw-   1 gabriel  staff   63779 Dec 19 11:38 map.xml.dist

~/Projects/Playground/magento2-migration.dev/vendor/magento/data-migration-tool/etc/ce-to-ce/1.9.2.4 » cp config.xml.dist config.xml     gabriel@Gabriels-MacBook-Air

~/Projects/Playground/magento2-migration.dev/vendor/magento/data-migration-tool/etc/ce-to-ce/1.9.2.4 » cat config.xml          gabriel@Gabriels-MacBook-Air
<?xml version="1.0" encoding="UTF-8"?>
<!--
/**
 * Copyright © 2015 Magento. All rights reserved.
 * See COPYING.txt for license details.
 */
-->
<config xmlns:xs="http://www.w3.org/2001/XMLSchema-instance" xs:noNamespaceSchemaLocation="../../config.xsd">
    <steps mode="settings">
        <step title="Settings Step">
            <integrity>Migration\Step\Settings\Integrity</integrity>
            <data>Migration\Step\Settings\Data</data>
        </step>
        <step title="Stores Step">
            <integrity>Migration\Step\Stores\Integrity</integrity>
            <data>Migration\Step\Stores\Data</data>
            <volume>Migration\Step\Stores\Volume</volume>
        </step>
    </steps>
    <steps mode="data">
        <step title="Data Integrity Step">
            <integrity>Migration\Step\DataIntegrity\Integrity</integrity>
        </step>
        <step title="EAV Step">
            <integrity>Migration\Step\Eav\Integrity</integrity>
            <data>Migration\Step\Eav\Data</data>
            <volume>Migration\Step\Eav\Volume</volume>
        </step>
```

Open `config.xml` in your favorite editor and locate the `<source>` tag:

```
        <step title="Customer Attributes Step">
            <delta>Migration\Step\Customer\Delta</delta>
            <volume>Migration\Step\Customer\Volume</volume>
        </step>
        <step title="Map Step">
            <delta>Migration\Step\Map\Delta</delta>
            <volume>Migration\Step\Map\Volume</volume>
        </step>
        <step title="Log Step">
            <delta>Migration\Step\Log\Delta</delta>
            <volume>Migration\Step\Log\Volume</volume>
        </step>
        <step title="OrderGrids Step">
            <delta>Migration\Step\OrderGrids\Delta</delta>
            <volume>Migration\Step\OrderGrids\Volume</volume>
        </step>
        <step title="SalesIncrement Step">
            <delta>Migration\Step\SalesIncrement\Delta</delta>
            <volume>Migration\Step\SalesIncrement\Volume</volume>
        </step>
    </steps>
    <source>
        <database host="localhost" name="magento1" user="root"/>
    </source>
    <destination>
        <database host="localhost" name="magento2" user="root"/>
    </destination>
    <options>
        <map_file>etc/ce-to-ce/1.9.2.4/map.xml.dist</map_file>
        <eav_map_file>etc/ce-to-ce/map-eav.xml.dist</eav_map_file>
        <eav_document_groups_file>etc/ce-to-ce/eav-document-groups.xml.dist</eav_document_groups_file>
        <eav_attribute_groups_file>etc/ce-to-ce/eav-attribute-groups.xml.dist</eav_attribute_groups_file>
        <log_map_file>etc/ce-to-ce/map-log.xml.dist</log_map_file>
        <log_document_groups_file>etc/ce-to-ce/log-document-groups.xml.dist</log_document_groups_file>
        <settings_map_file>etc/ce-to-ce/settings.xml.dist</settings_map_file>
        <customer_map_file>etc/ce-to-ce/map-customer.xml.dist</customer_map_file>
        <customer_document_groups_file>etc/ce-to-ce/customer-document-groups.xml.dist</customer_document_groups_file>
        <customer_attribute_groups_file>etc/ce-to-ce/customer-attribute-groups.xml.dist</customer_attribute_groups_file>
        <delta_document_groups_file>etc/ce-to-ce/deltalog.xml.dist</delta_document_groups_file>
        <order_grids_document_groups_file>etc/ce-to-ce/order-grids-document-groups.xml.dist</order_grids_document_groups_file>
        <map_document_groups>etc/ce-to-ce/map-document-groups.xml.dist</map_document_groups>
        <class_map>etc/ce-to-ce/class-map.xml.dist</class_map>
        <tier_price_map_file>etc/ce-to-ce/map-tier-price.xml.dist</tier_price_map_file>
search hit TOP, continuing at BOTTOM
```

Customize the node to match the information in the Magento 1 and Magento 2 databases. Take into account that you should add the following to each of the database tags to specify the database password: `password="<database password>"` Now, locate the `<crypt_key />` tag.

It's mandatory to add the encryption key from your Magento 1 configuration file. The key can be found in the `app/etc/local.xml` file under the `<key>` tag:

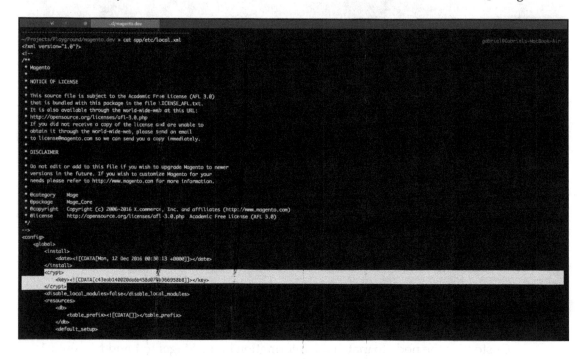

Copy and paste that key into the Data Migration Tool configuration file, as follows:

```
</source>
<destination>
    <database host="localhost" name="magento2migration" user="root"/>
</destination>
<options>
    <map_file>etc/ce-to-ce/1.9.2.4/map.xml.dist</map_file>
    <eav_map_file>etc/ce-to-ce/map-eav.xml.dist</eav_map_file>
    <eav_document_groups_file>etc/ce-to-ce/eav-document-groups.xml.dist</eav_document_groups_file>
    <eav_attribute_groups_file>etc/ce-to-ce/eav-attribute-groups.xml.dist</eav_attribute_groups_file>
    <log_map_file>etc/ce-to-ce/map-log.xml.dist</log_map_file>
    <log_document_groups_file>etc/ce-to-ce/log-document-groups.xml.dist</log_document_groups_file>
    <settings_map_file>etc/ce-to-ce/settings.xml.dist</settings_map_file>
    <customer_map_file>etc/ce-to-ce/map-customer.xml.dist</customer_map_file>
    <customer_document_groups_file>etc/ce-to-ce/customer-document-groups.xml.dist</customer_document_groups_file>
    <customer_attribute_groups_file>etc/ce-to-ce/customer-attribute-groups.xml.dist</customer_attribute_groups_file>
    <delta_document_groups_file>etc/ce-to-ce/deltalog.xml.dist</delta_document_groups_file>
    <order_grids_document_groups_file>etc/ce-to-ce/order-grids-document-groups.xml.dist</order_grids_document_groups_file>
    <map_document_groups>etc/ce-to-ce/map-document-groups.xml.dist</map_document_groups>
    <class_map>etc/ce-to-ce/class-map.xml.dist</class_map>
    <tier_price_map_file>etc/ce-to-ce/map-tier-price.xml.dist</tier_price_map_file>
    <!--
    In case bulk_size=0 it will be auto-detected for every document.
    -->
    <bulk_size>0</bulk_size>
    <!--
    Set direct_document_copy = 1 for better performance.
    NOTE: 'source' and 'destination' databases MUST be placed on the same MySQL instance
    and 'destination' user MUST be granted with 'SELECT' permissions on 'source' database
    -->
    <direct_document_copy>0</direct_document_copy>
    <source_prefix />
    <dest_prefix />
    <auto_resolve_urlrewrite_duplicates>0</auto_resolve_urlrewrite_duplicates>
    <log_file>migration.log</log_file>
    <progress_bar_format>%percent% [%bar%] Remaining Time: %remaining%</progress_bar_format>
    <upgrade_customer_password_hash>1</upgrade_customer_password_hash>
    <edition_migrate>ce-to-ce</edition_migrate>
    <edition_number>1.9.2.4</edition_number>
    <init_statements_source>SET NAMES utf8;</init_statements_source>
    <init_statements_destination>SET NAMES utf8;</init_statements_destination>
    <crypt_key>c43eab140020da6b458d07db366058b8</crypt_key>
</options>
</config>
-- INSERT --
```

6. **Data Migration Tool mapping**: The tool uses mapping files to perform custom database mappings between the Magento 1 and Magento 2 databases.

The mapping files are located in the same directories that we described before. There, we will see the mapping file templates:

```
~/Projects/Playground/magento2-migration.dev/vendor/magento/data-migration-tool/etc/ce-to-ce » ls          gabriel@Gabriels-MacBook-Air
1.6.0.0          1.8.1.0              1.9.2.2               customer-document-groups.xml.dist    map-eav.xml.dist
1.6.1.0          1.9.0.0              1.9.2.3               deltalog.xml.dist                    map-log.xml.dist
1.6.2.0          1.9.0.1              1.9.2.4               eav-attribute-groups.xml.dist        map-tier-price.xml.dist
1.7.0.0          1.9.1.0              1.9.3.0               eav-document-groups.xml.dist         order-grids-document-groups.xml.dist
1.7.0.1          1.9.1.1              1.9.3.1               log-document-groups.xml.dist         settings.xml.dist
1.7.0.2          1.9.2.0              class-map.xml.dist    map-customer.xml.dist
1.8.0.0          1.9.2.1              customer-attribute-groups.xml.dist    map-document-groups.xml.dist

~/Projects/Playground/magento2-migration.dev/vendor/magento/data-migration-tool/etc/ce-to-ce » cd ../ce-to-ee && ls     gabriel@Gabriels-MacBook-Air
1.6.0.0          1.8.1.0              1.9.2.2               customer-document-groups.xml.dist    map-eav.xml.dist
1.6.1.0          1.9.0.0              1.9.2.3               deltalog.xml.dist                    map-log.xml.dist
1.6.2.0          1.9.0.1              1.9.2.4               eav-attribute-groups.xml.dist        map-tier-price.xml.dist
1.7.0.0          1.9.1.0              1.9.3.0               eav-document-groups.xml.dist         order-grids-document-groups.xml.dist
1.7.0.1          1.9.1.1              1.9.3.1               log-document-groups.xml.dist         settings.xml.dist
1.7.0.2          1.9.2.0              class-map.xml.dist    map-customer.xml.dist
1.8.0.0          1.9.2.1              customer-attribute-groups.xml.dist    map-document-groups.xml.dist

~/Projects/Playground/magento2-migration.dev/vendor/magento/data-migration-tool/etc/ce-to-ee » cd ../ee-to-ee && ls     gabriel@Gabriels-MacBook-Air
1.11.0.0         1.13.1.0             class-map.xml.dist                   map-eav.xml.dist
1.11.0.1         1.14.0.0             customer-attr-document-groups.xml.dist    map-log.xml.dist
1.11.0.2         1.14.0.1             customer-attr-map.xml.dist           map-sales.xml.dist
1.11.1.0         1.14.1.0             customer-attribute-groups.xml.dist    map-tier-price.xml.dist
1.11.2.0         1.14.2.0             customer-document-groups.xml.dist    order-grids-document-groups.xml.dist
1.12.0.0         1.14.2.1             deltalog.xml.dist                    settings.xml.dist
1.12.0.1         1.14.2.2             eav-attribute-groups.xml.dist        visual_merchandiser_attribute_groups.xml.dist
1.12.0.2         1.14.2.3             eav-document-groups.xml.dist         visual_merchandiser_document_groups.xml.dist
1.13.0.0         1.14.2.4             log-document-groups.xml.dist         visual_merchandiser_map.xml.dist
1.13.0.1         1.14.3.0             map-customer.xml.dist
1.13.0.2         1.14.3.1             map-document-groups.xml.dist

~/Projects/Playground/magento2-migration.dev/vendor/magento/data-migration-tool/etc/ee-to-ee » ▮                       gabriel@Gabriels-MacBook-Air
```

The `map.xml.dist` file will be the one that you will use most of the time. Besides that, Magento provides a set of additional mapping files:

- **General**:
    - `class-map.xml.dist`: Class mappings between Magento 1 and Magento 2
    - `config.xml.dist`: Main configuration file for the Data Migration Tool
    - `deltalog.xml.dist`: List of tables for the setup of database routines
    - `settings.xml.dist`: Configuration file for the `core_config_data` table migration

- **EAV step in Data Migration Tool**:
    - `map-eav.xml.dist`: Map file
    - `eav-attribute-groups.xml.dist`: List of attributes
    - `eav-document-groups.xml.dist`: List of tables

- **Log step in Data Migration Tool**:
    - `map-log.xml.dist`: Map file
    - `log-document-groups.xml.dist`: List of tables
- **Map step in Data Migration Tool**:
    - `map.xml.dist`: Map file
- **Customer Attributes step in Data Migration Tool**:
    - `map-customer.xml`: Map file
    - `customer-attribute-groups.xml`: List of attributes
    - `customer-document-groups.xml`: List of tables
    - `customer-attr-map.xml.dist`: Map file for custom customer attributes (EE only)
    - `customer-attr-document-groups.xml.dist`: List of tables for custom customer attributes (EE only)
- **Other steps in Data Migration Tool**:
    - `order-grids-document-groups.xml`: List of tables for the `OrderGrids` step
    - `map-sales.xml.dist`: Map file that is used in `SalesOrder` step (EE only)

In order to map your data, you should rename the files from `.xml.dist` to `.xml` and edit the `<options>` node in `config.xml` to match the new name of the file. Once the data is mapped, you can proceed to the next step.

7. **Migrate Settings**: In this step, you will migrate the stores and store the configuration. In order to do that, you should go the the Magento 2 directory from the command line and run the following command:

```
php bin/magento migrate:settings <path to Data Migration Tool
configuration file>
```

In the previous command, `<path to Data Migration Tool configuration file>` is the path to the `config.xml` file that we created before: `vendor/magento/data migration-tool/etc/ce-to-ce/1.9.2.4/config.xml`

The final command to run is then:

```
php bin/magento migrate:settings vendor/magento/data-migration-
tool/etc/ce-to-ce/1.9.2.4/config.xml
```

Running this command takes just seconds, and you will be able to migrate the store configuration to Magento 2.

8. Migrate the rest of the data: In this step, you will migrate all the other data, such as the customers, orders, products, and so on.

The command is really similar to the previous one:

```
php bin/magento migrate:data <path to Data Migration Tool
configuration file>
```

The final command to run is then:

```
php bin/magento migrate:data vendor/magento/data-migration-
tool/etc/ce-to-ce/1.9.2.4/config.xml
```

This command takes the most time to run and will map all the data from the Magento 1 database to the new database.

9. **Migrate changes**: If you didn't put your store in maintenance mode, then there might be new registered customers and new orders since the last time you migrated the data. Fortunately, the Data Migration Tool allows you to migrate those changes to the new Magento 2 database as well. If you put the store in maintenance mode, then this step is not necessary since there won't be any new orders or customers.
Take into account that this step will migrate new customers and orders, but catalog changes won't be migrated. That is why it's important to not make changes to the catalog when you decide to move forward with the migration. As in the previous commands, we'll use the Magento Command Line Tool and we'll specify the path to the Data Migration Tool configuration file:
```
php bin/magento migrate:delta <path to Data Migration Tool
configuration file>
```
The final command to run is then:

```
php bin/magento migrate:delta vendor/magento/data-migration-
tool/etc/ce-to-ce/1.9.2.4/config.xml
```

The delta migration will map the changes between your Magento 1 and Magento 2 databases in real time. You can stop the delta migration by pressing *Ctrl + C*.

Summary

In this chapter, we reviewed the process of migrating from Magento 1 to Magento 2, including preparing custom and third-party extensions for Magento 2, and migrating all the information from the database to the new version of Magento. In the next chapter, we will review the process of creating a product in Magento 2.

4

Creating Your First Product, Images, Inventory, and Prices

In this chapter, you will be adding your first product to Magento 2, which is one of the most frequent tasks for a Magento administrator.

We will cover:

- Adding a product to the Magento catalog
- Working with images
- Working with Magento's pricing possibilities

Adding your first product

Congratulations! You are about to add your first product in Magento 2, which is a big step forward in the learning curve of Magento.

First, you should log in to the admin panel using your username and password. Once you do that, you should see the **PRODUCTS** menu item on the left sidebar:

You should go to the **PRODUCTS | Catalog** submenu item to open the **Catalog** grid. When the page loads, you will see the **Add Product** button in the top-right of the screen:

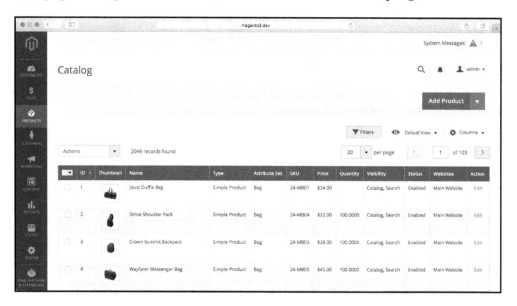

When you click on that button, you will be redirected to the **New Product** form. You should see the following form on screen:

We will go through each of the fields on that page to describe how to add the information for your new product:

- General information:
    - **Enable Product**: This is the status for the product.
    - **Attribute Set**: This refers to the group of attributes that are assigned to this product. We will cover this in detail in the next chapter.
    - **Product Name**: This is the name of the product.
    - **SKU**: This is the unique identifier of the product.
    - **Price**: This is the regular price of the product.
    - **Tax Class**: This refers to the tax rules associated to this product.
    - **Quantity**: This is the number of items in the inventory for the product.

- **Stock Status**: This is a setting to mark the product as **in-stock** or **out-of-stock**.
- **Weight**: This is the weight of the product (if applicable).
- **Visibility**: This marks the product as visible in the catalog and/or search.
- **Categories**: These set categories associated with the module.
- **Set Product as New From**: This marks the product as new in between the selected date.
- **Country of Manufacture**: This specifies the country of manufacture for the product.

- **Content**:
  - **Description**: This is the description of the product.
  - **Short Description**: This is a short version of the description for the product.

- **Configurations**:
  - **Create configurations**: This creates a configurable product. This will be described in a chapter later in the book.

- **Images and Videos**:
  - **Add video**: This can be used to add a video for the product.
  - **Browse to find or drag images here**: This is used to add multiple images to the product.

- **Search Engine Optimization**:
  - **URL Key**: This specifies the URL for this product. For example, if you specify `sample-product` as the URL Key, then the URL for the product will be `http://magento2-playground.dev/sample-product.html`.
  - **Meta Title**: This is the title meta tag for the product. This will be the title displayed in the search results in search engines, such as Google.
  - **Meta Keywords**: These are the keywords meta tag for the product. They are the keywords that the search engines will consider for the product detail page.

- **Meta Description**: This is the description meta tag for the product. This will be the description below the title in the search engine results.

- **Related Products, Up-Sells, and Cross-Sells**:
  - **Related Products**: The related products are a set of product recommendations that the customer may want to buy based on the product that he/she is currently viewing.

    Those products are displayed in the product detail pages, as shown in the following screenshot:

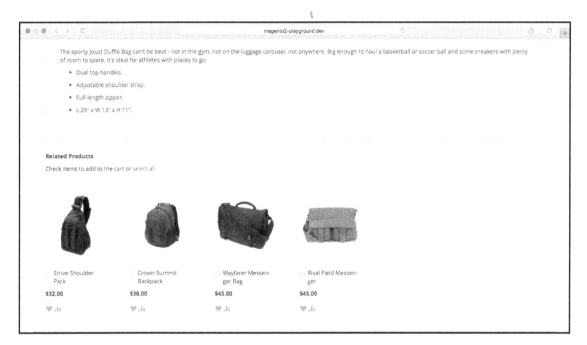

- **Up-Sell Products**: The up-sell products are more expensive products from the same product family. For example, if the customer is viewing a monitor, the up-sells will suggest more expensive monitors in the product detail page.

- The up-sells are associated to the current product and are displayed in the product detail page, as follows:

- **Cross-Sell Products**: Cross-sells are displayed to the customer in the shopping cart page. A cross-sell can be seen in the supermarket waiting line, right before placing the order. At that time, you will see products that the supermarket places in that specific location to try to convince you to buy more. Just like the supermarket, the cross-sell products in Magento are intended to convince the customer to buy more products before placing the order.

The cross-sell products are displayed in the shopping cart, as follows:

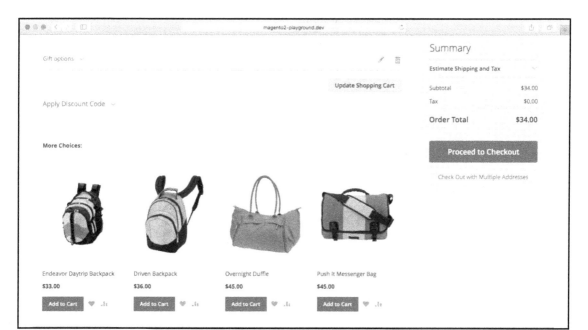

- **Customizable options**:
  - **Add Option**: This adds custom options to the product. The following field types are available for the customizable options:
    - Text field
    - Text area
    - File
    - Dropdown
    - Radio buttons
    - Checkbox
    - Multiple select
    - Date
    - Date and time
    - Time

- **Product in Website**:
  - **Websites**: If your Magento store has multiple views, you can set the product to be associated with specific views.

- **Design**:
    - **Layout**: This is used to set a specific layout for the product detail page:
        - **Empty**
        - **1 column**
        - **2 columns with left bar**
        - **2 columns with right bar**
        - **3 columns**
    - **Display Product Options In**: This sets a specific location for the product options:
        - **Product Info Column**
        - **Block after Info Column**
    - **Layout Update XML**: This adds custom XML configuration for the product layout, such us custom style sheets for the product detail page
- **Schedule Design Update**:
    - **Schedule Design From – To**: This is a schedule custom design to be applied in a specific range of dates
    - **New Theme**: This sets a specific theme for the product detail page on the scheduled date
    - **New Layout**: This sets a specific layout for the product detail page on the scheduled date:
        - **Empty**
        - **1 column**
        - **2 columns with left bar**
        - **2 columns with right bar**
        - **3 columns**
- **Gift Options**:
    - **Allow Gift Message**: This allows the customer to set a gift message on this product

- **Downloadable Information**:
    - **Is this a downloadable Product?**: This option is only available if the weight property for the product has been set to **The item has no weight**. You can add links and samples if the product is a downloadable product.

Now that we have reviewed all the fields for the **New Product** page, we will create our first product.

We will create a simple product with the following information:

General Information:

- **Enable Product: Yes**
- **Attribute Set: Default**
- **Product Name:** Red Shirt
- **SKU**: Red-shirt
- **Price**: $50.00
- **Tax Class: Taxable goods**
- **Quantity**: 100
- **Stock Status: In stock**
- **Weight**: 25 **lbs**
- **Visibility: Catalog, Search**
- **Categories: Default Category | Men | Tops**

Content:

- **Description**: This is the long description of the product
- **Short Description**: This is the short description of the product

- **Images and Videos**:
  - Upload two images for this product
    After filling this information for the product, click on **Save**. You will see the following message on screen:

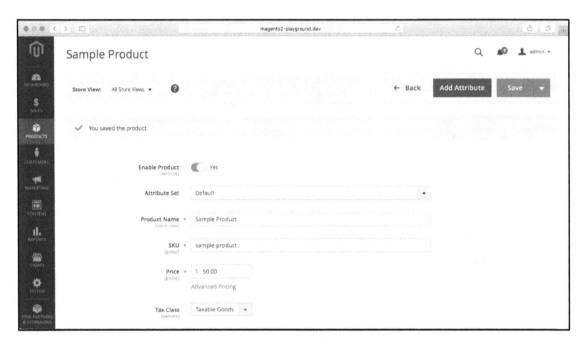

Now, it is time to see our product on the website.
First, go to the home page: `http://magento2-playground.dev/`.

Next, go to the **Men | Tops** category (the new product was associated with that category). You will see the new product as the first one in the grid:

If you click on that product, you will be redirected to the product detail page. There, you will see all the information that we added to the product in the new product form:

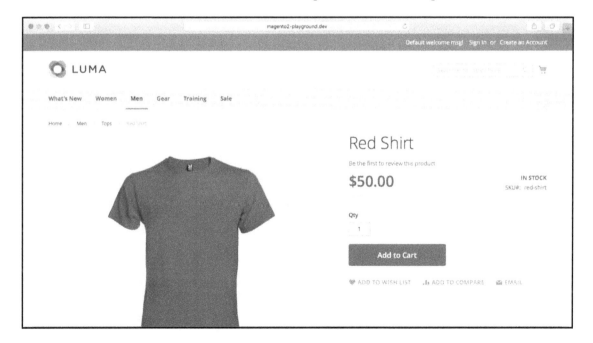

Working with images

In the last section, you created your first product in Magento 2. You might be wondering how you can assign different images for the product listing page, product detail page, and shopping cart. Magento 2 provides the ability to specify a different image for each of those locations, and we will cover this concept in this section.

If you go back and open the product that you created in the admin panel, you will see something similar to the following screenshot:

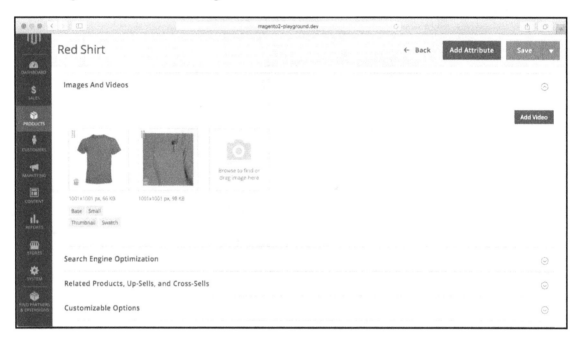

On the top of each image thumbnail, you will see two icons:

- **Eight dots in the top-left of the thumbnail**: You can simply drag and drop the thumbnails to set the order of the images on the product detail page
- **Trash icon in the bottom-left of the thumbnail**: You can remove the image by clicking on this icon

Below each image thumbnail, you will see the following things:

- General information for the image, such us the image size and resolution.

- Labels indicating the location of the image. These labels can be as follows:
    - **Base**
    - **Small**
    - **Thumbnail**
    - **Swatch**

Now, let's review each of the locations to understand what they mean:

- **Base image**: The base image is displayed as the main image on the product detail page. The zoom is activated if the uploaded image is larger than the image container.
- **Small image**: The small image is used in several places, including the product listing page, search results page, related products, and up-sells block.
- **Thumbnail**: The thumbnail image is displayed on the shopping cart page and the cross-sells block.
- **Swatch**: The swatch image is an illustrative image that represents a color, texture, or pattern for the product.

If you click on the image thumbnail, the **Image Detail** model will appear from the left with the configuration for that specific image, as seen in the following screenshot:

In the **Image Detail** model, you can update the following image configuration:

- **Alt Text**: The **Alt Text** is an attribute that is recommended for SEO. It helps the search engines to understand the content of your image. In addition, the **Alt Text** is displayed in the browser as a popover on mouseover.
- **Role**: You can associate the image with the specific roles that we described before, such as **Base**, **Small**, **Thumbnail**, and **Swatch**.
- **General Information for the Image**: This refers to **Image Size** and **Image Resolution**.
- **Hide from Product Page**: You can mark this image to not be displayed on the product detail page.

Working with Magento's pricing possibilities

You may have seen the **Advanced Pricing** link on the **New Product** page. If you haven't, you can see that link right below the **Price** field:

If you click on that link, the **Advanced Pricing** model will be displayed on screen, allowing you to set advanced pricing rules for the product:

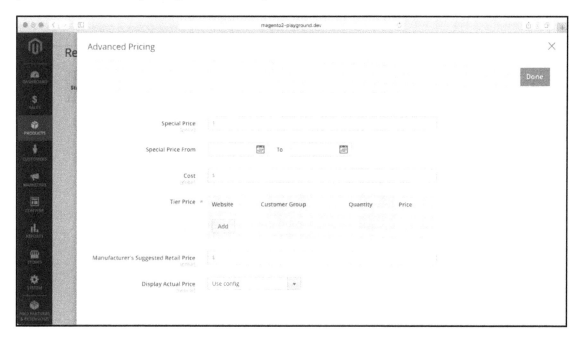

We will review each of the advanced pricing fields:

- **Special Price**: This refers to discounted price for a specific period of time. This is the way price is displayed in the product listing page:

And this is the way the price is displayed in the product detail page:

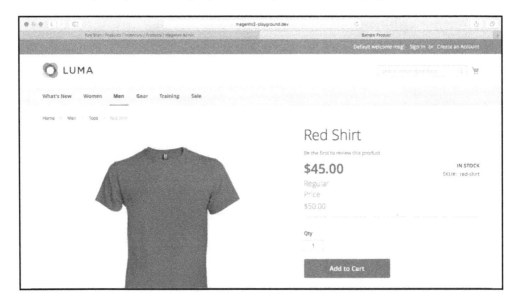

- **Cost**: This is the information for the administrator representing the cost of the product.
- **Tier Price**: This is the discounted price for the product based on the website, customer group, and purchased quantity.
- **Manufacturer's Suggested Retail Price**: This is the Minimum Advertised Price for the product.
- **Display Actual Price**: With this option, you can select where the **Manufacturer's Suggested Retail Price** (**MSRP**) should be displayed:
    - **On Gesture**: When this option is selected, the MSRP is displayed in the product listing and product detail pages. In addition, a **Click for price** link is added next to the MSRP price, which opens a popover that includes more information about the price of the product. This is what the **On Gesture** option looks like in the product listing page:

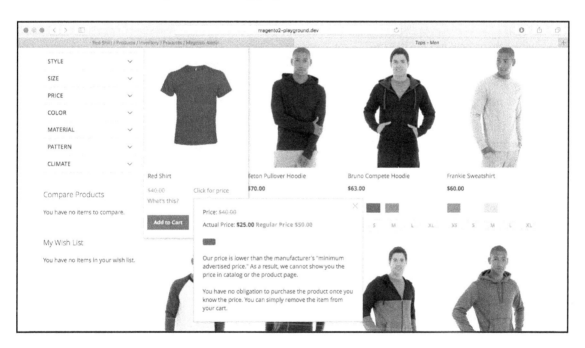

This is the way that option is displayed in the product detail page:

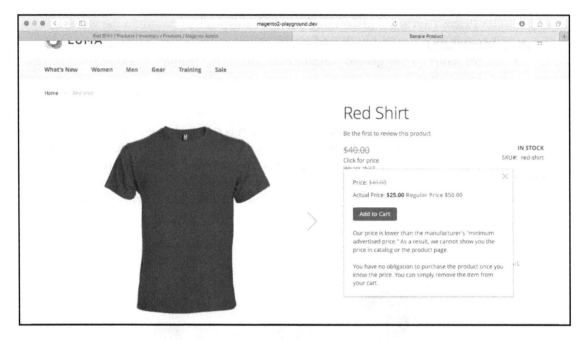

- **In Cart**: The final price is displayed in the shopping cart. The MSRP and a message are displayed in the product listing and product detail pages to notify the customer about the price information in the shopping cart. Here's how it looks on the product listing page:

And this is how it looks in the product detail page:

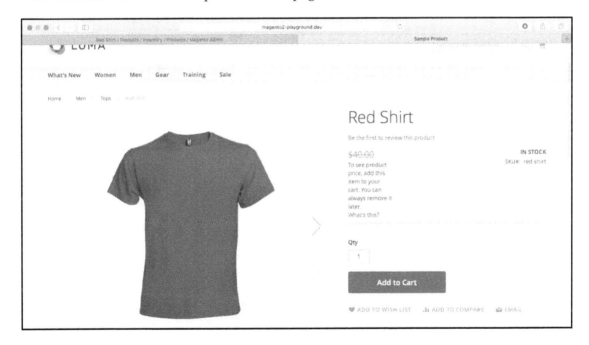

- **Before Order Confirmation**: The final price is displayed in the last step of the checkout. The MSRP and a message are displayed in the product listing, product details, and **Shopping Cart** pages to notify the customer about the price information in the checkout. Here's the way the MSRP and message are displayed in the product listing page:

Here is how it looks in the product detail page:

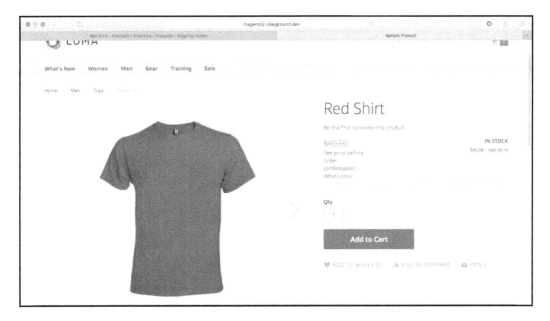

And here you can see the**Shopping Cart** page:

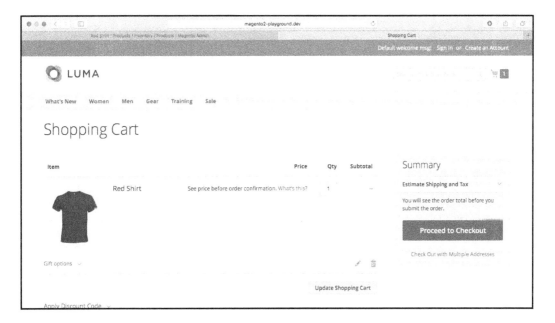

Summary

In this chapter, we learned how to add a new product, including setting up advanced pricing options and product images.

In the next chapter, we will cover attributes and attribute sets to add more information to your products.

5
Attribute Sets and Custom Attributes

Magento is a really flexible platform and allows the creation of different types of attributes for the products in the catalog.

In this chapter, we will cover the following concepts:

- Product attributes
- Attribute sets
- Associating attribute sets with products

Product attributes

An attribute is a property of a product, for example, the product color, the size, or the description. You can add, edit, or remove product attributes in Magento to customize your products. In order to manage the product attributes, you should go to the **STORES** | **Attributes** | **Product** section in the Magento admin panel.

In the following screenshot, you can see the location of the menu item for the **Product** attributes section:

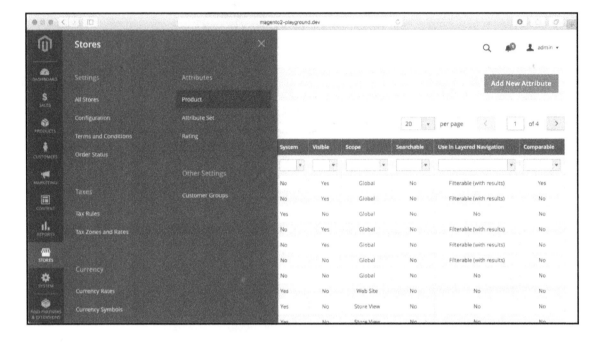

The **Product** attributes are part of the core of the catalog. Even though you can manage the attributes, you can't remove the system attributes that are included in Magento by default. In order to see a list of system attributes, you should filter the grid by **System: Yes**, as seen in the following screenshot:

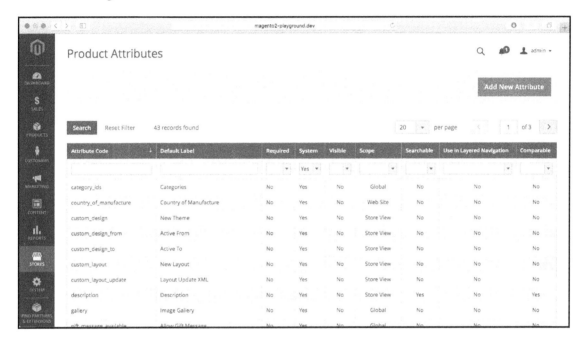

As you can see, there are 43 system attributes in Magento. You must be familiar with most of them since these attributes are part of the **New Product** form field that we reviewed in the last chapter.

Creating a product attribute

You can create custom product attributes in Magento to add custom information to the products in your catalog. You can see the **New Product Attribute** form by following these steps:

1. Click on **Add New Attribute** in the top-right of the **Product** attributes grid.
2. You will see the following form on screen:

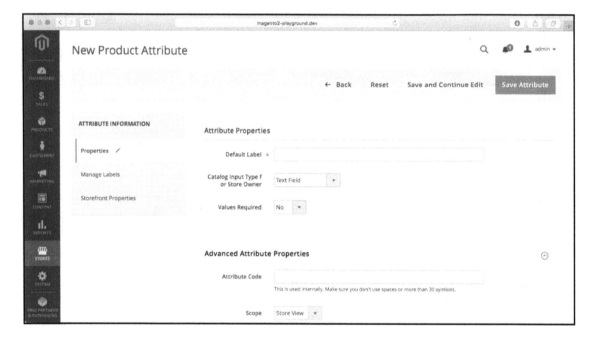

We will go through each of the fields on the form:

- **Properties | Attribute Properties**:
  - **Default Label**: This is the label that describes the new attribute during data entry.
  - **Catalog Input Type for Store Owner**: This sets the data type and input control for the **Product** attribute. It's important to mention that once the attribute type is created, it cannot be changed. The following options are available:
    - **Text Field**
    - **Text Area**
    - **Date**
    - **Yes/No**
    - **Multiple Select**
    - **Dropdown**
    - **Price**
    - **Media Image**
    - **Fixed Product Tax**
    - **Visual Swatch**
    - **Text Swatch**
  - **Values Required**: This defines whether the value for the **Product** attribute is mandatory or not.
- **Properties | Advanced attribute properties**:
  - **Attribute Code**: This specifies a unique identifier for the **Product** attribute for internal use. Only letters (a-z), numbers (0-9), and underscores are allowed for the code, and the first character should be a letter. The code must be less than thirty characters and it shouldn't contain any spaces.
  - **Scope**: This defines whether the attribute can be customized at a global, website, or store view level.
  - **Default Value**: This is the value that will be declared for the attribute by default during data entry.
  - **Unique Value**: This sets whether the value for this **Product** attribute should be unique within the context of scope setting. For example, SKU is a system attribute that must have a unique value identifying each product.
  - **Input Validation for Store Owner**: This sets validation for the attribute value when the product is created from the admin panel.

- **Add to Column Options**: This includes the attribute in the list of column options in the product grid.
- **Use in Filter Options**: This includes the attribute in the list of filter options in the product grid.

- **Manage Labels**:
  - **Manage Titles (Size, Color, etc.)**: This customizes the label for the **Product** attribute by store view. For example, if you have three store views with different languages, you can translate the label for each of the store views.

- **Storefront Properties**:
  - **Use in Search**: If **Yes**, the attribute will be included in the search queries and customers will be able to search in the catalog based on the values for the attribute:
    - **Search Weight**: If **Use in Search** is set to **Yes**, then this field will be displayed. You can set the priority for the search query by setting a number between **1** and **10**, where **10** has the highest priority.
    - **Visible in Advanced Search**: If **Use in Search** is set to **Yes**, then you can specify whether the **Product** attribute should be included in the **Advanced Search** form.

 Note: Including many attributes in the Magento search can slow down the search performance.

- **Comparable on Storefront**: Include the **Product** attribute in the **Compare Products** page.
- **Use in Layered Navigation**: If the attribute type is Dropdown, Multiple Select, or Price, you can add the attribute to the layered navigation (left sidebar) in the product listing page.
- **Use in Search Results Layered Navigation**: If the attribute type is Dropdown, Multiple Select, or Price, you can add the attribute to the layered navigation (left sidebar) in the search results page.

Note: Including many attributes in the Magento layered navigation can slow down the performance in the product listing and search result pages.

- **Position**: This sets the position for the attribute in the layered navigation in relation to other attributes in the block.
- **Use for Promo Rule Conditions**: This adds an attribute to the list of the available conditions for the promo rules.
- **Allow HTML Tags on Storefront**: This is used to define whether the attribute value can include HTML for formatting.
- **Visible on Catalog Pages on Storefront**: This includes the **Product** attribute in the **Additional Information** tab of the product detail page. This configuration is only applicable to simple and virtual products.
- **Used in Product Listing**: This includes attributes in the product listing page. This attribute configuration depends on the theme.
- **Used for Sorting in Product Listing**: This includes attributes in the **Sort By** option in the product listing page. This attribute configuration depends on the theme.

Now that we reviewed the **New Product Attribute** form, we are ready to create a custom attribute for the product that we created in the last chapter.

We will create a new product attribute for the **Red Shirt** that we created before–**Sleeve Length**.

Set the following information for the attribute in the **New Product Attribute** form:

- **Properties | Attribute Properties**:
  - **Default Label**: `Sleeve Length`
  - **Catalog Input Type for Store Owner**: Dropdown
  - **Values Required**: No

- **Manage Options (Values of Your Attribute)**: In the case of **Manage Options (Values of Your Attribute)**, since the input type for the attribute is **Dropdown**, we must specify the options, as seen in the following screenshot:

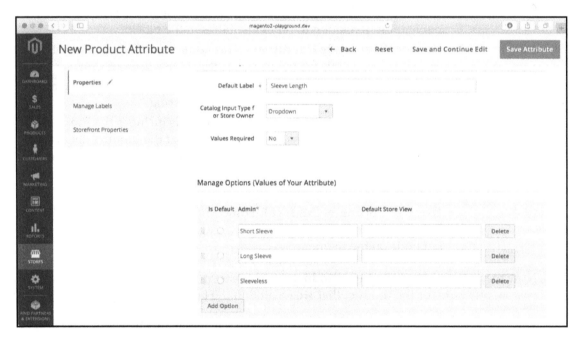

- **Properties | Advanced attribute properties**:
  - **Attribute Code**: `sleeve_length`
  - **Scope: Store View**
  - **Unique Value: No**
  - **Add to Column Options**: Yes
  - **Use in Filter Options**: Yes
- **Manage Labels**:
  - **Manage Titles (Size, Color, etc.) | Default Store View**: `Sleeve Length`
- **Storefront Properties**:
  - **Use in Search: Yes**
  - **Search Weight: 10**
  - **Visible in Advanced Search: Yes**
  - **Comparable on Storefront: Yes**

- **Use in Layered Navigation**: Filterable (with results)
- **Use in Search Results Layered Navigation**: Yes
- **Use for Promo Rule Conditions**: Yes
- **Allow HTML Tags on Storefront**: Yes
- **Visible on Catalog Pages on Storefront**: Yes
- **Used in Product Listing**: Yes
- **Used for Sorting in Product Listing**: Yes

When you have added all the information for the attribute, you should click on **Save Attribute** at the top-right of the screen.

You will see the following popup when the attribute is saved:

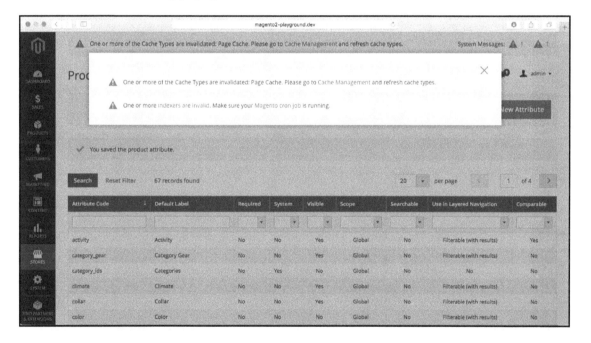

That message is notifying that a reindex is necessary for the database. Indexing is the way Magento prepares the data, such us Products and Attributes, to increase the performance of the store. When the data changes, a reindex is necessary to update the information in the database.

For example, when you change the price of a product, you must reindex the price change to show the updated price in the product detail page. Without indexing, Magento will have to calculate the price for every product on-the-fly, including all the calculations for the advanced price rules, promotions, and so on.

In order to avoid a manual reindex, you should set up a Magento cron job to run every minute. Since we didn't configure the cron job, we should manually run the reindex process.

In order to reindex, you can click on the **Indexers are Invalid** link on the popup from the latest screenshot or go to the **System | Tools | Index Management** menu item.

There, you will see a list of indexers, and you will see the **Index product EAV** indexer requiring the reindex, as can be seen in the following screenshot:

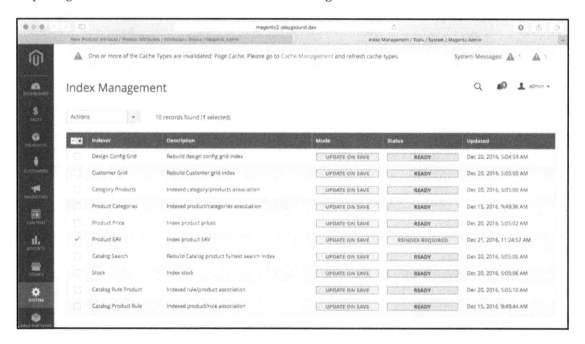

If the cron job is not running in your website, you can manually run the reindex from the Magento command-line tool:

1. Open the terminal and go to the project folder.
2. Run the following command:

```
php bin/magento indexer:reindex
```

You will see the following output from the command:

```
~/Projects/magento2-playground.dev » php bin/magento indexer:reindex
Design Config Grid index has been rebuilt successfully in 00:00:00
Customer Grid index has been rebuilt successfully in 00:00:00
Category Products index has been rebuilt successfully in 00:00:00
Product Categories index has been rebuilt successfully in 00:00:00
Product Price index has been rebuilt successfully in 00:00:02
Product EAV index has been rebuilt successfully in 00:00:01
Catalog Search index has been rebuilt successfully in 00:00:03
Stock index has been rebuilt successfully in 00:00:00
Catalog Rule Product index has been rebuilt successfully in 00:00:03
Catalog Product Rule index has been rebuilt successfully in 00:00:00

~/Projects/magento2-playground.dev » ▮
```

If you reload the page in the admin panel, you will see that the indexer does not require an update anymore:

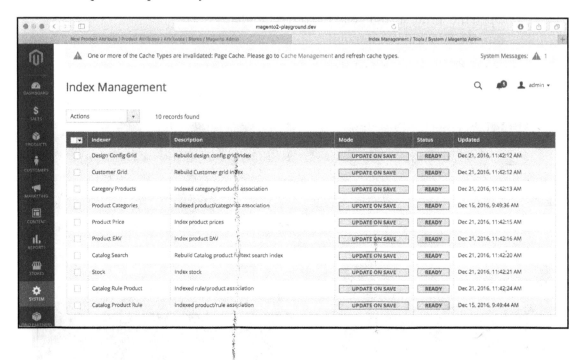

Attribute sets

As we saw in the preceding section, you can define new properties for the products by adding new attributes. When you create an attribute, it's not immediately available in the **New Product** form. For example, the **Sleeve Length** attribute that we created is not available yet when you edit the **Red Shirt** product or any other product.

Attributes are grouped by attribute sets. The attribute sets represent a list of attributes that are related to a specific product family. For example, the **Sleeve Length** attribute should be part of the **Shirt** attribute set. Therefore, that specific attribute for clothing is available only for products that are associated with the **Shirt** attribute set.

If you add a new attribute and you want the attribute to be available for most of the products, then you can associate it with the **Default** attribute set.

You can see a list of attribute sets by going to the next section in the admin panel, that is, **Stores** | **Attributes** | **Attribute Sets**, as shown:

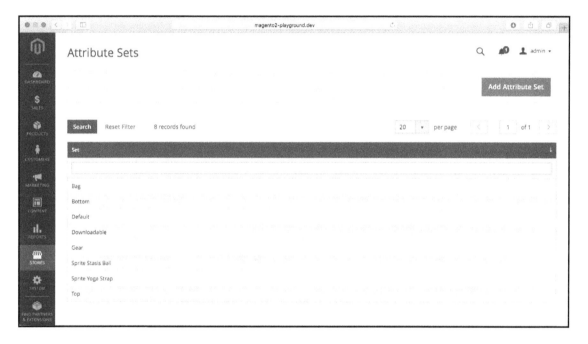

If you click on the **Default** attribute set, you will open the form to edit that attribute set specifically:

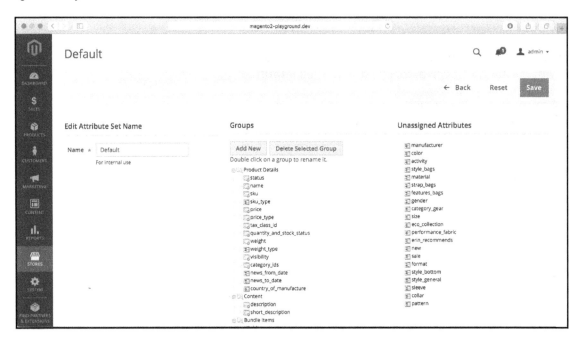

You will see a form with the following three columns:

- **Edit Attribute Set Name**: This updates the name for the attribute set.

- **Groups**: This specifies the list of attributes that are associated with this attribute set. These attributes are contained in different groups for easier product management.

- **Unassigned Attributes**: This is a list of attributes that are not associated with this attribute set. You can drag and drop the attributes from this list to the **Groups** list to associate them with an attribute set.

We will create the first custom attribute set for the **Shirt** that we created in the first chapter.

Go back to the **Attribute Sets** grid and click on **Add Attribute Set** in which you will be able to find the following:

- **Name**: Type in `Shirt` here
- **Based On**: You can select the attributes from an existing attribute set that will be included in the new attribute set by default. We will select the **Default** attribute set:

After clicking on **Save**, you will be redirected to the next page in the new attribute set creation process. Drag and drop the **sleeve_length** attribute from the **Unassigned Attributes** column to the **Groups** column to include the attribute that we created in the preceding section in the new attribute set:

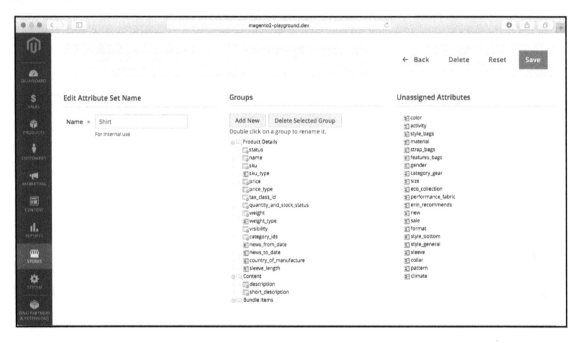

Click on **Save** to finish the attribute set setup.

If the cron is not configured, you will see the following message on screen:

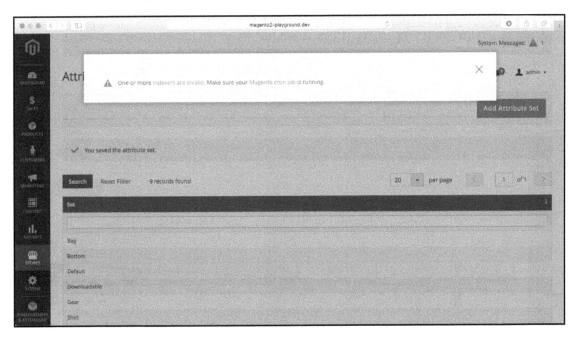

As we saw earlier, we should reindex the database using the Magento command-line tool:

```
php bin/magento indexer:reindex
```

Associating attribute sets with products

Now that we have a new attribute set that includes a new attribute, let's move on to associate the attribute set with a product.

1. Navigate to the **Catalog** page, that is, **PRODUCTS | Catalog**.
2. Select the **Red Shirt** that we created in the last chapter:

3. Select **Shirt** from the **Attribute Set** dropdown:

4. You will see the new attribute in the **New Product** form. Take into account that the attribute will be displayed in the group that you selected when you moved the attribute from the **Unassigned Attributes** to the **Group** column in the preceding section. Select **Short Sleeve** from the list:

5. Click on **Save** at the top-right of the screen.

Now, the product has been associated with the new attribute set and contains the new attribute that we created in this chapter.

Let's see how it looks on the product details page:

Now, let's check whether the attribute can be seen in different locations as well.

Compare Products page:

The **Compare Products** page shows the attribute as follows:

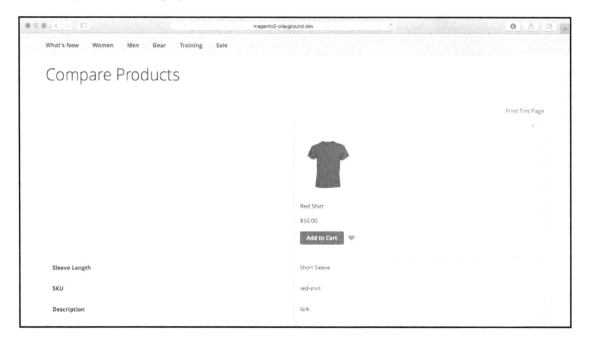

The following is a view of the layered navigation in the product listing page (left sidebar):

Take a look at the following view of the layered navigation in the search results page (left sidebar):

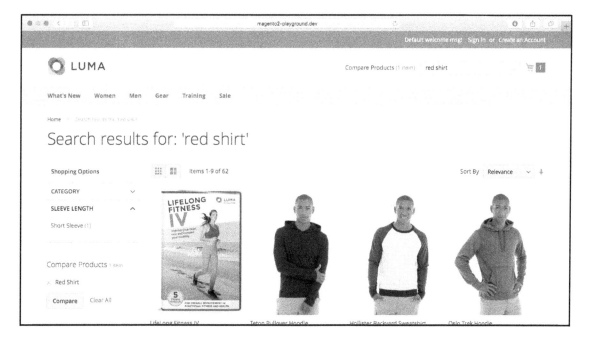

The following screenshot displays the **Sort By** dropdown in the product listing Page:

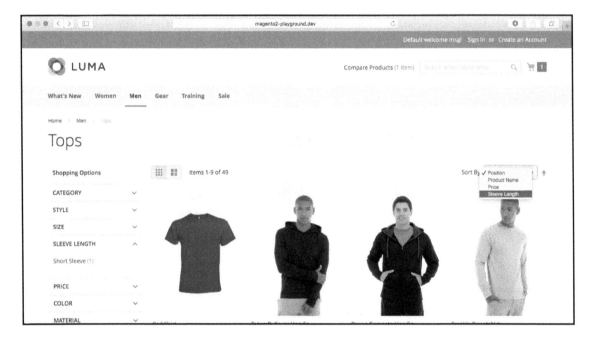

The **Advanced Search** form
(`http://magento2-playground.dev/catalogsearch/advanced/`) is as follows:

The following screenshot shows the promo rule conditions in the admin panel:

Summary

In this chapter, we created an attribute and an attribute set, and associated the attribute set with a product. Now you are able to customize products by adding new properties through attributes and grouping them by attribute sets. In the next chapter, we will go through the different product types in Magento and the product relations.

6
Product Types

We will go through the following sections in this chapter:

- Introduction to the different product types in Magento
- Simple products
- Configurable products
- Grouped products
- Virtual products
- Bundle products
- Downloadable products

Introduction to the different product types in Magento

One of the most important features of Magento are the product types. The different product types allow you to set up products in different ways, for example, by offering a group of products in the product details page or by allowing the customer to buy downloadable products.

There are six product types in Magento:

- Simple products
- Configurable products
- Grouped products
- Virtual products
- Bundle products
- Downloadable products

You can see the list with the help of the following steps:

1. Go to the following section in the admin panel:
   Products | Inventory | Catalog
2. Click on the arrow inside the **Add Product** button on the top-right corner of the screen:

It's important to mention that Magento can set the correct product type based on the information from the product. For example, if you add a new product with no weight, Magento will create a virtual product.

We will review each of the product types including examples to show the way these products are created and how they are displayed on the Storefront.

Simple products

This is the most basic and popular product type. Simple products are products that are not customizable by the customer, for example, a book that has a specific set of properties, such as pages and author.

When you click on the **Add Product** button in the **Products | Inventory | Catalog** page, you are actually adding a simple product. This means that we have already added a simple product, **Red Shirt**:

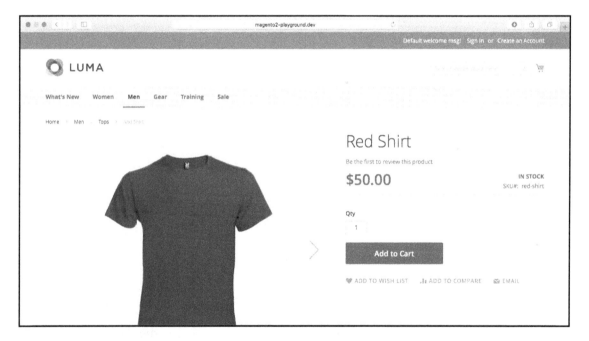

We are going to complete the information for that product by adding the color and size available as attributes.

Go to the **STORES** | **Attributes** | **Attribute Set** page, select the **Shirt** attribute set that we created in the previous chapter, and edit that attribute set as follows:

1. Drag and drop the following attributes from the **Unassigned Attributes** list to the **Groups** list:

   - **color**
   - **size**
   - **gender**

   As a result, the attribute set will include the attributes from the page shown in the following screenshot:

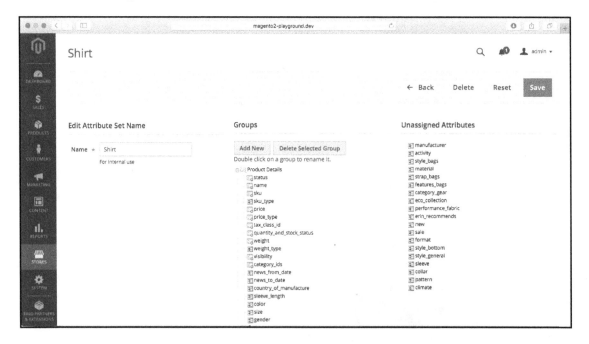

2. The next step is editing the **Red Shirt** product by going to the **PRODUCTS** | **Inventory** | **Catalog** page and selecting that product from the grid.

You will see the new attributes that we included in the previous step:

3. We will update the information on the product as follows:

- **Product Name:** Red Shirt - Men - L
- **Color: Red**
- **Size: L**
- **Gender: Men**

4. Next, click on **Save**, and then re-index the catalog as we saw in the previous sections.

If we go back to the Storefront and open the product details page for the **Red Shirt** product, we will see the updated product showing all the information that we need for that simple product:

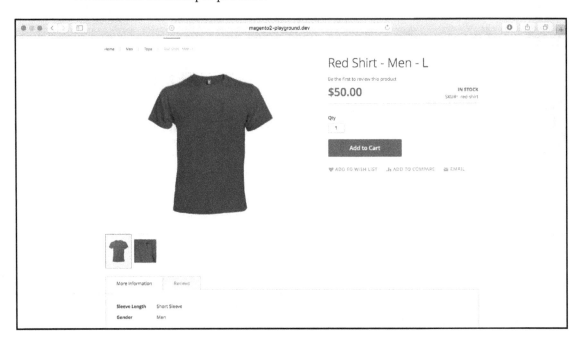

Configurable products

Now, imagine if you have shirts in different sizes and colors. If you add all of them as simple products and display them in the catalog, the result would be several red shirts that look exactly the same in the product listing page. It would be difficult to find the shirt that you need, and it would be visually confusing.

Fortunately, Magento allows you to create products that can be configured from the product details page. In our example, you will have a shirt product with multiple options to select the color and size from the product details page.

This is the concept of a **configurable product**. Configurable products are made of simple products that are associated. When the customer chooses a combination in the configurable product, the customer is actually choosing which simple product will be added to the cart from the configurable product page.

Let's create the first configurable product: Shirt. In order to do that, we will follow these steps:

1. Go to the **PRODUCTS** | **Inventory** | **Catalog** page and select **Red Shirt**.
2. Click on the arrow inside the **Add Product** button, and select **Configurable Product**.

3. Set the following information for the configurable product:

   General Information:

   - **Enable Product: Yes**
   - **Attribute Set: Shirt**
   - **Product Name:** Shirt
   - **SKU:** shirt
   - **Price:** $50
   - **Tax Class: Taxable Goods**
   - **Quantity:** 100
   - **Stock Status: In Stock**
   - **Weight:** 1 lbs.

- **Visibility: Catalog, Search**
- **Categories: Default Category** | **Men** | **Tops**
- **Sleeve Length:** None
- **Color:** None
- **Size:** None
- **Gender:** None

Configurations:

- **Create Configurations**: Click on this button to open the **Create Product Configurations** window, as shown in the following screenshot:

4. Follow these steps to create different configurations (simple products) for the configurable product:

- **Step 1: Select Attributes**: Choose the configurable attributes for the product. The list of configurable attributes from the selected attribute set will be displayed in the list. Select **color** and **size**, and click on the **Next** button on the top-right corner of the screen:

- **Step 2: Attribute Values**: In this step, you can select which combinations will be available for the product. Each unique combination will create a new simple product.

    Select the following colors:

    - **Black**
    - **Blue**
    - **Green**
    - **White**

Then, select the following sizes:

- **S**
- **M**
- **L**
- **XL**

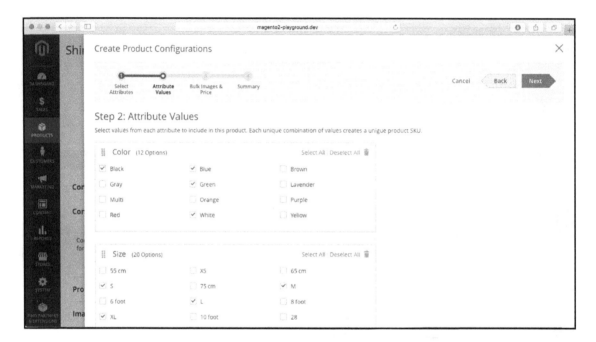

- **Step 3: Bulk Images, Price, and Quantity**: Right below the title of the step, you will see the number of simple products that will be created based on the selection you made in the previous step.
  In this step, you can customize the images, price, and quantity for each of the product combinations.

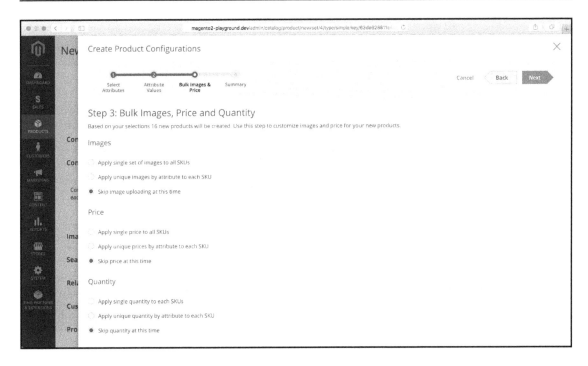

You can choose from the following options:

Images:

- **Apply a single set of images to all SKUs**: If you select this option, you will be able to upload a set of images that will be applied to all the product combinations.
- **Apply unique images by attribute to each SKU**: By selecting this option, you will be able to select one of the configurable attributes, and then upload an image for each attribute value. For example, we can select **Color**, and then upload the image for each color of the product.
- **Skip image uploading at this time**: You can skip this step and upload the images later.

Price:

- **Apply single price to all SKUs**: Set the same price for all product combinations.
- **Apply unique prices by attribute to each SKU**: You can select a specific configurable attribute, and then set a price for each configurable attribute value. For example, given a specific watch model, the price will be different depending on the case material: white gold versus stainless steel.
- **Skip price at this time**: You can skip the pricing on the wizard.

Quantity:

- **Apply single quantity to all SKUs**: Set the same quantity for all the product combinations.
- **Apply unique quantity by attribute to each SKU**: Just like the price, you can select a configurable attribute and set the stock depending on the attribute value. In the example that we gave before, you may have 10 gold, and 150 stainless steel watches.
- **Skip quantity at this time**: You can skip this step on the wizard.

For this example, we will apply the following settings:

Images:

- **Apply unique images by attribute to each SKU**: Select **Color** as a configurable attribute, and upload an image for each of the colors

Price:

- **Apply single price to all SKUs**: Set $50 as the price for all product combinations

Quantity:

- **Apply single quantity to each SKUs**: Set 100 as the quantity for all product combinations
- **Step 4: Summary**: In this step, you can review all the product combinations that will be created for the configurable product. Once you review the list of products, you can click on **Next** to finish the product configuration:

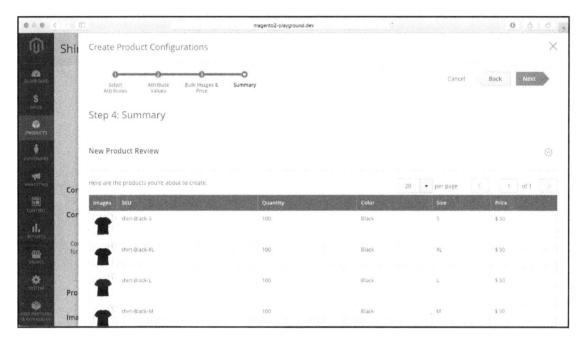

5. Lastly, we will upload an image for the configurable product. The process is the same as the one we followed when we uploaded images for **Red Shirt** in Chapter 4, *Creating Your First Product, Images, Inventory, and Prices*.

For this configurable product, I created a special image showing the different colors in just one image:

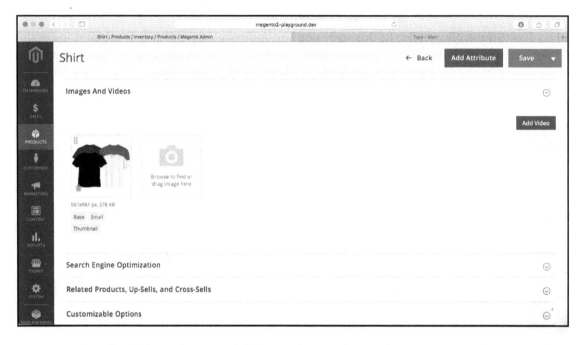

6. Finally, click on **Save** to add the product to the catalog. We are ready to save the configurable product and review how it looks on the Storefront.

Here is how the configurable product looks in the product listing page:

If you click on the blue swatch, you will see that the image is updated in the product listing page:

Here is how the product looks in the product details page:

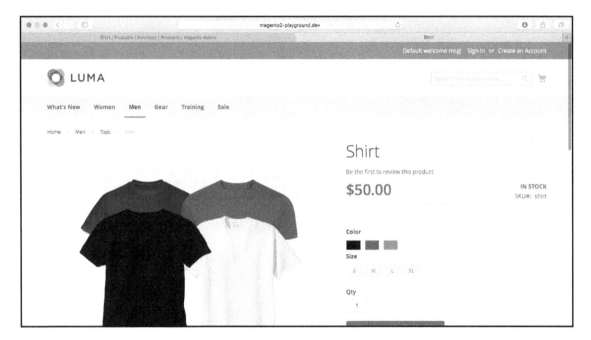

And just like the product listing page, the image of the product is updated when you click on a color swatch:

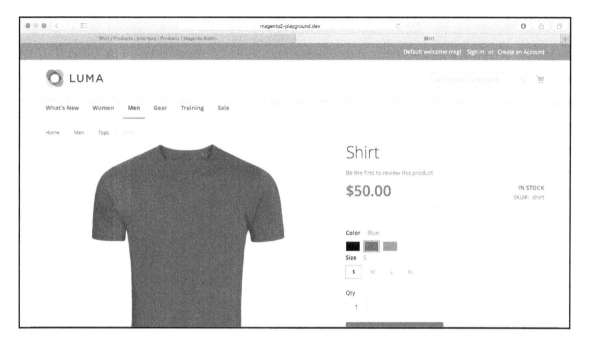

If you add the configurable product to the cart, then you will see the details for the selected combination in the cart item:

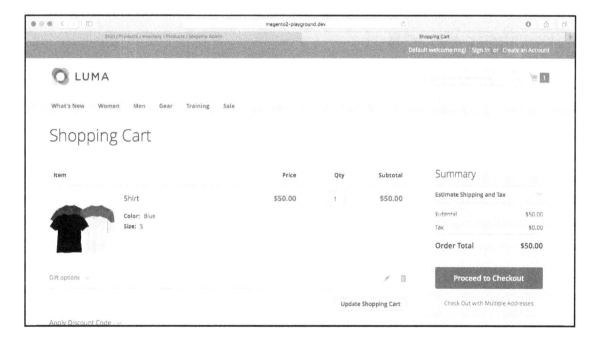

Here, you can see the details in the checkout page:

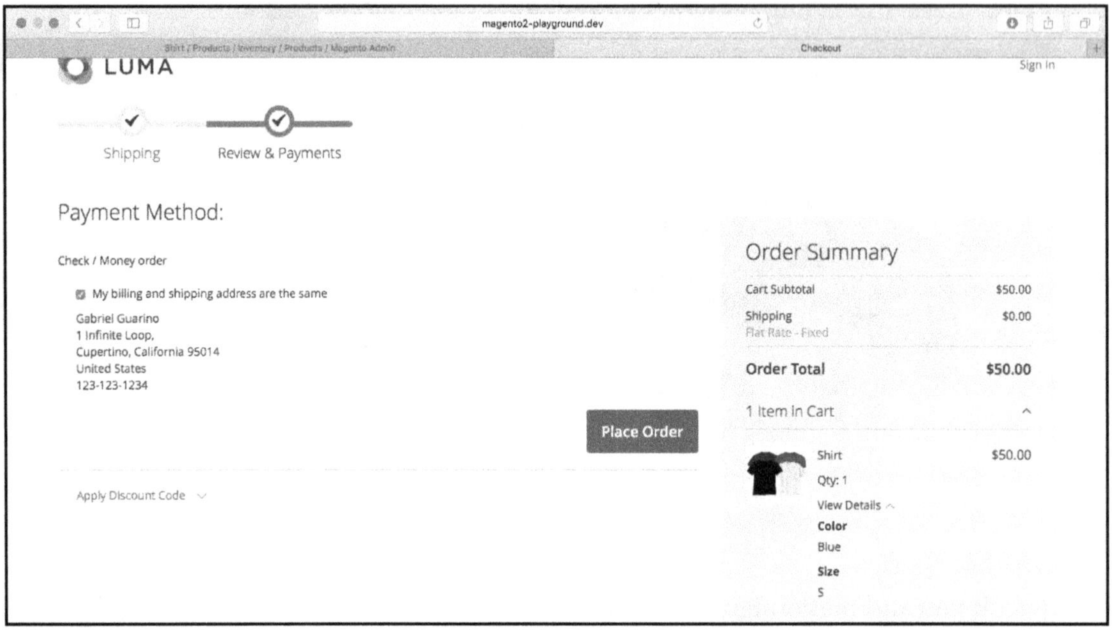

Grouped Product

Grouped Product are simple products that are presented in the product details page together. Let's say you want to display accessories in addition to the main product:

- Digital camera
- Memory card
- Tripod

By doing this, you have the opportunity of presenting one set of products together to increase the probability of selling all of them.

There are multiple ways of doing this and the **Grouped Product** type is one of them.

Let's create a **Grouped Product**:

1. Go to the **PRODUCTS** | **Inventory** | **Catalog** page.
2. Click on the arrow inside the **Add Product** button and select **Grouped Product**:

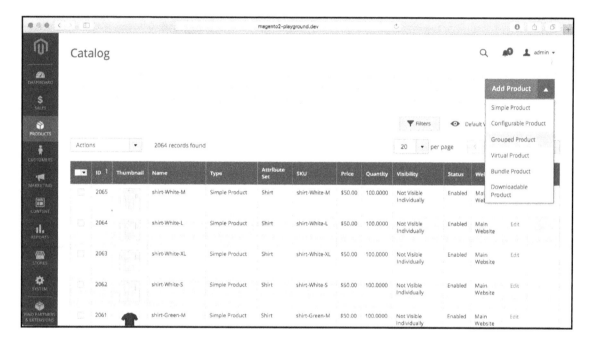

3. Once you open the **New Product** page, you will see that the form is almost identical to the other forms that we have seen before in that page.
   The difference is that there is a new section in the form: **Grouped Products**

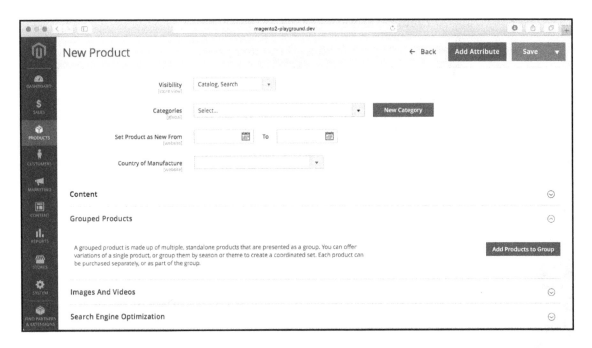

4. If you click on the **Add Products to Group** button, the following window will be displayed in the page:

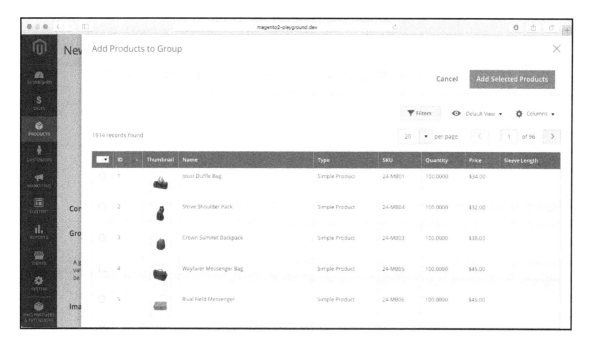

5. For the grouped product, we will select the existing products from the Magento 2 sample data.

Select the products with the following IDs:

- **1**: **Joust Duffle Bag**
- **4**: **Wayfarer Messenger Bag**
- **8**: **Voyage Yoga Bag**

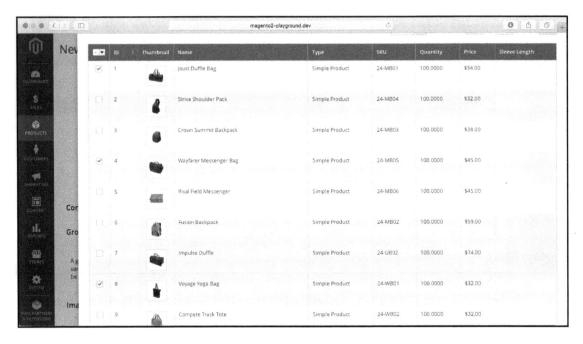

6. Now, click on the **Add Selected Products** button on the top-right corner of the screen. Finally, append the additional information for the product as well:

General Information:

- **Enable Product**: Yes
- **Attribute Set**: **Default**
- **Product Name**: Bag Collection
- **SKU**: bag-collection
- **Stock Status**: **In Stock**
- **Visibility**: **Catalog, Search**
- **Categories**: **Default Category | Collections | Erin Recommends**

For the grouped product, I uploaded each of the images from the associated simple products:

7. Now, save the product by clicking on the **Save** button on the top-right corner of the screen.

Let's see how the product is displayed on the Storefront. We have associated the product with the **Erin Recommends** category. You can't access that category from the main navigation menu; you should click on the banner in the middle of the page that contains the **Shop Erin Recommends** link:

You will find the product in the last page of the product listing page:

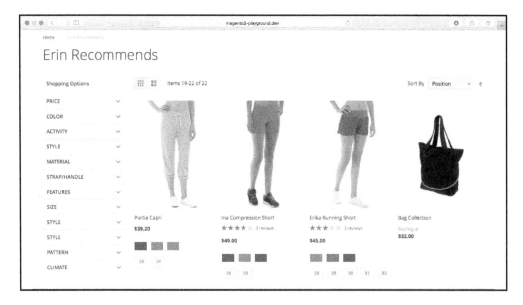

Let's click on the product to review the product details page:

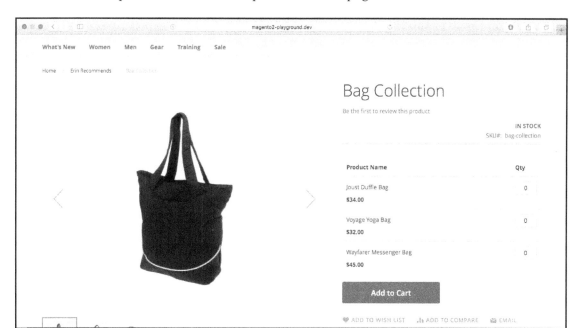

As you can see on the page, you can add any number of items from each of the products. If you add some of these products to the cart, they will be individually displayed there.

Bundle Product

A **Bundle Product** is very similar to a **Grouped Product**; the only difference is that the customer can choose the products to include into the bundle. The final price will depend on the options that have been chosen.

A very good example of **Bundle Product** is a computer. The customer will be able to choose which components to include in the computer; for example, the customer will be able to select between 8 GB and 16 GB for memory or between 256 GB and 512 GB for SSD storage. The price of the product will be updated at the time of the selection, depending on the selection.

We will create a **Bundle Product** using the Magento 2 sample data:

1. Go to the **PRODUCTS** | **Inventory** | **Catalog** page.
2. Click on the arrow inside the **Add Product** button and select **Bundle Product**.

   You will see that the form will be similar to the other products but there will be a new section, **Bundle Items**:

3. We will add the following information on this product:

   General Information:

   - **Enable Product**: Yes
   - **Attribute Set**: Default
   - **Product Name**: Bags
   - **Dynamic SKU**: Yes
   - **Dynamic Price**: Yes
   - **Stock Status**: In Stock
   - **Dynamic Weight**: Yes
   - **Visibility**: Catalog, Search
   - **Categories**: Default Category | Collections | Erin Recommends

By enabling the **Dynamic Price**, **Dynamic Weight**, and **Dynamic SKU**, the customer will get the information for each of the options in the product details page.

Ship Bundle Items:

With this setting, you can specify if the bundle products will be shipped together or separately.

- **Ship Bundle Items**: Together

4. Now, click on **Add Option** in that section:

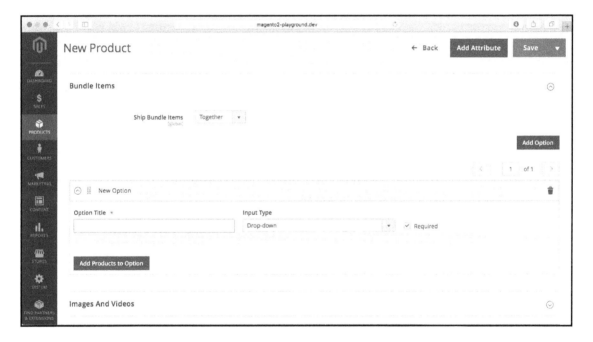

The following screen will be displayed:

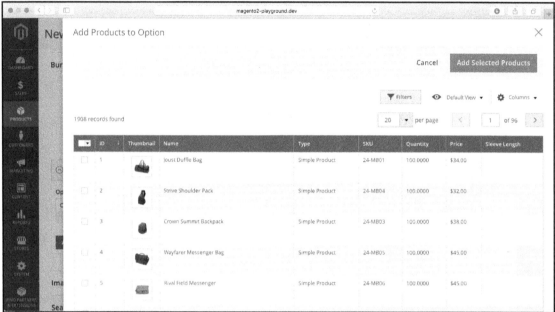

Here, you can set the **Option Title**, **Input Type** (**Drop-down**, **Radio Buttons**, **Checkbox**, or **Multiple Select**), and set whether the option is mandatory or not. Each of the options in a bundle product will have a set of products to select. You can add those products to the option by clicking on the **Add Product to Option** button.

We will set the following information for the option:

- **Option Title:** `Choose your collection`
- **Input Type: Radio Buttons**
- **Required**: Yes

5. Now, if you click on **Add Product to Option**, the following modal will be displayed:

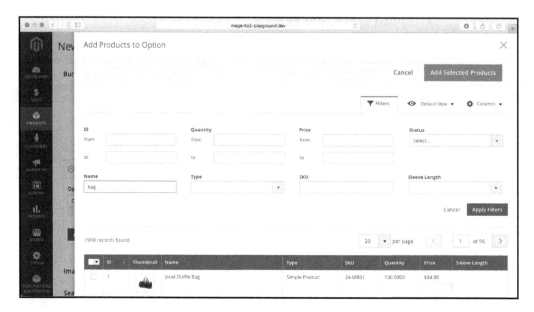

Filter the grid to show bags by using the **Name** filter, as follows:

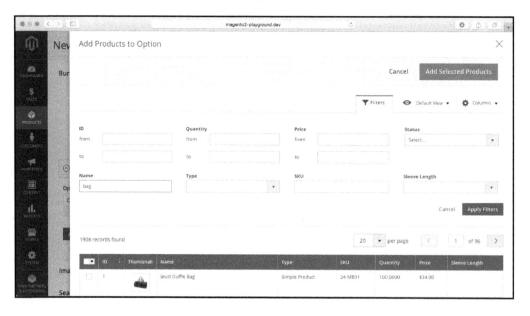

We will select all the products from the filtered grid:

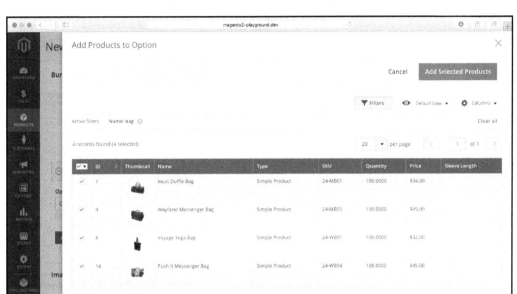

6. Click on **Add Selected Products** to associate the products, and then, set the default quantity to 1 for the bundled items, as you can see in the following screenshot:

7. We will associate an image from one of the bundled items for our new product:

8. Finally, click on **Save** to save the bundle product.

Let's review the new product on the Storefront. This is how the product looks in the product listing page:

Here is how the product is presented in the product details page:

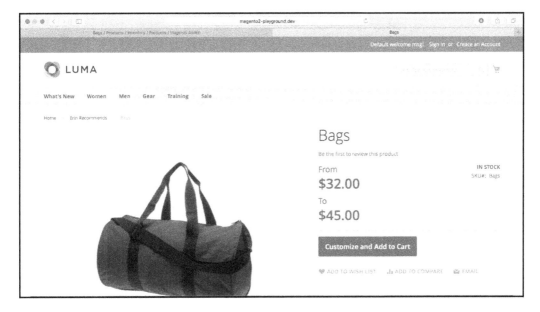

If you click on **Customize and Add to Cart**, a smooth scroll will be performed in the page to reveal the section, as follows:

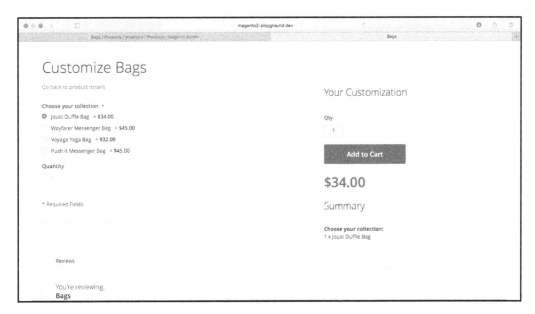

Virtual Product

Magento allows you to create non-tangible products for your catalog, such us memberships or professional services. These products can be displayed individually or included as part of grouped or bundle products.

Virtual products are very similar to the simple products in Magento, the only difference being that the virtual products don't have weight as an attribute and they don't require shipping information.

We will create a **Virtual Product** by following these steps:

1. Go to the **Products | Inventory | Catalog** page.
2. Click on the arrow inside the **Add Product** button and select **Virtual Product**.
3. We will set the following information for this product:

    General Information:

    - **Enable Product: Yes**
    - **Attribute Set: Default**
    - **Product Name:** Membership
    - **SKU:** membership
    - **Price:** $100
    - **Tax Class: Taxable Goods**
    - **Quantity:** 50
    - **Stock Status: In Stock**
    - **Visibility: Catalog, Search**
    - **Categories: Default Category | Collections | Erin Recommends**

4. Add a sample image for this product:

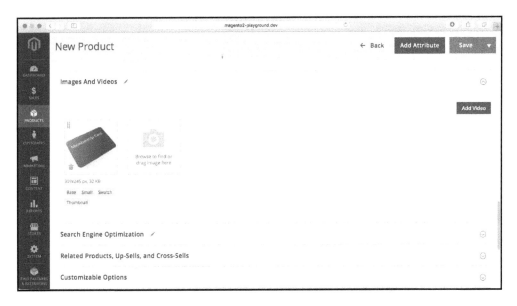

5. Click on **Save** to finish the setup for the virtual product.

Now, let's review how the product looks on the Storefront. Here is the product listing page:

Here is the product details page:

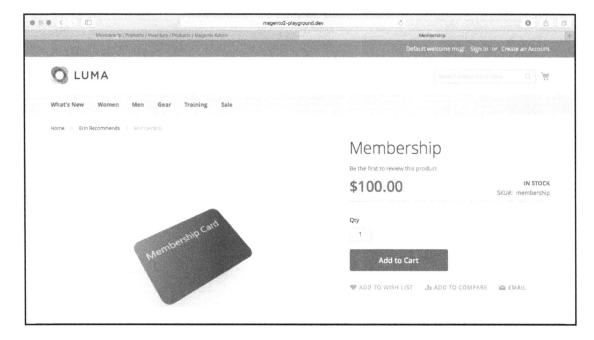

Downloadable Product

A **Downloadable Product** is a digital file that can be sent to a downloadable file, for example, e-books, software, music videos, and so on.

Since the downloadable file is not available before purchase, you can add samples to the product details page, such as the introduction for the e-book, a trial version for the software, or a short clip for the music video.

Let's create a **Downloadable Product** by following these steps:

1. Go to the **Products | Inventory | Catalog** page.
2. Click on the arrow inside the **Add Product** button and select **Downloadable Product**.

As you can see in the following screenshot, the downloadable product form has a special section named **Downloadable Information**:

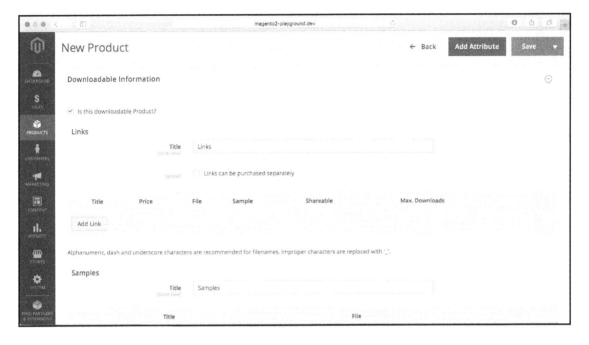

3. We will set the following information for this product:

General Information:

- **Enable Product**: Yes
- **Attribute Set**: Default
- **Product Name**: Sample Training Program
- **SKU**: sample-training-program
- **Price**: $25
- **Tax Class: Taxable Goods**
- **Quantity**: 100
- **Stock Status: In Stock**
- **Visibility: Catalog, Search**
- **Categories: Default Category | Collections | Erin Recommends**

4. Add a sample image for this product:

5. You can now add the specific details for the downloadable product. The **Downloadable Information** section contains the following:

- **Links**: This allows you to specify the downloadable links for this product. The links are displayed when the product is purchased.
- **Samples**: This allows you to add samples for the downloadable product that will be displayed in the product details page.

6. Let's add a link and a sample for the downloadable product. Click on **Add Link** in the **Links** container, and set the following information:

- **Title**: Sample Link
- **File: URL** | http://url.dev/file
- **Sample: URL** | http://url.dev/sample
- **Shareable: No**
- **Max. Downloads**: 100

As you can see in the details, you can set a sample for the individual links as well.

If you set the **Shareable** setting to **Yes**, then the customer will receive the link through an e-mail and will be able to share the link with other people.
If you set the **Shareable** setting to **No**, the customer will have to log in to the customer account in order to access the download link.

Finally, you can set a limit to the number of downloads, and you have a checkbox to set unlimited downloads as well, as you can see in the following screenshot:

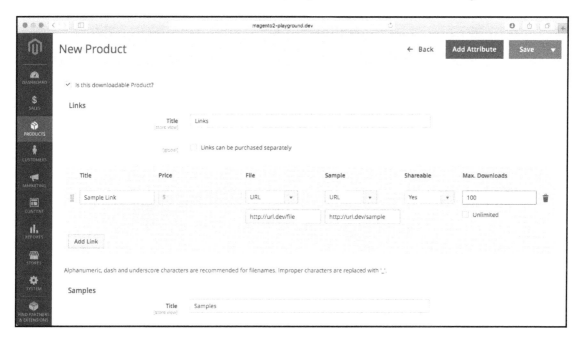

7. Now, let's add a sample for the product in the **Samples** container:

   - **Title**: Product Sample
   - **File**: **URL** – http://url.dev/product-sample

8. Finally, click on **Save** to finish the downloadable product setup.

We will review the downloadable product now, going through each of the pages from the product details page to the customer account:

- Product listing page:

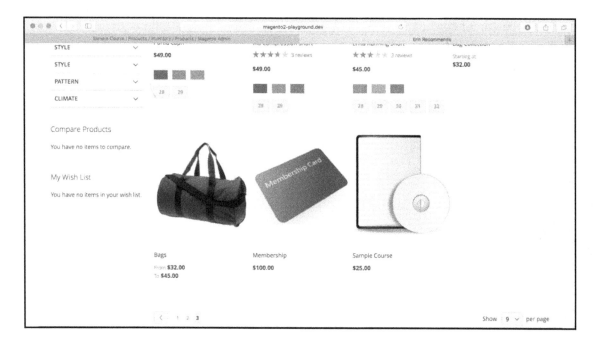

- Product details page:

- Shopping Cart:

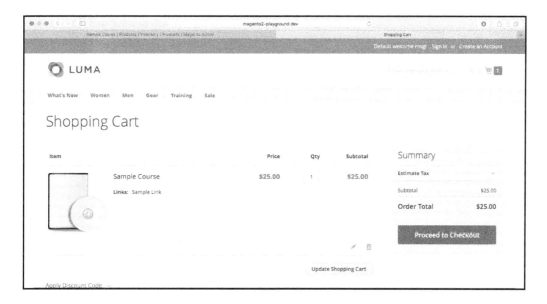

- Checkout:

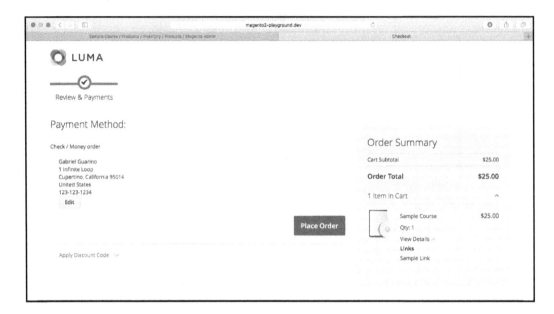

- Customer account:

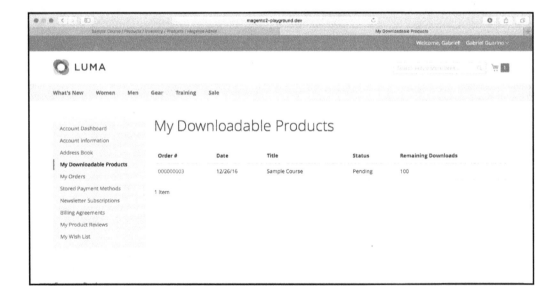

Summary

In this chapter, you learned about the different product types in Magento and you created a sample product for each product type.

In the next chapter, we will go through the process of managing categories in Magento 2 to be able to set up our main navigation menu and the category tree for our stores.

7
Categories

We will cover the following concepts in this chapter:

- Categories
- Hierarchy
- Top navigation

Categories

Magento provides a way of organizing your catalog into different categories and subcategories. You can organize your catalog internally in the admin panel and offer to the customers a clear way of browsing your products on the Storefront.

You can manage the categories in your store by going to the **PRODUCTS | Inventory | Categories** section in the admin panel:

Once that section is loaded in the admin panel, you will see the category tree on the left, and the form to add and the edit categories on the right:

On top of the category tree, you will see two buttons:

- **Add Root Category**: You can add root categories. This is useful to set up multiple store views, for example, a store for clothing and another store for electronics and computers. These stores will be separated store views, each one of them with a specific catalog contained in different root categories. An example of two root categories can be seen in the following screenshot:

- **Add Subcategory**: You can add a subcategory for the current category. In the preceding screenshot, the **Alternative Store** root category was selected, so if we click on **Add Subcategory**, then the subcategory will be created, as you can see in the following screenshot:

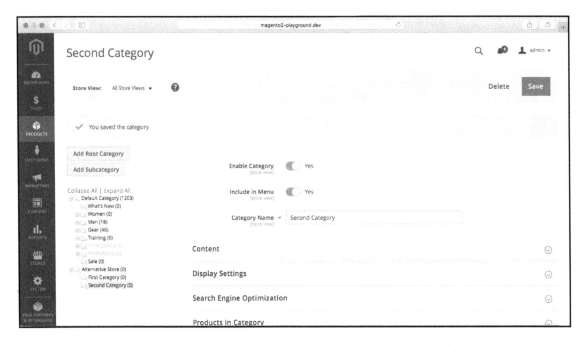

We added a root category and a subcategory, but we haven't reviewed the form to create them. We will create a new category, and we will go through the process step by step:

1. Click on the **Default Category** in the category tree to select it:

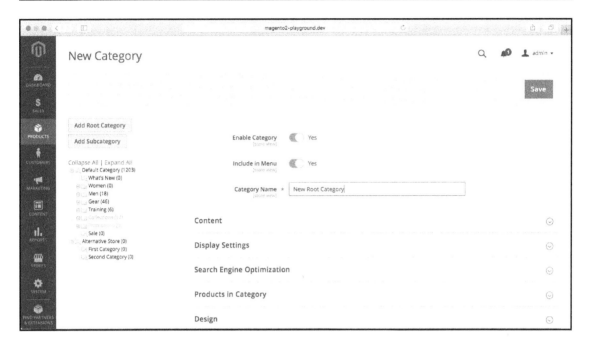

2. Click on **Add Subcategory** on the top-left corner of the screen.

3. Add the following information to the top section of the form:
   - **Enable Category**: **Yes**
   - **Include in Menu**: **Yes**
   - **Category Name**: Sample Category

These fields are self-explanatory. The **Include in Menu** field allows you to set whether the category should be included in the main navigation menu in the Storefront or not:

4. Set the following information for the **Content** section:
   - **Category Image**: Add a banner image for the category, as shown in the following screenshot:

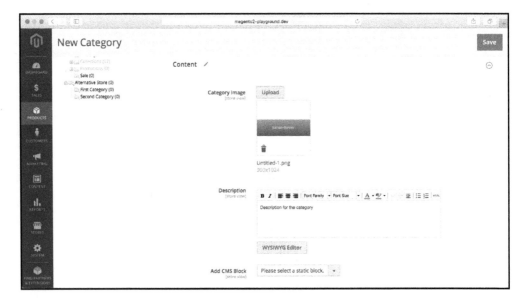

- **Description**: Add a sample description for the category
- **Add CMS Block**: You can add a static block to be displayed in the category

5. Set the following section in **Display Settings**:

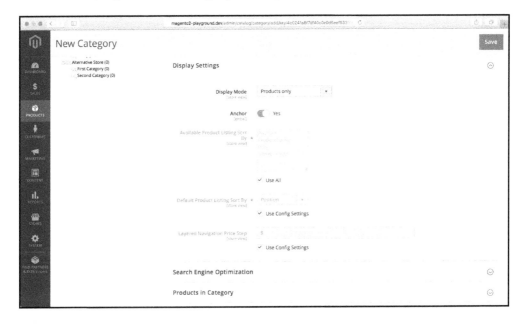

In this section, you can set:

- **Display Mode**: You can choose between showing only products, only the selected static block, or both. For this category, we will select **Products only**.
- **Anchor**: If you select **Yes**, then the category will have a layered navigation filter on the left sidebar. The layered navigation is the block that lets you filter the category by attribute, for example, by color or size. We will choose **Yes** for this category.

6. Next, we will find the **Search Engine Optimization** section:

The following settings are available in this section:

- **URL Key**: You can set the specific URL key for the category. We will leave this empty for this category, and Magento will create the URL key based on the category title.
- **Meta Title**: You can set the title meta tag for search engine optimization.
- **Meta Keywords**: You can set the keywords meta tag for search engine optimization.
- **Meta Description**: You can set the description meta tag for search engine optimization.

We will leave the fields for **Meta Title**, **Meta Keywords**, and **Meta Description** empty, and Magento will assign the meta tags based on the category title.

7. You can select the products that will be associated with this category in the **Products in Category** section:

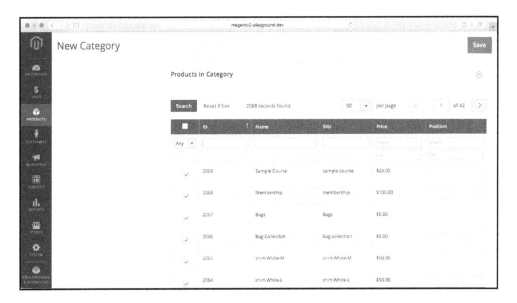

As per the preceding screenshot, select all the products that we created in the previous chapter.

8. The next section is **Design**. Just like the products, you can set a specific design for the categories as well:

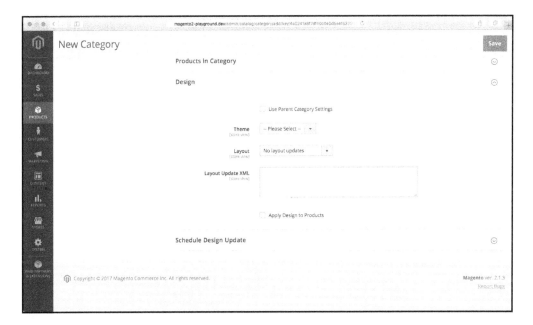

We will go through each of the fields, but we will keep the default values for all of them:

- **Use Parent Category Settings**: If you click on this checkbox, the category will inherit the design configuration from the parent category
- **Theme**: You can choose a specific theme for the category
- **Layout**: You can set a specific layout for the category:
    - **Empty**
    - **1 column**
    - **2 columns with left bar**
    - **2 columns with right bar**
    - **3 columns**
- **Layout Update XML**: Add a custom XML configuration for the category layout, such as a custom style sheet
- **Apply Design to Products**: If you click on this checkbox, the associated products will inherit the design configuration from this category

9. The section at the end of the form is **Schedule Design Update**. Here, you can specify a range of dates for the design update from the previous section. We will leave this empty as well for this category.
10. Click on **Save** to add the new category.

When the category is saved, you will see the message confirmation and the category as a child of **Default Category**:

If you go to the Storefront, you will see the new category in the main navigation menu:

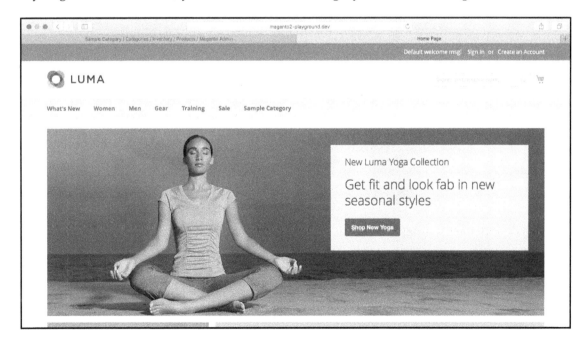

If you go to that category, you will see the configuration and the products that we set in the category form before:

Hierarchy

As we have seen before, you can set the hierarchy for the categories by selecting the parent category before creating the subcategory. Magento allows you to manage the hierarchy for the categories easily, and we will review how to update the category tree to change the parent and child categories.

On the category tree, you will see that there is a plus icon next to some of the categories:

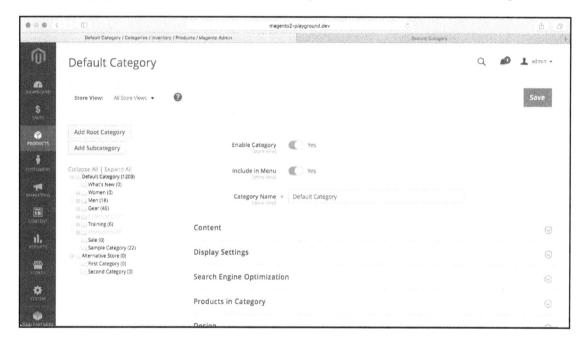

If you click on any of the plus icons, you will be able to expand that category to reveal its subcategories:

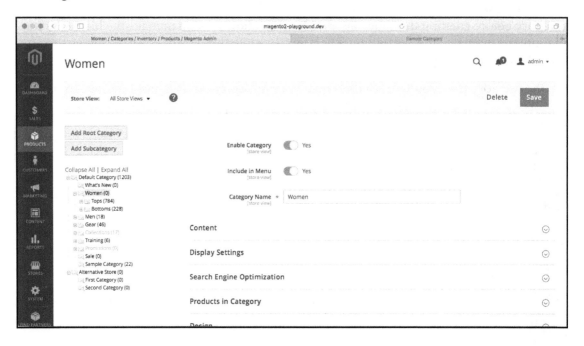

Now, let's say we want to change the hierarchy for the category tree by moving the **Sample Category** to become a child category of the **Woman** category.
If you want to do that, Magento allows you to simply drag and drop the category, just like you do in your favorite operating system to manage your folders.

Let's go ahead and drag the **Sample Category** from its current location and drop it on top of the **Women** category.

You will see the following message on screen:

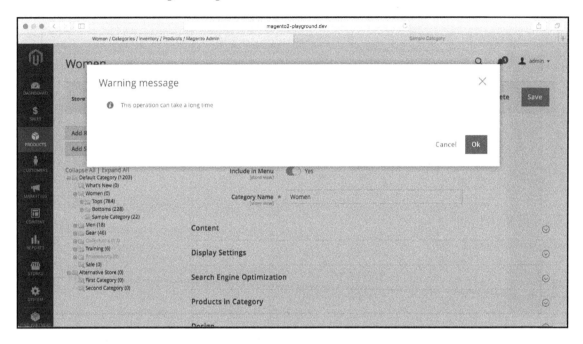

The process of updating the hierarchy for the categories takes a lot of resources for Magento, and that is why a warning is presented on screen. Let's move forward and press **Ok** to proceed with the operation.

Once the category is moved, you will see the confirmation message and the updated category tree on screen:

Now, if you go to the Storefront, you will see the updated navigation menu on the screen:

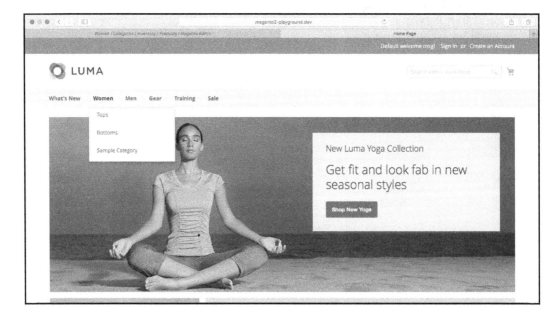

Top navigation

Let's take another look at the category tree in the admin panel:

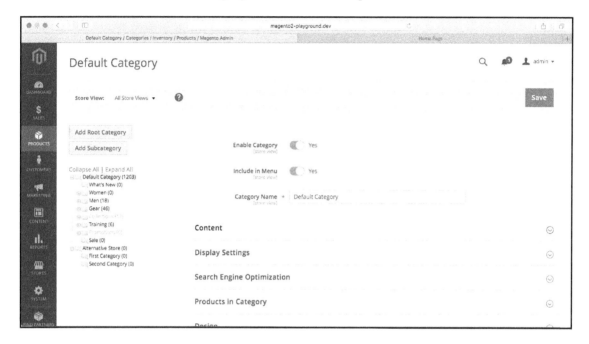

As you can see there, the color for some of the categories is light gray. This means that these categories are disabled, and that is why **Collections** and **Promotions** are not visible in the main navigation menu in the Storefront.

Even though that is correct, there could be a second reason why a category is not visible in the main navigation menu. If you look at the preceding screenshot, you will see that there is an **Include in Menu** setting in the form. It is a very important setting since you can keep the category enabled but not included in the main navigation menu.

Let's go ahead and select **Sample Category**, which we created before. Once you are there, update the **Include in Menu** setting to **No**, as shown in the following screenshot:

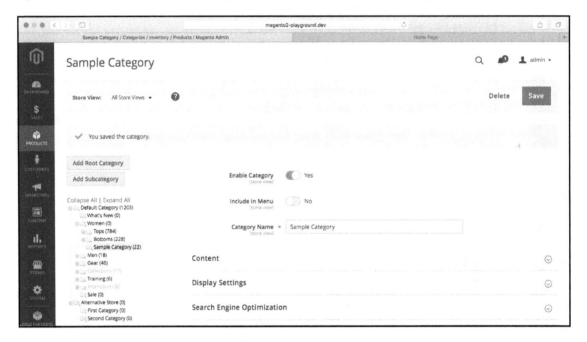

If you go to the Storefront now, you will see that the **Women** menu item is not including the **Sample Category** submenu item in the dropdown:

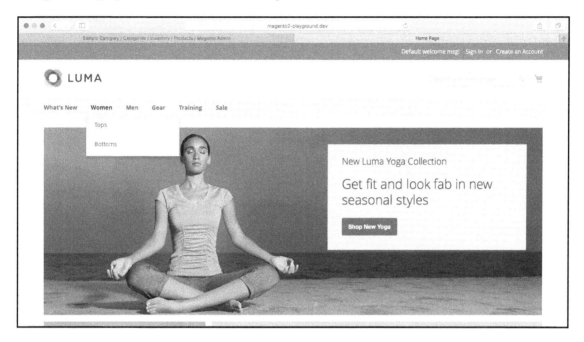

This allows you to specify the menu items that you want to keep visible in the main navigation menu, which is really important to customize the way your catalog is presented to the customer on the Storefront.

Summary

In this chapter, you learned to manage the categories in your Magento store and now you can associate products into different categories and update the main navigation menu. In the next chapter, we will cover CMS pages, blocks, and widgets to continue customizing your store.

8

CMS Pages, Blocks, and Widgets

In this chapter, we will cover the following topics:

- CMS Pages
- Static blocks
- Widgets

CMS Pages

If you are wondering whether you can add additional pages with static content, this is the right section for you. We will cover the process of managing static pages in Magento, such as *Privacy Policy* or *Terms and Conditions*, allowing you to create additional pages to add more information to your store.

You can manage these pages from the **CONTENT** I **Elements** I **Pages** section in the admin panel:

If you go to the section, you will see the list of pages that are currently available in your store:

As you can see in the previous screenshot, there are six pages included in the Magento 2 sample data. One important aspect of CMS Pages is the **URL Key**, which is unique for each page from the same store view.

You can access the CMS Pages by combining the Base URL for the store and the URL Key. For example, to access the **About us** page, you should go to
`http://magento2-playground.dev/about-us`.

You will see the following page on the screen:

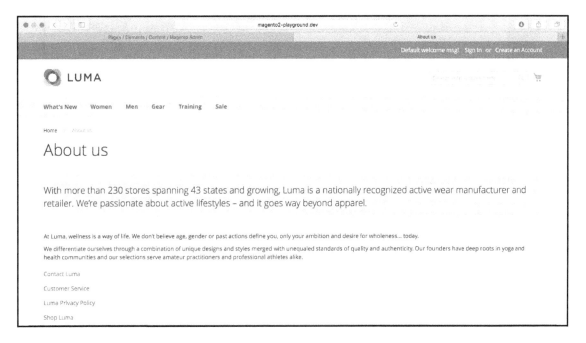

Now, let's say you want to edit the page to update the subtitle. Then, you should click on **Select** on the row for that page in the pages grid and click on **Edit**:

You will be redirected to the following form:

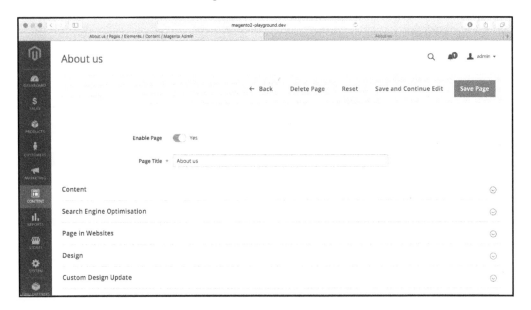

Let's go through each of the fields in the form:

- **General:**
  - **Enable Page**: Set the page to be visible in the Storefront.
  - **Page Title**: This is the title for the CMS Page. You will be able to see the title for the page in the admin grid, and it will be the `Title` meta tag and the title in the breadcrumbs as well.

- **Content:**
  - **Content Heading**: This will be the title on the Storefront, right below the breadcrumbs
  - **WYSIWYG Editor**: You can edit the content for the page using the WYSIWYG editor

- **Search Engine Optimization:**
  - **URL Key**: You can set the specific URL key for the CMS Page
  - **Meta Title**: You can set the title meta tag for search engine optimization
  - **Meta Keywords**: You can set the keywords meta tag for search engine optimization
  - **Meta Description**: You can set the description meta tag for search engine optimization

- **Page in Websites:**
  - **Store View**: The page will be accessible from the selected store views

- **Design:**
  - **Layout**: Set a specific layout for the CMS page:
    - Empty
    - 1 column
    - 2 columns with left bar
    - 2 columns with right bar
    - 3 columns
  - **Layout Update XML**: Add custom XML configuration for the page layout

- **Custom Design Update:**
  - **From – To**: Schedule custom design to be applied in a specific range of dates
  - **New Theme**: Set a specific theme on the scheduled date

- **New Layout**: Set a specific layout on the scheduled date:
  - Empty
  - 1 column
  - 2 columns with left bar
  - 2 columns with right bar
  - 3 columns

We will edit the **About Us** page by updating the following fields:

- **General:**
  - **Page Title:** `About this company`
- **Content:**
  - **Content Heading:** `The company`
  - **WYSIWYG Editor:** Replace `230 stores` with `300 stores` and add an image below the subtitle

Now, if you try to access the same page as before, you will see the changes that we made:

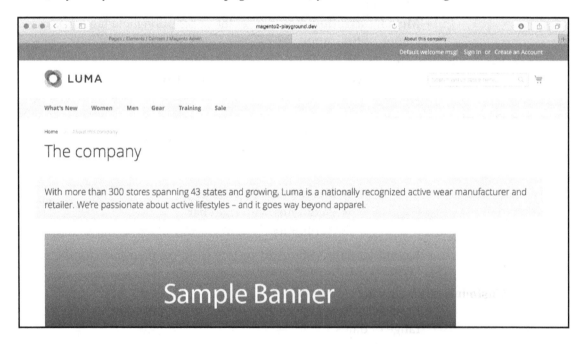

In order to add a new CMS Page, you should go to the pages grid (**CONTENT** | **Elements** | **Pages**), and click on the **Add New Page** button on the top-right corner of the screen:

The form is the same as the one we saw before when we edited the **About Us** page, so it's really easy to add a new page as well:

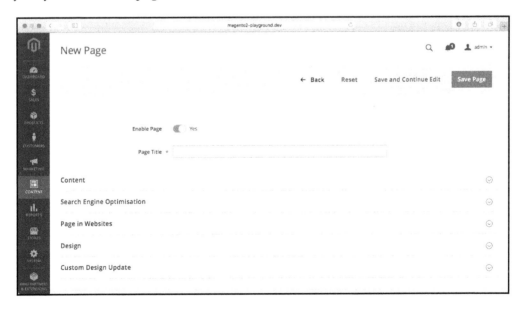

Static blocks

If you have information that you want to display in different places, for example, a promotional banner, or the *Business Hours* for your business location, then you should have a way of editing the information from one section in the admin panel and implementing it in different areas of your websites.

Magento allows you to do the same through static blocks. Static blocks are a powerful way of managing content in your Magento store as you can add HTML content to display in different pages and manage them from the static blocks section in the admin panel.

You can access the static blocks section through the **CONTENT** I **Elements** I **Blocks** menu item in the admin panel:

There, you will see the following grid with the existing blocks:

There are 18 static blocks included in the Magento 2 sample data. Let's review the static block **Training Block**. Click on **Select** on the row of that static block in the **Blocks** grid and click on **Edit**:

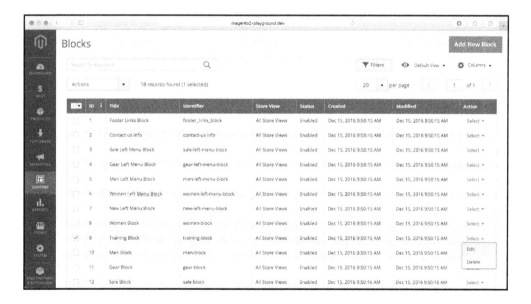

You will be redirected to the following form:

As you can see, the form is simpler than New/Edit page from the CMS Pages. There are a few fields:

- **Enable Block**: Set the static block to be active in order to be included in other pages
- **Block Title**: Title for the static block
- **Identifier**: Unique identifier for the static block
- **Store View**: The page will be visible in the selected store views
- **WYSIWYG Editor**: You can edit the content of the static block using the WYSIWYG editor

This is the banner included in the **Training** category page. You can see the banner if you click on the **Training** category in the main navigation menu:

The Static Blocks can be included in the following places:

- Template files in the theme (included programmatically)
- Categories
- CMS Pages and other static blocks through widgets

Widgets

Widgets are modules that can be included in different pages to display the information based on different configurations through different widget types.

The following widgets are available in Magento for content management:

- CMS Page Link
- CMS Static Block
- Catalog Category Link
- Catalog New Products List

- Catalog Product Link
- Catalog Products List
- Orders and Returns
- Recently Compared Products
- Recently Viewed Products

You can manage your widgets by going to the **CONTENT** | **Element** | **Widgets** section in the admin panel:

There are 18 widgets included in the Magento 2 sample data. As you can see in the following screenshot, all of them are CMS Static Blocks that are included in different places on the Storefront:

We will create a new widget by clicking on the **Add Widget** button on the top-right corner of the screen. The following form will be displayed:

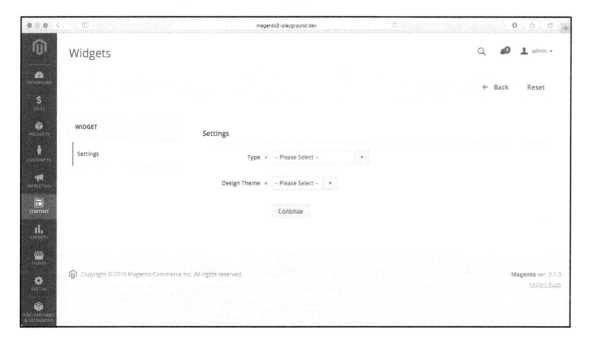

As you can see, the first step is to select the widget type and the design theme. For this example, we will choose the **Catalog Products List** widget in **Type**. In the **Design Theme** dropdown, you should select the theme that is currently applied to your store. Since we are using the Luma theme, we will select it as an option in the dropdown:

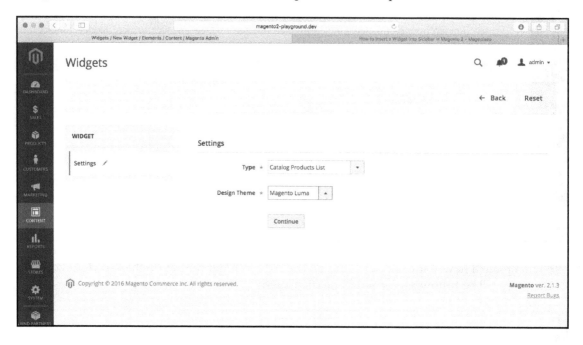

In the next step, you will see two tabs on the left side of the screen:

- **Storefront Properties**
- **Widget Options**

The first tab contains the same form for all the widget types. The form for the second tab, **Widget Options**, depends on the **Widget Type** that you selected in the previous step.

Let's review all the fields from the **Storefront Properties** tab:

- **Type**: This field is non-editable and displays the widget type that has been selected in the previous step.
- **Design Package/Theme**: This field is non-editable and displays the theme that has been selected for the widget in the previous step.
- **Widget title**: This is the title of the widget for reference.

- **Assign to Store Views**: The widget will be visible in the selected store views.
- **Sort Order**: This is the order of widgets if there are multiple widgets in the same container.
- **Layout Updates**: You can select the place where the widget will be displayed. You can add as many places as you need, and you can also manually add the widget to other pages later, such as categories, CMS Pages, and more.

The **Widget Options** form depends on the widget type, so I suggest you review all the widget types to see the configuration of all of them.

For our widget, we will set the following information in the **Storefront Properties** tab:

- **Widget Title**: `Sample products`
- **Assign to Store Views**: **All store views**
- **Sort Order**: `0`
- **Layout updates**:
    - **Display on**: **Anchor Categories**
    - **Categories**: **All**
    - **Container**: **Main Content Top**

For the **Widget Options** tab, we will set the following information:

- **Title**: `List of Sample Products`
- **Display Page Control**: **No**
- **Number of Products to Display**: `10`
- **Cache Lifetime (Seconds)**: `Leave empty for default value`
- **Conditions**: You can select which products will appear in the list based on the conditions that you select. We will select the following condition:
    - **SKU is...**[select the products that we created before by clicking on the blue window icon]

You can see the conditions for the widget in the following screenshot:

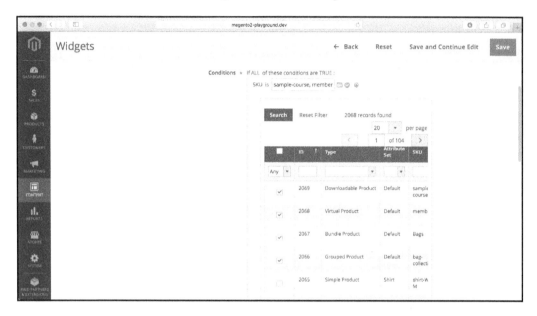

Finally, click on **Save** to enable the widget. You will see Magento notifying that you need to refresh the cache:

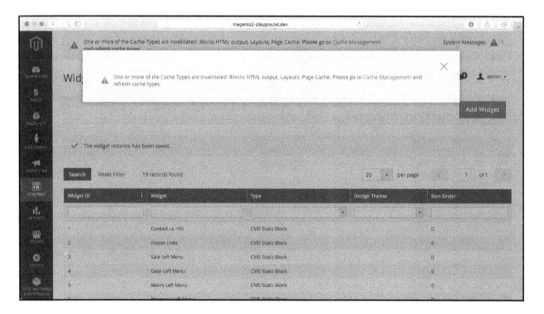

You should clear the cache types from the **Cache Management** page as we saw before. After that, you will see the widget in the anchor categories, for example, **Men** | **Tops**:

Summary

In this chapter, you learned how to manage the content in your Magento store, including CMS Pages, static blocks, and widgets. In the next chapter, we will review how to manage the scope of your websites, stores, and store views, and we will review how to configure the locale options in your Magento store.

9
Managing Scope and Locale Settings

In this chapter, we will cover:

- Magento scopes – websites, stores, and store views
- Reviewing how adding store views affects the catalog and CMS
- Languages

Magento scopes – websites, stores, and store views

One of the most important features of Magento is the ability to create multiple stores from a single Magento instance. Magento has implemented a hierarchical system that includes four levels:

- Default/global
- Website
- Store/store group
- Store view

The most common scenario of multistore configuration in Magento is found in retailers that separate their catalog by store view as follows:

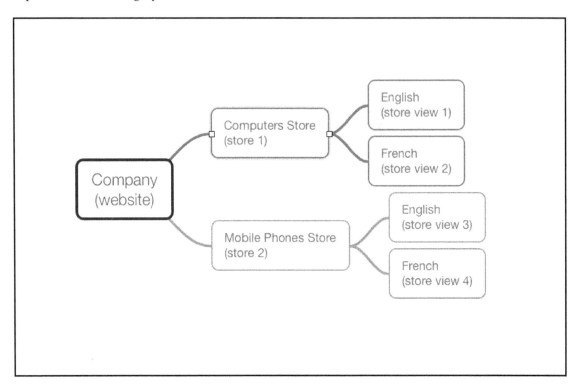

In the preceding example, the company has a website, but each product family has its own store to target different customers. Finally, each store has its own store views to be able to display the content in different languages.

With a single instance of Magento, you can implement a multistore configuration using:

- Multiple languages
- Multiple domain names
- Different categories

You can see the store configuration for your Magento instance in the **STORES** | **Settings** | **All Stores** section of the Magento admin panel. You will see the following grid on the screen:

There you will see the current store configuration of your Magento instance. Magento includes one website, one store, and one store view in the Magento 2 sample data. In the subsequent sections, we will review all the concepts, from websites to store views.

Websites

A website contains one or more stores. You can have a different set of customers in different websites, all of them managed from a single Magento instance.
If not, you can share the customer accounts between all the websites. In addition to that, you can set specific product prices, tax classes, currencies, and system configurations by website.

Stores/store groups

A store contains products and categories. Each store has an associated root category, allowing you to define different categories by store. In the previous example, we saw two stores with completely different product families:

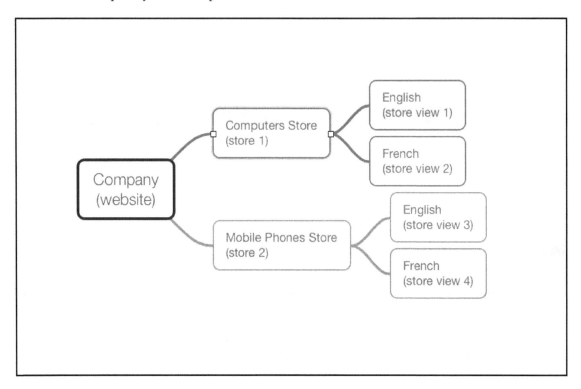

Magento allows you to do this by defining a root category per store. All the stores that are associated with the same website share the same customer accounts.

Store views

Store views are commonly used to define different languages for your website. By doing so, the merchants are able to target customers by their language.

All the store views that are associated with the same store share the same root category, shipping, and payment methods. By using store views, you can set different prices, titles, descriptions, and more.

We will review the **Web Site**, **Store**, and **Store View** that is included in the Magento 2 sample data.

We will go to the **STORES** section in the admin panel: **STORES** | **Settings** | **All Stores**.

There, you will see the grid that we described before:

We will start by clicking on the **Main Website** link on the first column. You will be redirected to the following screen:

There you can edit the **Name, Code, Sort Order,** and **Default Store**. Take into account that the multistore configuration can be set in the index.php file in the root of the project. If the multistore configuration has been set in that way and you change the website code, make sure to update the index.php file to specify the new code for the website.

If we go back to the **STORES** grid and click on the **Main Website Store** link in the second column, we will be redirected to the following page:

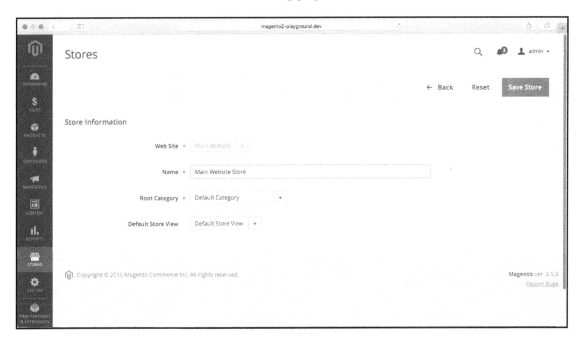

As you can see on that page, you can see the parent website for this store, edit the **Name**, and set the **Root Category** and the **Default Store View**.

Finally, if we go back to the grid and click on the **Default Store View** link in the third column, we will be redirected to the following form:

You can edit the parent store for the store view, set the **Name**, **Code**, **Status**, and **Sort Order**. It's important to mention that the multistore configuration can be set using the store view code in the `index.php` file. If that is the case, you should update the file every time you change the store view code in the admin panel.

Default/global scope

Besides the **Web Site**, **Store**, and **Store View**, we should mention that the default/global scope defines the default values for different configurations in the admin panel. By selecting this scope, you will set the specific configuration to be applied to all websites, stores, and store views.

When you are editing the Magento configuration, products, or categories, you will be able to select the scope for the values. You can define the values globally, or, specifically, on a website, store, or store view level.

You can find the drop-down menu to select the scope in the Magento admin panel. For example, for the system configuration values (**Stores** | **Settings** | **Configuration**), you will find the scope drop-down menu on the top-left corner of the screen:

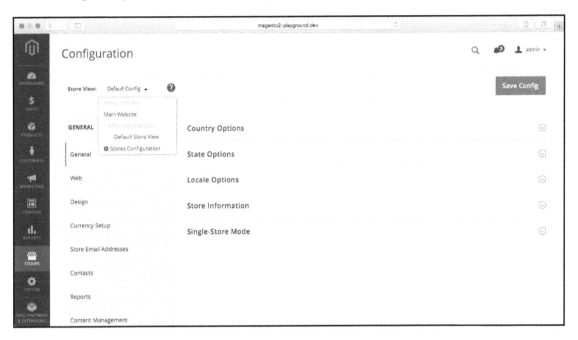

Summary

In this chapter, you learned about the hierarchical system that Magento implements for managing stores. We described the concepts of websites, stores, and store views, and you are now aware about the difference between those scopes. In the next chapter, we will go through the system configuration settings in Magento.

10
System Configuration

We will cover the following concepts in this chapter:

- General system configuration
- Catalog configuration
- Customer configuration
- Sales, shipping, and payment configuration
- Advanced configuration

System configuration sections and fields

The system configuration page is one of the most important pages in the admin panel. The reason for this is that you can configure all the Magento modules from there.

You can go to the system configuration page by selecting the **STORES** | **Settings** | **Configuration** menu item in the admin panel. You will see the following page on your screen:

The following sections are available in the **System Configuration** page:

- **GENERAL**:
    - **General**
    - **Web**
    - **Design**
    - **Currency Setup**
    - **Store Email Addresses**
    - **Contacts**
    - **Reports**
    - **Content Management**
    - **New Relic Reporting**

- CATALOG:
    - Catalog
    - Inventory
    - XML Sitemap
    - RSS Feeds
    - Email to a friend

- CUSTOMERS:
    - Newsletter
    - Customer Configuration
    - Wish List
    - Promotions
    - Persistent Shopping Cart

- SALES:
    - Sales
    - Sales Emails
    - PDF Print-outs
    - Tax
    - Checkout
    - Shipping Settings
    - Multishipping Settings
    - Shipping Methods
    - Google API
    - Payment Methods

- SERVICES:
    - Magento Web API
    - OAuth

- ADVANCED:
    - Admin
    - System
    - Advanced
    - Developer

We will go through the most important sections of the system configuration, describing what can be managed from each one of them.

GENERAL | General

You can update the following settings from this section:

- **Country Options**:
    - **Default Country**: This is the country where your business is located
    - **Allow Countries**: You can select the countries from where you accept orders
    - **Zip/Postal Code is Optional for**: You can specify the countries that don't need ZIP/postal code information
    - **European Union Countries**: You can select the countries in the EU where you conduct business
    - **Top destinations**: You can define specific countries to be displayed at the top of the **Country** dropdown in the Storefront. Based on this setting, the drop-down menu will include the top countries, as can be seen in the following screenshot:

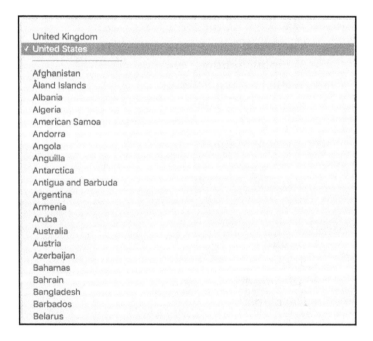

- **State Options**:
    - **State is Required For**: You can specify the countries that don't need state information
    - **Allow to Choose State if It is Optional for Country**: If this setting is set to **Yes**, the state will be included as an optional field in the Storefront. If this setting is set to **No**, then the field won't be displayed in the Storefront.
- **Locale Options**:
    - **Timezone**: Selects your timezone
    - **Locale**: Selects the language for the store
    - **Weight Unit**: Sets the weight unit for the store (lbs or kgs)
    - **First Day of Week**: Selects the day that is considered the first day of the week in your location
    - **Weekend Days**: Selects the days that are considered weekend days in your location
- **Store Information**: General information of your business, including:
    - **Store Name**
    - **Store Phone Number**
    - **Store Hours of Operation**
    - **Country**
    - **Region/State**
    - **ZIP/Postal Code**
    - **City**
    - **Street Address**
    - **Street Address Line 2**
    - **VAT Number**
- **Single-Store Mode:**
    - **Enable Single-Store Mode:** You can set this setting to **Yes** to simplify the display of the pages by turning off all store views and scope indicators

GENERAL | Web

- **Url Options**:
    - **Add Store Code to Urls**: If you set this setting to **Yes**, then the store URL will include the store code, for example, `http://www.magento2-playground.dev/[store-code]/url-key`
    - **Auto-redirect to Base URL**: Redirect to the base URL when the requested URL is different, for example, redirect from `http://magento2-playground.dev/store/` to `http://www.magento2-playground.com/store/`
- **Search Engine Optimization**:
    - **Use Web Server Rewrites**: When this setting is disabled, the URL includes `index.php` after the base URL, for example, `http://magento2-playground.dev/index.php/url-key`. When the setting is enabled, the URL doesn't include `index.php` after the base URL.
- **Base URLs**:
    - **Base URL**: Set the unsecure base URL, for example, `http://magento2-plaground.dev/`
    - **Base Link URL**: Set the placeholder that is used to create relative links to the unsecure base URL
    - **Base URL for Static View Files**: This is an optional field to set an alternative location for static view files
    - **Base URL for User Media Files**: This is an optional field to set an alternative location for user media files
    - **Base URLs (Secure)**:
        - **Secure Base URL**: Set the secure base URL, for example, `https://magento2-plaground.dev/`
        - **Secure Base Link URL**: Set the placeholder that is used to create relative links to the secure base URL
        - **Secure Base URL for Static View Files**: This is an optional field to set an alternative location for static view files

- **Secure Base URL for User Media Files**: This is an optional field to set an alternative location for user media files
- **Use Secure URLs on Storefront**: Enable this setting to serve all the pages on the Storefront over HTTPS
- **Use Secure URLs in Admin**: Enable this setting to serve all the pages on the Storefront over HTTPS
- **Offloader header**: Set the SSL offloader header value

- **Default Pages**:
    - **Default Web URL**: Relative path to the folder in the Magento instance that contains the landing page
    - **CMS Home Page**: Set the CMS page that will be displayed for the home page
    - **Default No-route URL**: Relative path to the folder in the Magento instance where the page is redirected when a 404 error occurs
    - **CMS No Route Page**: Set the CMS page that will be displayed for the 404 error page
    - **CMS No Cookies Page**: Set the CMS page that will be displayed when the cookies are disabled in the browser
    - **Show Breadcrumbs for CMS Pages**: Specify whether breadcrumbs should be displayed for CMS pages

GENERAL | Currency Setup

- **Currency Options**:
    - **Base Currency**: Set the primary currency for store transactions
    - **Default Display Currency**: Set the currency to be displayed in product prices on the Storefront
    - **Allowed Currencies**: Set the accepted currencies for store transactions

GENERAL | Store Email Addresses

- **General Contact / Sales Representative / Customer Support / Custom Email 1 / Custom Email 2**:
    - **Sender Name**: Set the sender name for each of the contact types
    - **Sender Email**: Set the e-mail address for each of the contact types

GENERAL | Contacts

- **Contact Us**:
    - **Enable Contact Us**: Enable the contact us page on the Storefront
- **Email Options**:
    - **Send Emails To**: Send the contact e-mails to the specified email addresses
    - **Email Sender**: Set the contact type that will be the sender of the contact e-mails
    - **Email Template**: Set the e-mail template for the contact e-mails

GENERAL | Contact Management

- **WYSIWYG Options**:
    - **Enable WYSIWYG Editor**: When this setting is dissabled, the WYSIWYG editor won't be displayed and plain text will be used for the text area fields in the admin panel

CATALOG | Catalog

- **Storefront**:
    - **List Mode**: Set the display mode for the product listing page. The possible values are:
        - **Grid Only**
        - **List Only**
        - **Grid (default) / List**
        - **List (default) / Grid**

- **Products per Page on Grid Allowed Values**: Set the allowed number of products per page in the grid mode of the product listing page.
- **Products per Page on Grid Default Value**: Set the default number of products per page in the grid mode of the product listing page.
- **Products per Page on List Allowed Values**: Set the allowed number of products per page in the list mode of the product listing page.
- **Products per Page on List Default Value**: Set the default number of products per page in the list mode of the product listing page.
- **Product Listing Sort by**: Set sorting criteria for the products in the product listing page.
- **Allow All Products per Page**: Allow the customer to display all products at once in the product listing page.
- **Use Flat Catalog Category**: Turn this setting on to enable flat tables for categories. This setting improves the performance of the store by combining all the category information in a flat table to fetch the data in a single query.
- **Use Flat Catalog Product**: Turn this setting on to enable flat tables for products. This setting improves the performance of the store by combining all the product information in the flat table to fetch the data in a single query.
- **Allow Dynamic Media URLs in Products and Categories**: When this setting is enabled, you can add relative references to images and other media assets. For example, you can reference an image in the media folder by using `{{media url="path/to/image.jpg"}}`. Enabling this setting has an impact on the catalog performance.

- **Product Reviews**:
  - **Allow Guests to Write Reviews**: If this setting is set to **No**, then authentication will be required on the Storefront to write reviews

- **Product Image Placeholders**: Set default image placeholder when the image for the product is missing. You can specify a different placeholder with a different size for each of the Magento product types:
  - **Base**
  - **Small**
  - **Swatch**
  - **Thumbnail**

- **Recently Viewed/Compared Products**:
    - **Show for Current**: Set the scope of the list of recently viewed or compared products
    - **Default Recently Viewed Products Count**: Set the number of products to be displayed in the recently viewed products block
    - **Default Recently Compared Products Count**: Set the number of products to be displayed in the recently compared products block
- **Layered Navigation**:
    - **Display Product Count**: Display the number of products in each item of the layered navigation
    - **Price Navigation Step Calculation**: By configuring this setting, you will be able to distribute products by price range in the layered navigation
- **Category Top Navigation**:
    - **Maximal Depth**: Set the limit for the number of subcategories that should be displayed in the top navigation menu on the Storefront

CATALOG | Inventory

- **Stock Options**:
    - **Decrease Stock When Order is Placed**: Specify whether the available quantity for the product should be decreased as soon as the customer places the order
    - **Set Items' Status to be In Stock When Order is Cancelled**: Increase the available quantity of products and change the status back to in stock if the order is cancelled
    - **Display Out of Stock Products**: Indicates whether out of stock products should be displayed on the Storefront
    - **Only X left Threshold**: Set the quantity to display the Only X left label on the Storefront
    - **Display Products Availability in Stock on Storefront**: If you enable this setting, the **Out of Stock** label will be displayed on the Storefront

CATALOG | Email to a Friend

- **Email Templates**:
    - **Enabled**: Specify whether the **Email to a Friend** feature should be available in the Storefront.
    - **Select Email Template**: Choose the e-mail template for the **Email to a Friend** feature.
    - **Allow for Guests**: If you set this setting to **Yes**, then the link to share the product will be available to all the customers. If you set the setting to **No**, then only logged in customers will be able to see the link.
    - **Max Recipients**: Set the maximum number of recipients for the shared product.
    - **Max Products Sent in 1 Hour**: Set a limit to the number of products that the customer can share per hour.
    - Limit Sending By: Specify whether the customer should be identified by a cookie or the IP address. The limitation on the number of products per hour will depend on this setting. If you select **Cookie (unsafe)**, then there will be X number of products allowed per cookie to be sent in an hour. If you select **IP address**, then the specific IP address can share X number of products per hour. The **IP address** option is recommended since the cookies can be cleaned in the browser, and the customer would be able to continue sharing products.

CUSTOMERS | Newsletter

- **Subscription Options**:
    - **Allow Guest Subscription**: Allow guests to subscribe to the newsletter
    - **Need to Confirm**: Configure whether the e-mail address should be confirmed by the subscriber

- **Confirmation Email Sender / Success Email Sender / Unsubscription Email Sender**: Set the contact type for the confirmation/success/unsubscription e-mail
- **Confirmation Email Template / Success Email Template / Unsubscription Email Template**: Set the e-mail template for the confirmation/success/unsubscription e-mail

CUSTOMERS | Customer Configuration

- **Create New Account Options**:
    - **Enable Automatic Assignment to Customer Group**: Set whether the customer should be auto-assigned to a specific customer group
    - **Default Group**: If you enable the previous field, you can specify the customer group for the auto-assignment using this dropdown
    - **Default Welcome Email**: Specify the default transactional e-mail for the e-mail that is sent to the customer after registering
    - **Default Welcome Email Without Password**: Specify the default transactional e-mail for the e-mail that is sent when the customer was created without a password
    - **Email Sender**: Set the contact type as the sender for the **Welcome Email**
    - **Require Emails Confirmation**: Specify whether new customer accounts require validation to be active
    - **Confirmation Link Email**: Choose the transactional e-mail for the confirmation link e-mail
    - **Welcome Email**: If you specify the account validation, you can set the transactional e-mail that is sent when the account is confirmed
- **Login Options**:
    - **Redirect Customer to Account Dashboard after Logging in**: If you set this setting to **No**, the customer will stay on the current page after logging in

- **CAPTCHA**:
    - **Enable CAPTCHA on Storefront**: You can enable and configure CAPTCHA for the following forms:
        - Create user
        - Login
        - Forgot password
        - Checkout as guest
        - Register during checkout
        - Contact us
        - Change password

CUSTOMERS | Persistent Shopping Cart

- **General Options**:
    - **Enable Persistence**: If you enable this setting, the customers will be able to keep their products in the cart after leaving the website or logging out from their account. The customers will still have the products in the cart the next time they visit the store.
    - **Persistence Lifetime (seconds)**: This is the time period for which the cookie that saves the customer data will be stored. 31,536,000 seconds is equal to 1 year, and that's the maximum value allowed.
    - **Enable "Remember Me"**: Display the **Remember Me** checkbox in the login page
    - **"Remember Me" Default Value**: Indicates whether or not the **Remember Me** checkbox should be checked by default.
    - **Clear Persistence on Sign Out**: Clear the products that are in the customer's shopping cart after customer logout.
    - **Persist Shopping Cart**: Keep the persistent cookie after the session expires. For example, if a guest user adds products to the cart and the session cookie expires, then the shopping cart items will be still there.

SALES | Sales

- **Reorder:**
    - Allow Reorder: If this setting is enabled, the "Reorder" link will appear for the customer to be able to place the same order again
- **Gift Options:**
    - Allow Gift Messages on Order Level: Allow customers to specify gift messages for orders
    - Allow Gift Messages for Order Items: Allow customers to specify gift messages for order items

Sales – Tax

- **Calculation Settings:**
    - Tax Calculation Method Based On: There are three calculation methods for taxes:
        - Unit Price: The tax will be calculated for each unit
        - Row Total: The tax will be calculated for each item
        - Total: The tax will be calculated from the order total
    - Tax Calculation Based On: You can select which address type to consider as the location to calculate the taxes
        - Shipping Address
        - Billing Address
        - Shipping Origin
    - Catalog Prices: Specify if the prices in the catalog include taxes or not
    - Shipping Prices: Specify whether the shipping prices entered from the Magento admin panel or retrieved from gateways include taxes or not
    - Apply Customer Tax: Specify whether taxes should be calculated before or after discount
    - Apply Discount On Prices: If "Apply Customer Tax after Discount" is selected in the previous field, then you can specify if the discount on prices should include taxes or not

- Apply Tax On: Specify if the taxes should be applied on the original price or custom price if available
- Enable Cross Border Trade: If you enable this setting and the prices in the catalog include taxes, then the price will be fixed, no matter the customer's tax rate

Sales – Checkout

- **Checkout Options:**
    - Enable One-page Checkout: If this setting is set to "No", then the default checkout won't be available on the Storefront (you can still enable multi-shipping checkout)
    - Allow Guest Checkout: Allow guest users to place orders on the Storefront
    - Enable Terms and Conditions: Enable the terms and conditions checkbox in the checkout page

Sales – Shipping Settings

- **Origin:** Set the address from where the items for the orders are delivered. These are the available fields in this section:
    - Country
    - Region/State
    - ZIP/Postal Code
    - City
    - Street Address
    - Street Address Line 2
- **Shipping Policy Parameters:**
    - Apply custom shipping policy: You can add your custom shipping policy to display in the checkout

Sales – Multishipping Settings

- **Options:**
    - Allow Shipping to Multiple Addresses: Enable multishipping checkout
    - Maximum Qty Allowed for Shipping to Multiple Addresses: Set the maximum allowed quantity for multishipping checkout

Sales – Shipping Methods

Configure the available shipping methods for the customers in the checkout page. The available shipping methods are:

- Flat Rate
- Free Shipping
- Table Rates
- UPS
- USPS
- FedEx
- DHL

Sales – Google API

- **Google Analytics:**
    - Enable: Enable Google Analytics to keep a track of the web traffic in your Magento store
- **Google AdWords:**
    - Enable: Enable Google Adwords Conversion Tracking

Sales – Payment Methods

Configure the available payment methods for the customers in the checkout page. We will review the process of setting up payment methods in Chapter 15, Processing Payments.

The available payment methods are:

- Paypal
- Braintree
- Check/Money Order
- Bank Transfer Payment
- Cash On Delivery Payment
- Zero Subtotal Checkout
- Purchase Order
- Authorize.net Direct Post

Advanced – Admin

- **Startup Page:**
    - Startup Page: Set the page that will be displayed after the administrators log in to the admin panel
- **Admin Base URL:**
    - Use Custom Admin URL: Set the custom base URL for the admin panel, for example, `http://magento-playground.dev/magento/`
    - Use Custom Admin Path: Append the custom path after the base URL, for example, `sample_admin`

Advanced – System

- **Scheduled Backup Settings:**
    - Enable Scheduled Backup: If this setting is set to **Yes**, then Magento will perform the specified backup on a regular basis.
    - Backup Type: Select the type of backup that will be automatically done by Magento. The available backup types are:
        - Database
        - Database and Media
        - System
        - System (excluding Media)

- Start Time: Set specific time in the day to automatically start backup
    - Frequency: Set the frequency of automatic backup
    - Maintenance Mode: Specify whether the store should be put into maintenance mode during backup (recommended)

Advanced – Advanced

- **Disable Modules Output:** You can disable specific modules from your Magento instance from this section. By disabling the modules in this section, you are specifically disabling the output and not the entire module functionality. For example, an event observer will still be running after the module is disabled from this section.
    - Magento_AdminNotification
    - Magento_AdvancedPricingImportExport
    - Magento_Authorization
    - Magento_Authorizenet
    - Magento_Backup
    - Magento_Braintree
    - Magento_Bundle
    - Magento_BundleImportExport
    - Magento_BundleSampleData
    - Magento_CacheInvalidate
    - Magento_Captcha
    - Magento_Catalog
    - Magento_CatalogImportExport
    - Magento_CatalogInventory
    - Magento_CatalogRule
    - Magento_CatalogRuleConfigurable
    - Magento_CatalogRuleSampleData
    - Magento_CatalogSampleData
    - Magento_CatalogSearch
    - Magento_CatalogUrlRewrite

- Magento_CatalogWidget
- Magento_Checkout
- Magento_CheckoutAgreements
- Magento_Cms
- Magento_CmsSampleData
- Magento_CmsUrlRewrite
- Magento_Config
- Magento_ConfigurableImportExport
- Magento_ConfigurableProduct
- Magento_ConfigurableSampleData
- Magento_Contact
- Magento_Cookie
- Magento_Cron
- Magento_CurrencySymbol
- Magento_Customer
- Magento_CustomerImportExport
- Magento_CustomerSampleData
- Magento_Deploy
- Magento_Developer
- Magento_Dhl
- Magento_Directory
- Magento_Downloadable
- Magento_DownloadableImportExport
- Magento_DownloadableSampleData
- Magento_Eav
- Magento_Email
- Magento_EncryptionKey
- Magento_Fedex
- Magento_GiftMessage
- Magento_GoogleAdwords
- Magento_GoogleAnalytics
- Magento_GoogleOptimizer
- Magento_GroupedImportExport
- Magento_GroupedProduct

- Magento_GroupedProductSampleData
- Magento_ImportExport
- Magento_Indexer
- Magento_Integration
- Magento_LayeredNavigation
- Magento_Marketplace
- Magento_MediaStorage
- Magento_Msrp
- Magento_MsrpSampleData
- Magento_Multishipping
- Magento_NewRelicReporting
- Magento_Newsletter
- Magento_OfflinePayments
- Magento_OfflineShipping
- Magento_OfflineShippingSampleData
- Magento_PageCache
- Magento_Payment
- Magento_Paypal
- Magento_Persistent
- Magento_ProductAlert
- Magento_ProductLinksSampleData
- Magento_ProductVideo
- Magento_Quote
- Magento_Reports
- Magento_RequireJs
- Magento_Review
- Magento_ReviewSampleData
- Magento_Rss
- Magento_Rule
- Magento_Sales
- Magento_SalesInventory
- Magento_SalesRule
- Magento_SalesRuleSampleData
- Magento_SalesSampleData
- Magento_SalesSequence

- Magento_SampleData
- Magento_Search
- Magento_Security
- Magento_SendFriend
- Magento_Shipping
- Magento_Sitemap
- Magento_Store
- Magento_Swagger
- Magento_Swatches
- Magento_SwatchesLayeredNavigation
- Magento_SwatchesSampleData
- Magento_Tax
- Magento_TaxImportExport
- Magento_TaxSampleData
- Magento_Theme
- Magento_ThemeSampleData
- Magento_Translation
- Magento_Ui
- Magento_Ups
- Magento_UrlRewrite
- Magento_User
- Magento_Usps
- Magento_Variable
- Magento_Vault
- Magento_Version
- Magento_Webapi
- Magento_WebapiSecurity
- Magento_Weee
- Magento_Widget
- Magento_WidgetSampleData
- Magento_Wishlist
- Magento_WishlistSampleData

Summary

In this chapter, we went through the most important system configuration fields in Magento. In the next chapter, we will go through the process of managing customer accounts and customer groups to be able to create, edit, and delete accounts, and associate them with different groups.

11
Working with Customers

In this chapter, we will cover the following topics:

- Working with customer accounts
- Customer groups

Working with customer accounts

Customers have the ability to register an account on the Storefront to keep track of their orders, save their personal information for future orders, and more.

You can manage the customer accounts in your store from the **CUSTOMERS** | **All Customers** section in the admin panel.

You will see the following page on the screen:

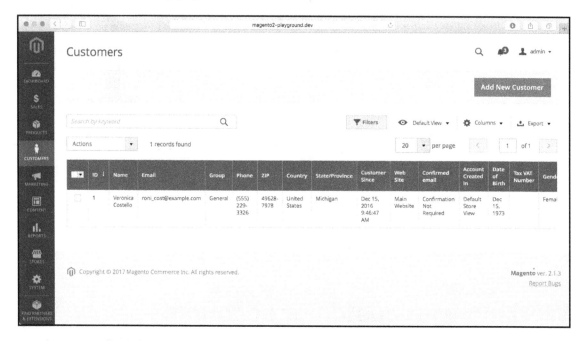

One of the most useful elements from the grids in the Magento admin panel is the **Actions** dropdown. The dropdown contains mass actions to apply a specific action to the items that are selected in the grid.

The following mass actions are available from the **Customers** grid:

- **Delete**
- **Subscribe to Newsletter**
- **Unsubscribe from Newsletter**
- **Assign a Customer Group**
- **Edit**

In addition to that, you can filter and sort the list of customers in the grid, set the number of customers to display per page, select the columns to display, search by keyword, and export the customer list to CSV and Excel XML.

You can view and edit the customer information by clicking on the **Edit** link in the last column from the **Action** grid.

If you click on that link, you will be redirected to the **Customer** edit page:

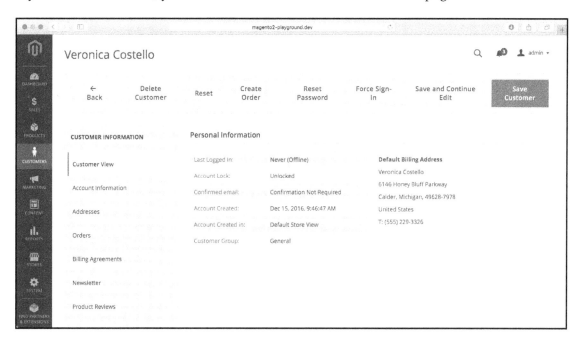

We can see that there are several buttons on top to perform different actions on the customer account:

- **Delete Customer**
- **Reset**: Resets all changes that have been made in the customer information since you opened the **Customer** edit page
- **Create Order**: Creates an order for the customer
- **Reset Password**
- **Force Sign-In**: Revokes the API token for the customer account

On the left sidebar, the following sections are available:

- **Customer View**: Take a look at the following screenshot:

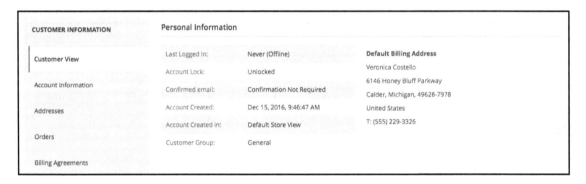

You can see the personal information of the customer, including:

- The last time the customer logged in
- Whether the account is locked or unlocked (Magento locks the account after six failed login events)
- If a confirmation e-mail was required, then you can see whether the account has been verified
- The date that the account was created on
- The store view from which the account was created
- The customer group of the customer account
- The default billing and shipping addresses

- **Account Information**: You can edit the personal information in this section and specify the customer group for the customer account:

- **Addresses**: You can add new addresses for the customer account and specify which one of them should be the default billing and shipping addresses:

- **Orders**: You can see the list of orders placed by the customer. You can open the order to see all the details and even reorder directly from the grid (if reorder is enabled in the system configuration–**SALES** | **Sales** | **Reorder** | **Allow Reorder**):

- **Billing Agreements**: To make the checkout process simpler, customers can enter into a billing agreement with PayPal as the payment service provider. The customer chooses the billing agreement as the payment method in the checkout, and PayPal identifies the billing agreement by its unique number and proceeds with the charge. The **Billing Agreements** section contains all the billing agreements for the customer:

- **Newsletter**: You can check if the customer is subscribed to the newsletter and see the list of newsletters with the ability to filter by **ID**, **Start date**, **End Date**, **Receive Date**, **Subject**, and **Status**:

- **Product Reviews**: You can see the list of product reviews written by the customer:

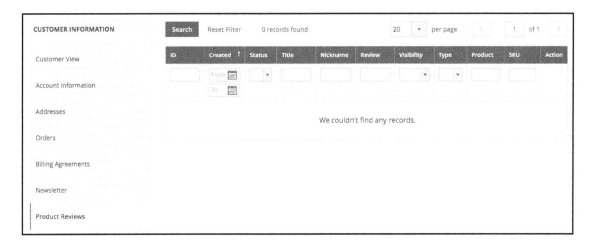

- **Wish List**: You can review the list of products that are in the wish list of the customer, including important information such as the number of days since the product was added to the wish list:

Adding a new customer

Even though the customer can create the account from the Storefront, the administrator can create the account from the admin panel as well. You can add a new customer by clicking on the **Add New Customer** button in the **Customers** page (**Customers | Customers | All Customers**):

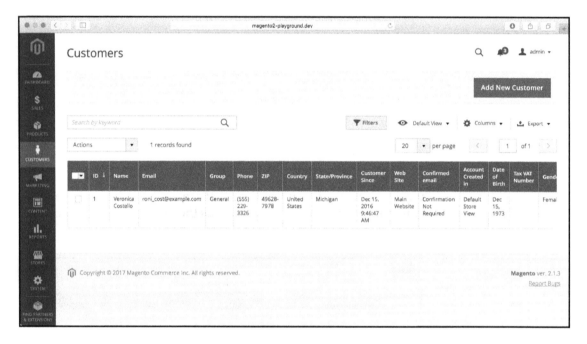

You will be redirected to the **New Customer** page:

We will add just the basic account information for the new customer:

- **Associate to Website**: **Main Website**
- **Group**: **General**
- **First Name**: Your first name
- **Last Name**: Your last name
- **Email**: Your e-mail
- **Send Default Email from**: **Default Store View**

Now, click on the **Save Customer** button on the top-right corner of the screen. You will be redirected to the **Customers** page, and you will see the success message as confirmation that the account has been created:

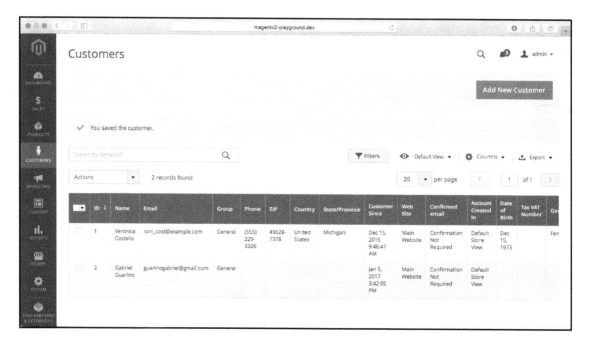

Summary

You saw that managing customers in Magento is really simple, from the ability to see the list of all customers to applying useful mass actions such as *Subscribe to Newsletter*. Creating and editing customers is an easy process as well, and you can review all the information of customers, including their orders, reviews, and more.

In the next chapter, we will go through the process of setting up and managing taxes for your Magento store.

12
Admin Users and Roles

In this chapter, we will cover the following concepts:

- Managing admin users
- Managing roles and granting permissions

Managing admin users

When managing an e-commerce website, you need different administrators that have access to different pages in the admin panel. For example, if a person from your team is in charge of adding and updating products in your Magento store, then you need that person to access only the **PRODUCTS** | **Catalog** page. If another team member is in charge of marketing, then you can create a new admin user with a specific role to access just the **MARKETING** and **CONTENT** sections.

You can create users for the Magento admin panel and grant specific privileges to each of the user roles. You can see a list of existing admin users by opening the **SYSTEM** | **Permissions** | **All Users** page in the admin panel:

You can add new users by clicking on the **Add New User** button on the top-right corner of the screen. You will be redirected to the following form:

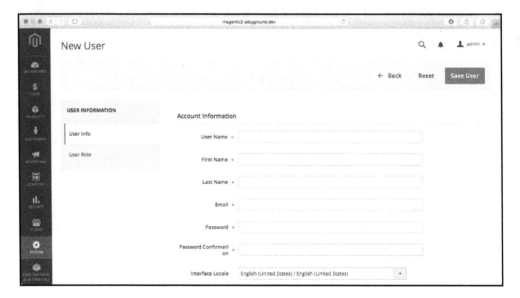

There, you can set the personal information for the new admin user, the password, the interface language, the account status, and the admin role.

If we take a look at the **User Role** tab, we can see that Magento includes only one user role by default, that is, **Administrators**:

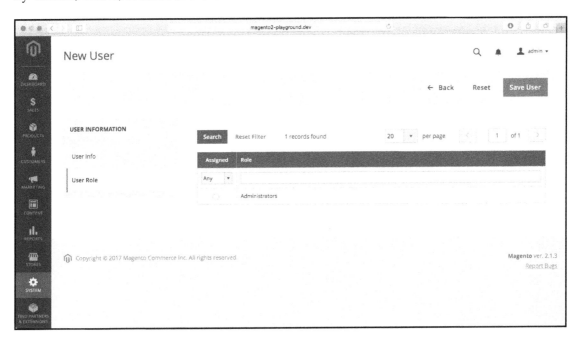

Let's create a sample admin user by adding the following information to the form:

User Info:

- **First Name**: Your first name
- **Last Name**: Your last name
- **Email**: Your e-mail address
- **Password**: Set a password for the account
- **Password Confirmation**: Repeat the same password for the account
- **Interface Locale**: **English (United States)** / **English (United States)**
- **Your Password**: Password for the current admin user

User Role:

- **Role**: **Administrator**

After filling out this information in the form, click on **Save User**. You will be redirected to the **Users** grid, and you will see the following message on the screen:

Managing roles

You can create new roles for your admin users to grant specific permissions to different admin pages. You can manage user roles by going to the **SYSTEM** | **Permissions** | **User Roles** page in the admin panel. You will be redirected to the following page:

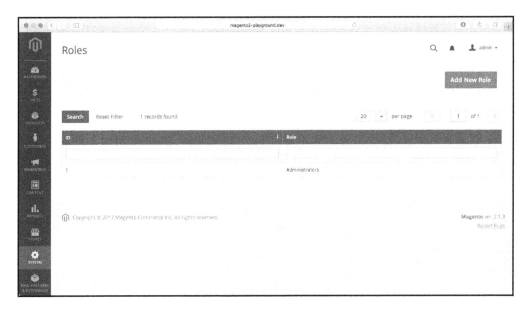

We can see the only admin role that is available in Magento by default, which has all the permissions in the admin panel. We will create a new user role by clicking on **Add New Role** in the top-right corner of the screen. After clicking the button, you will see the following page on the screen:

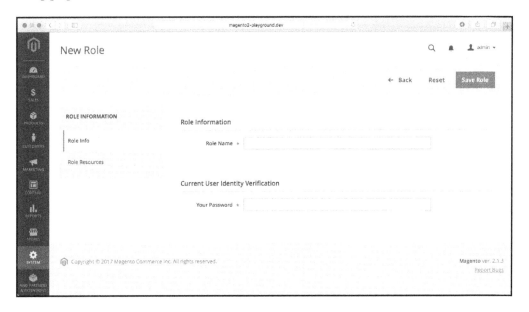

In the first tab, **Role Info**, you can set the role name and specify the password for your current admin user to be able to save the changes. In the second tab, **Role Resources**, you will see a list of all resources to assign to the user role:

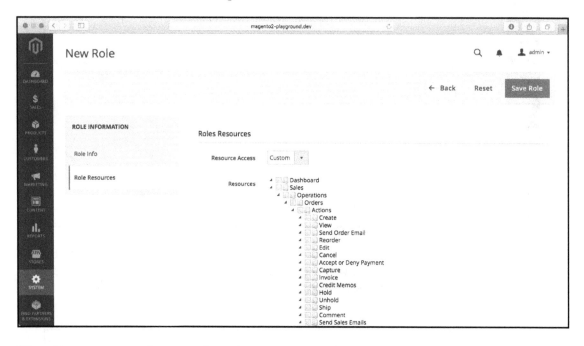

We will create a sample user role with access to just the **Dashboard** and **Sales** sections in the admin panel.

First, we will set the name as `Sample User Role`, and we will specify the password for our current admin user in the **Role Info** tab.

Then, we will check the **Dashboard** and **Sales** checkboxes in the **Role Resources** tab, as you can see in the following screenshot:

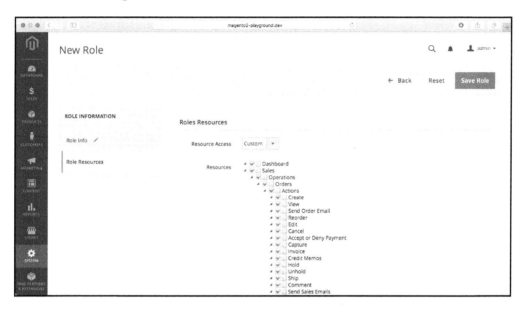

Finally, click on **Save Role** to add the new admin user role to Magento. You will see a confirmation message in the **Roles** grid:

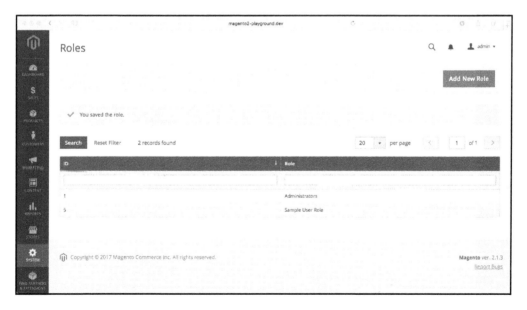

If we go back to the **Users** grid (**SYSTEM | Permissions | All Users**) and click on the user that we have just created, we will be able to assign the user to the new user role:

If we save the changes, sign out from the current admin user account, and log in as the new user, we will see that we will just have access to the **Dashboard** and **Sales** sections:

Summary

In this chapter, you learned how to create new admin users and grant specific permissions to the different admin sections. In the next chapter, we will go through the tax configuration in Magento, including tax classes, tax rules, tax zones, and rates.

13
Taxes

In this chapter, we will cover the following topics:

- Tax classes and rules
- Tax zones and rates

Tax classes and rules

One of the tasks that should be done by the store owner before the website launch is setting up taxes for the store.

Magento allows you to set up taxes based on your business needs. The general configuration for the taxes is located in the system configuration page that we reviewed before (**STORES** | **Configuration** | **Sales** | **Tax**):

As you can see in the preceding screenshot, there are tax classes that you can assign to shipping, products, and customers. This means that we will be able to assign specific tax rules through tax classes. New tax classes can be created when a new tax rule is defined.

You can review all the existing tax rules in the **STORES** | **Taxes** | **Tax Rules** section:

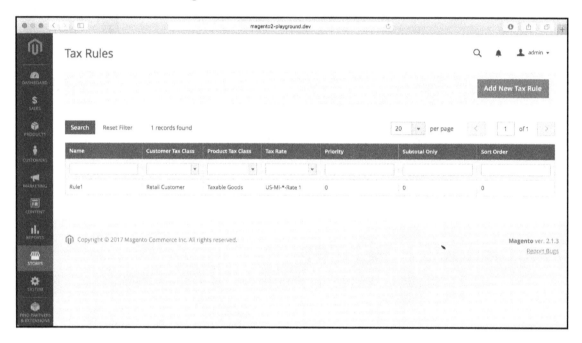

As you can see in the preceding screenshot, the default tax rule that is included in the Magento 2 sample data is **Rule1**. There you can see two tax classes that are associated with that rule:

- **Retail Customer**
- **Taxable Goods**

Let's create a new tax rule by clicking on the **Add New Tax Rule** button in the top-right corner of the screen.

You will be redirected to the following form:

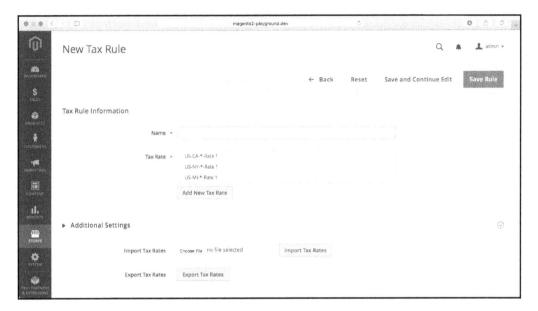

If you click on **Additional Settings**, the following additional fields will be visible in the form:

As you can see, you can add new tax classes for customers and products. These new classes will be available later for selection from the system configuration page.

Let's go through each of the fields in the **New Tax Rule** form:

- **Tax Rule Information**:
    - **Name**: Name of the tax rule
    - **Tax Rate**: This will be the rate percent for the tax rule, based on location. You can select existing rates or create a new tax rate for selection. We will cover this later.

- **Additional Settings**:
    - **Customer Tax Class**: The customer tax class is used in specific scenarios when the purchase is not retail.
    - **Product Tax Class**: Since different products have different taxes, you can add product tax classes for each of the product families of your store.
    - **Priority**: Priority is used when there are multiple tax classes. Tax rates of the same priority are added, and other tax rates are compounded.
    - **Calculate Off Subtotal Only**: Override the priority order for compound taxes and calculate the tax based on the subtotal of the order.
    - **Sort Order**: This is the order that the taxes are displayed in. The lower the sort order, the higher it will appear in the list.
    - **Import Tax Rates**: Import tax rates from a CSV file.
    - **Export Tax Rates**: Export tax rates to a CSV file. This is useful to get the right CSV format for the import in the previous field.

Let's move on and create a new tax rule. We will add the following information to the form:

- **Tax Rule Information**:
    - **Name**: `Sample Rule`
    - **Tax Rate**: For this rule, we will select the following tax rates:
        - **US-CA-*-Rate 1**
        - **US-NY-*-Rate 1**

- **Additional Settings**:
  - **Customer Tax Class: Retail Customer**
  - **Product Tax Class: Taxable Goods**
  - **Priority**: 0
  - **Calculate Off Subtotal Only**: Unchecked
  - **Sort Order**: 0

Now, click on **Save Rule**. When you are redirected to the **Tax Rules** grid, you will see a confirmation message and the new rule in the grid:

Now, let's modify the **Customer Tax Class** and the **Product Tax Class** for the rule that we just created. We will click on the **Sample Rule** item in the grid to be redirected to the edit form.

There, we will click on the **Additional Settings** link, and we will click on the **Add New Tax Class** button.

A new field will appear to specify a name for the new tax class:

Add `Sample Customer Tax Class` and `Sample Product Tax Class`, and select those tax classes from the multiselect fields:

If you click on **Save Rule**, you will see the updated tax classes in the **Tax Rules** grid:

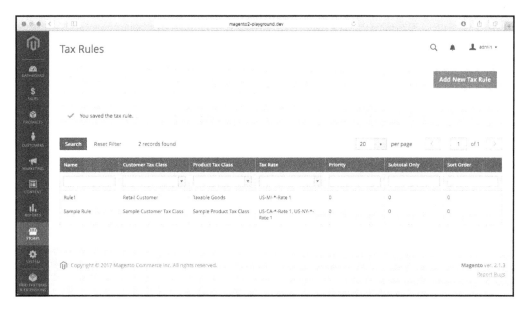

In addition to this, the new tax classes will be available for selection in the system configuration page for taxes (**STORES** | **Configuration** | **Sales** | **Tax**):

Tax zones and rates

We have seen in the **New Tax Rate** form that some tax rules were included in the list by default in the Magento sample data.

You can manage those rules from the **STORES** | **Taxes** | **Tax Zones and Rates** section. You will see the following grid on that page:

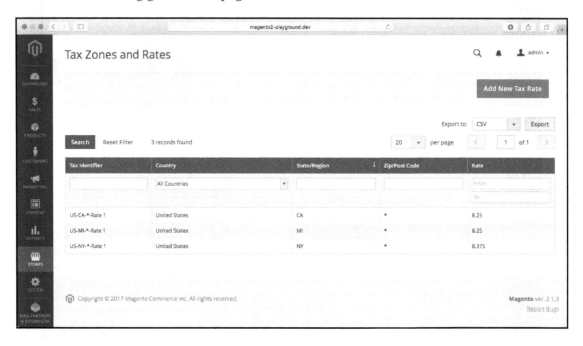

As you can see in the grid, you can set specific tax rates by **Country**, **State/Region**, and **Zip/Post Code**.

We will add a new tax rate by clicking on **Add New Tax Rate**. Once the page is loaded, you will see the following form:

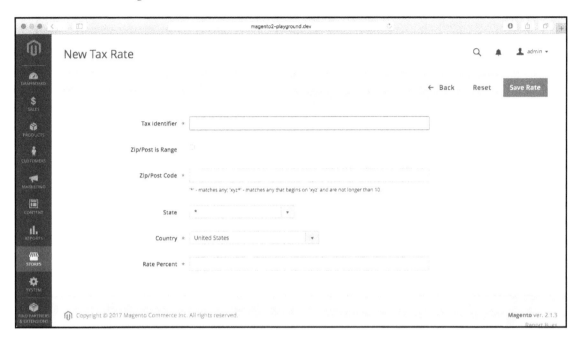

There, you can specify the following information:

- **Tax Identifier**: Name for the tax rate.
- **Zip/Post is Range**: You can specify a zip/post code range for the tax rate.
- **Zip/Post Code**: You can specify the specific post code, or use the asterisk character to specify a pattern for the zip code. For example, *bay**** will match any zip/post Code that begins with *bay*.
- **State**: Select all states or a specific state from the country that you choose in the next field.
- **Country**: Select the country for the tax rate.
- **Rate Percent**: Set the tax percent.

You can also add new tax rates from the **New / Edit Tax Rule** page by clicking on the **Add New Tax Rate** button:

When you click on that button, you will see the following window to add the information for the new tax rate:

Summary

In this chapter, we reviewed the process of creating tax classes, tax rules, and tax rates, based on the customer location. Now, you will be able to set prices and taxes accurately for the catalog in your Magento store. In the next chapter, you will learn about catalog and shopping cart price rules to create promotions and increase your sales.

14

Catalog and Shopping Cart Price Rules

We will cover the following concepts in this chapter:

- Catalog price rules
- Shopping cart price rules
- Generating coupons

Catalog price rules

One of the key elements of an online store is the ability to set up promotions in order to increase sales and keep visitors coming back to place new orders.

Magento allows you to set up promotions for your catalog. You can manage those promotions from the **MARKETING** | **Promotions** | **Catalog Price Rule** admin page:

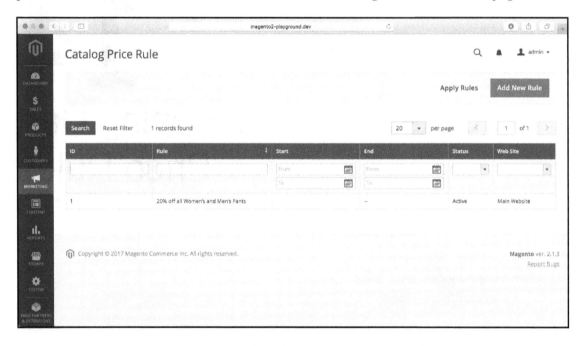

As you can see in the preceding screenshot, the Magento 2 sample data includes one catalog promotion– **20% off all Women's and Men's Pants**

You can add a new rule by clicking on **Add New Rule** in the top-right corner of the page.

The **New Catalog Price Rule** will be visible on the screen when the page loads:

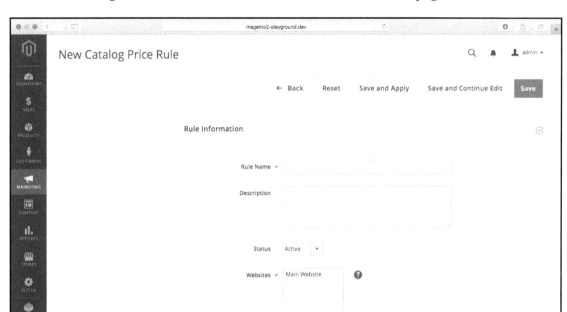

Here, you can specify the following information:

- **Rule Information**:
    - **Rule Name**: A name to help you remember the details of this catalog price rule.
    - **Description**: A description for the catalog price rule. This is an internal field for the administrator and won't be displayed on the Storefront.
    - **Status**: Set whether the catalog price rule is active or not.
    - **Websites**: Specify the websites for the catalog price rule.
    - **Customer Groups**: Set specific customer groups for the catalog price rule.
    - **From** (Select Date) – **To** (Select Date): Set a specific date range for the catalog price rule.
    - **Priority**: The matching catalog price rules will be applied in the order that is set in this field, the lower priority being the first to be applied.

- **Conditions**: Set conditions to apply the catalog price rule to specific products. If there are no conditions, then the catalog price rule will be applied to all products. You can set the conditions based on the product attributes:

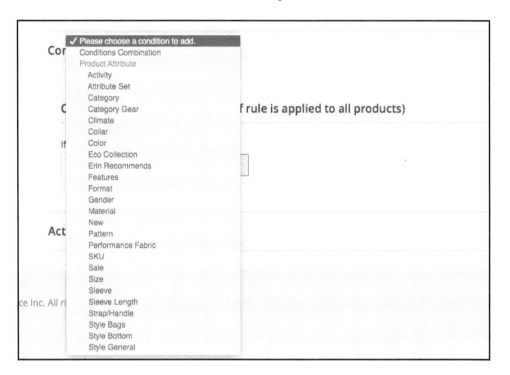

You can also set the catalog price rule to be valid if all the selected conditions are **True** or **False**:

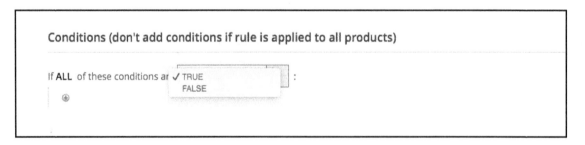

When you click on the green plus icon and select a product attribute, a new field and new icons will be visible, and you can choose the specific filter for the attribute:

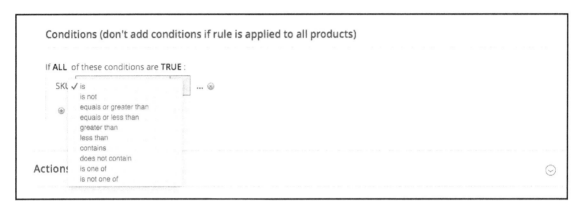

The preceding filter is for the **SKU** attribute; different filters apply for the attributes. For example, here is the filter dropdown for the color attribute:

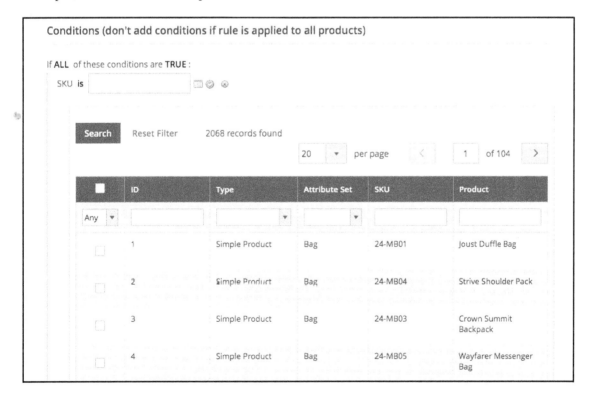

Finally, a blue window icon is available for some of the attributes. For example, if you select the **SKU** attribute and click on the blue window button, you will see a product grid to filter and choose products through that interface:

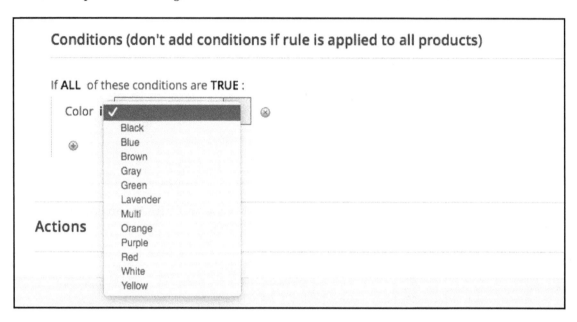

If you select the **Category** attribute and click on the blue window icon, you will be able to select categories through the category grid:

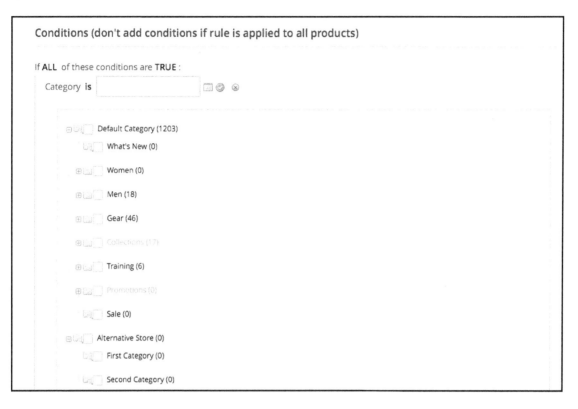

- **Actions**:
  - **Apply**: This will be the action that will be applied to all matching products, based on the rule information and conditions that form the previous fields. The available actions are:
    - **Apply as percentage of original**: The discount is calculated as a percentage of the product price. If the product price is $200 and the discount is 10%, then the final price with discount will be $190.
    - **Apply as fixed amount**: The discount will be a fixed amount. If the product price is $200 and the discount is 10%, then the final price with discount will be $190.

- **Adjust final price to this percentage**: The final price for the product will be the percentage of the product price (direct percentage calculation from the product price). If the product price is $200 and the discount is 10%, then the final price with discount will be $20.
- **Adjust final price to discount value**: The final price for the product will be the amount that you set as a discount. The original price doesn't matter; the price will always be the amount specified as the discount. If the product price is $200 and the discount is 10%, then the final price with discount will be $10.
- **Discount Amount**: Set the discount amount that will be applied in the way that you selected in the previous dropdown.
- **Discard subsequent rules**: If additional rules meet the same conditions, then you can discard those rules to prevent multiple discounts from being applied to the same purchase.

Shopping cart price rules

Magento allows you to create specific promotions that can be applied to the shopping cart. For example, customers love using coupon codes in online stores, and some of them even search for a coupon code for every online purchase that they make.

You can manage those promotions from the **MARKETING** | **Promotions** | **Cart Price Rules** section in the admin panel. You will be redirected to the following grid:

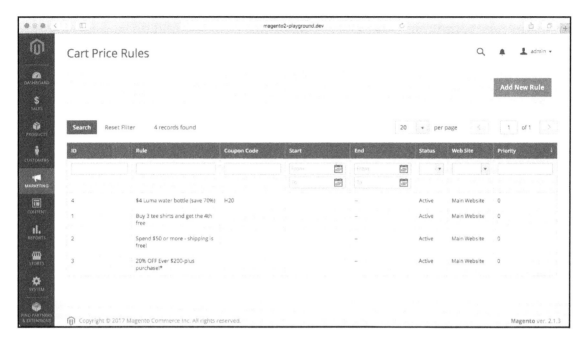

By default, the Magento 2 sample data includes four cart price rules:

- **$4 Luma water bottle (save 70%)**
- **Buy 3 tee shirts and get the 4th free**
- **Spend $50 or more – shipping is free!**
- **20% OFF Ever $200-plus purchase!***

If you click on the first row in the grid, you will be redirected to the form to edit that specific cart price rule:

If we collapse the first section, we will see that there are several sections to set up the cart price rules:

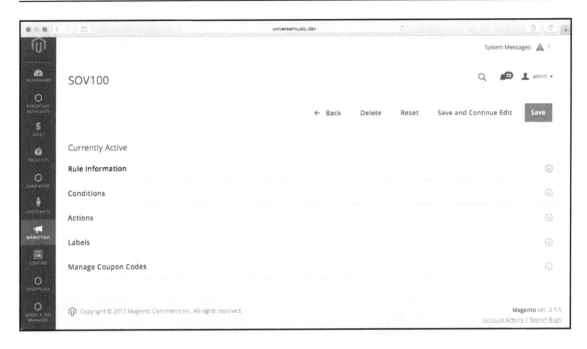

We will describe the fields from each of those sections:

- **Rule Information**:
    - **Rule Name**: A name to help you remember the details of the cart price rule.
    - **Description**: A description for the cart price rule. This is an internal field for the administrator and won't be displayed on the Storefront.
    - **Active**: Set whether the cart price rule is active or not.
    - **Websites**: Specify the websites for the cart price rule.
    - **Customer Groups**: Set specific customer groups for the cart price rule.
    - **Coupon**: Specify whether a coupon is required for this promotion to be applied.
    - **Coupon Code**: If you specify that a coupon is required for the promotion, then you can set the coupon code in this field.
    - **Use Auto Generation**: By using this checkbox, you can autogenerate the coupon codes from the last section of this form.
    - **Uses per Coupon**: Set a limit for the number of uses of the coupon.

- **Uses per Customer**: Set a limited number of times that the coupon can be used by the same customer (only for logged in customers).
- **From** (Select Date) – **To** (Select Date): Set a specific date range for the cart price rule.
- **Priority**: The matching cart price rules will be applied in the order that is set in this field, the lower priority being the first to be applied.
- **Public In RSS Feed**: Set whether the cart price rule should be public in the Magento RSS Feed.

- **Conditions**: Set conditions that should match for the cart price rule to be applied. If there are no conditions, then the cart price rule will always be applied if the properties defined in the **Rule Information** section are met.

We can find the following conditions to apply:

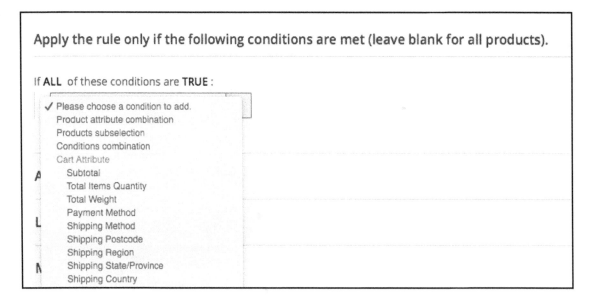

- **Actions**:
    - **Apply**: This will be the action that will be applied for the cart price rule. The available actions are:
        - **Percent of product price discount**
        - **Fixed amount discount**
        - **Fixed amount discount for whole cart**
        - **Buy X get Y free (discount amount is Y)**
    - **Discount Amount**: Set the discount amount that will be applied in the way that you selected in the previous dropdown
    - **Maximum Qty Discount is Applied To**
    - **Discount Qty Step (Buy X)**
    - **Apply to Shipping Amount**
    - **Free Shipping**
    - **Apply the rule only to cart items matching the following conditions**: You can set conditions that should be met for the promotion to be applied to the shopping cart items. The following conditions are available:

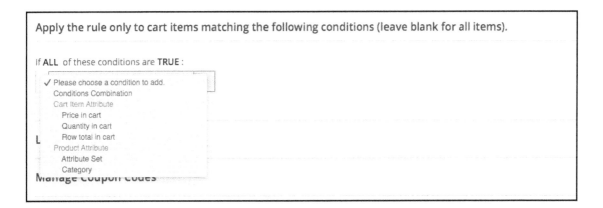

- **Labels**: From this section, you can manage the default and specific labels for each of the store views:

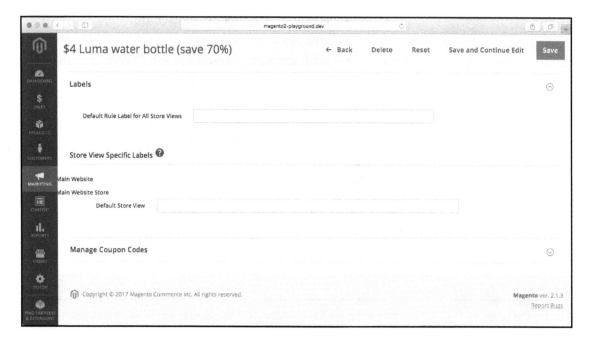

- **Manage Coupon Codes**: You can generate coupon codes for the promotion, based on specific properties, including length, code format, prefix, suffix, and dashes:

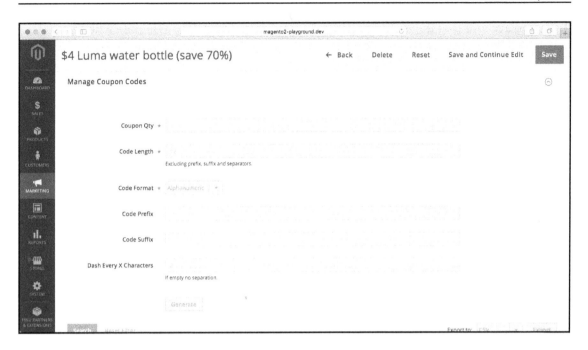

Then, you will be able to see the coupon codes and their usage from the following grid:

Take into account that the ability to generate coupon codes is only available when you check the **Use Auto Generation** checkbox in the **Rule Information** section:

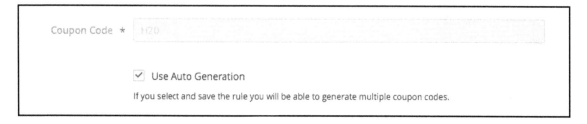

Then, if you go to the **Manage Coupon Code** section again, you will see that the form is active and you will be able to generate coupons based on the specific conditions that you set:

When you click on the **Generate** button, the coupons will be generated on the fly and the *X* **coupon(s) have been generated**. message will be displayed on the screen. In addition to that, you will be able to see the coupons that have been generated in the grid at the end of the page:

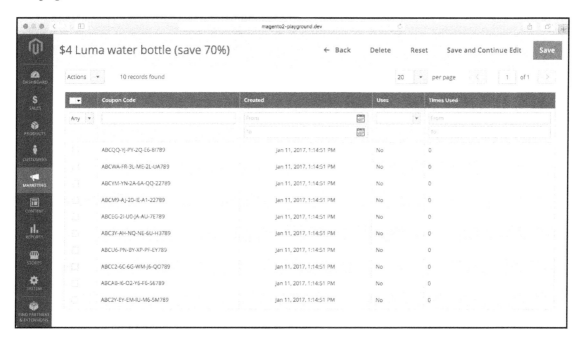

Summary

In this chapter, we reviewed the catalog and shopping cart price rules to create promotions for your store in order to boost sales.

In the next chapter, we will configure the default payment methods in Magento, and we will cover the concept of PCI compliance to keep your system secure, allowing customers to place orders using their credit cards with no risk.

15
Processing Payments

In this chapter, we will cover the following topics:

- Default Magento payment methods
- Setting up PayPal
- PCI compliance

Default Magento payment methods

Magento includes several payment methods by default:

- PayPal
- Braintree
- Check or money order
- Bank transfer payment
- Cash on delivery payment
- Zero subtotal checkout
- Purchase order
- Authorize.net direct post

You can see the configuration for those payment methods on the System Configuration page (**STORES | Configuration**) in the **SALES | Payment Methods** section:

Here, you can see that Magento recommends the following payment solutions:

- **PayPal Express Checkout**
- **Braintree**

However, in the **Recommended Solutions** section, you will see that there is a link located in the bottom-right corner–**Other PayPal Payment Solutions**. If you click on that link, you will see the other PayPal solutions that are included in Magento:

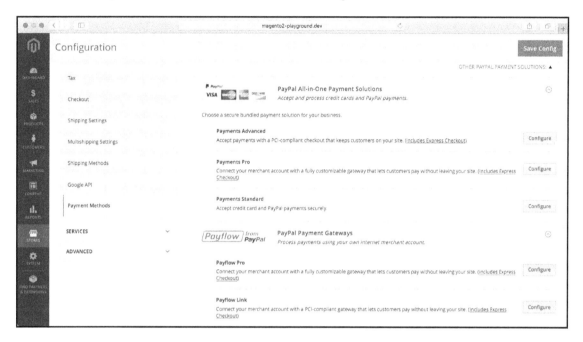

This makes a total of 13 payment solutions that are included in Magento out-of-the-box, which gives you a lot of alternatives to set up the payment methods that you prefer.

Setting up PayPal

PayPal Express Checkout is one of the most widely used payment methods for e-commerce. The customer will be able to log in using their PayPal account or pay with a credit or debit card as a PayPal guest.

We will describe the process of setting up **PayPal Express Checkout** for your Magento store. At the end of the setup, the PayPal button will be included on the Storefront as follows:

Product details page:

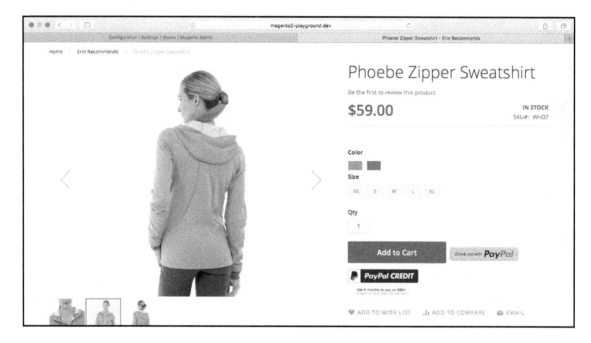

Mini cart in the header:

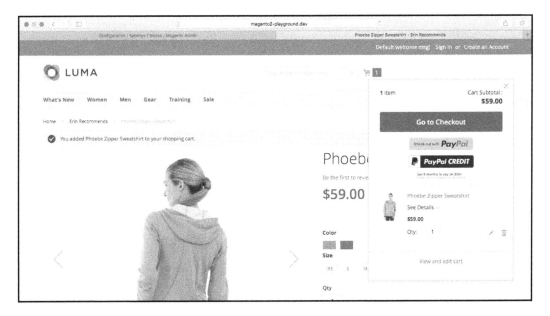

Shopping cart page:

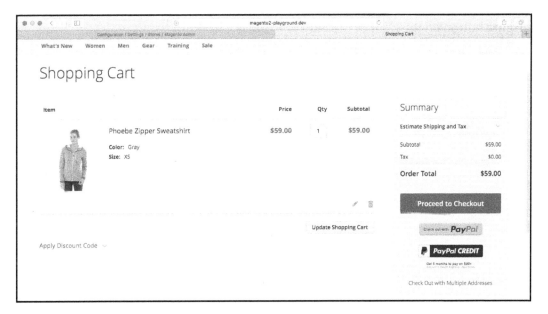

Checkout page:

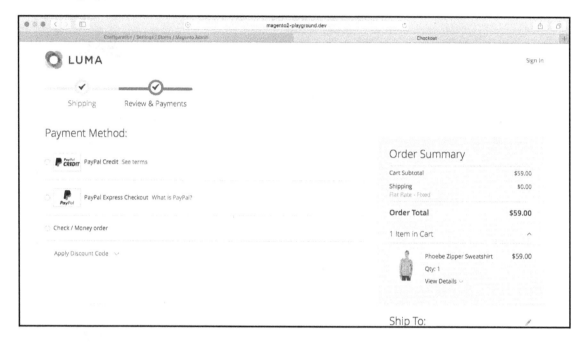

Now, if you go back to the **SALES | Payment Methods** section, you will see that there is a **Configure** button on the right of the **PayPal Express Checkout** section:

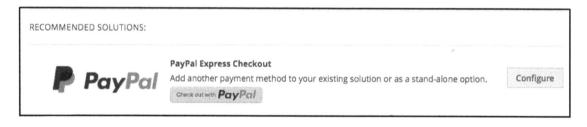

If you click on that button, the following form will be displayed:

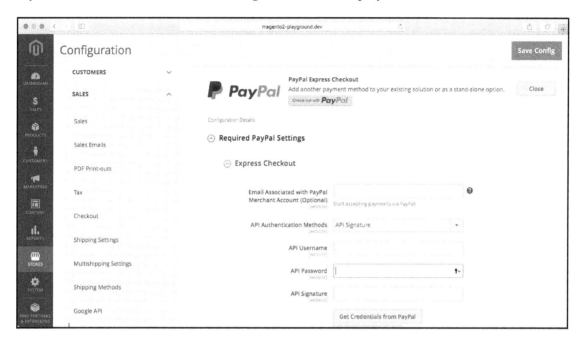

You will need the API username, password, and signature from your account in order to use PayPal Express Checkout.

You can get that information by following these steps:

1. Log in to your PayPal Business Account:

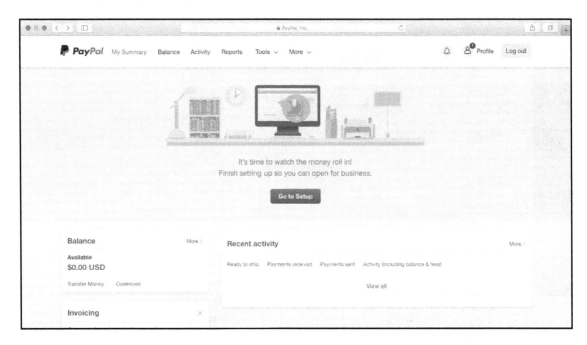

2. Click on the **Profile** link in the top-right corner of the screen and then on **Profile and Settings**.

3. Click on **My Setting Tools** and then on the **Update** link in the **API access** section:

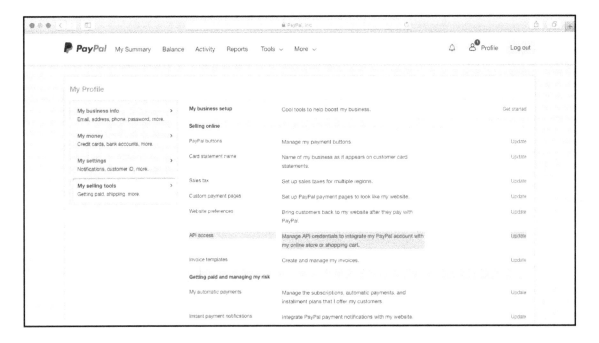

4. Click on the **Request API Credentials** link in the **NVP/SOAP API integration** section:

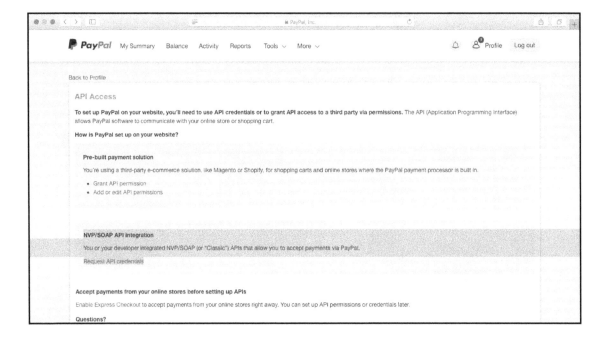

5. Click on the **Request API signature** link and click on **Agree and Submit**:

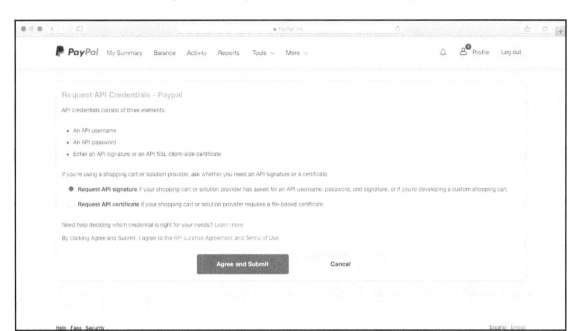

Now that you have the credentials, copy and paste that information in the **PayPal Express Checkout** form in Magento.

In addition to that, you will see the basic and advanced settings to configure at the end of the **PayPal Express Checkout** section:

You will see the following fields for the **Basic Settings** form:

- **Title**: You can customize the title that will be displayed for this payment method in the Storefront.
- **Sort Order**: You can set the specific order in the list of payment methods on the Storefront, *0* being the payment method that would be displayed at the top of the list.
- **Payment Action**: You can choose between the following actions for the purchase:
    - **Authorization**: In this action, the purchase is approved but the payment should be authorized by the merchant to charge the customer. The merchant is responsible for invoicing and then fulfilling the order.

- **Sale**: The customer will be charged immediately when the order is placed. Magento will create the invoice when PayPal confirms the payment.
- **Order**: The purchase represents an agreement between PayPal and the merchant. The total amount can be captured by the merchant at any time during the next 29 days.

- **Display on Product Details Page**: Select whether or not the PayPal buttons should be displayed on the **Product Details** page.

And you will see the following fields for the **Advanced Settings** form:

- **Display on Shopping Cart**: Select whether or not the PayPal buttons should be displayed on the shopping cart page and the mini shopping cart in the header
- **Payment Applicable From**: Restrict **PayPal Express Checkout** to only be available as a payment method in specific countries
- **Debug Mode**: Enable debug mode to log useful information for debugging during development
- **Enable SSL verification**: Enable SSL protection for **PayPal Express Checkout**
- **Transfer Cart Line Items**: Include details about the purchased items in PayPal
- **Transfer Shipping Options**: Include details about the shipping options in PayPal
- **Shortcut Buttons Flavor**: Choose between dynamic or static shortcut buttons
- **Enable PayPal Guest Checkout**: Allow customers who don't have a PayPal account to use **PayPal Express Checkout**
- **Require Customer's Billing Address**: Specify whether the customer should include a billing address for **PayPal Express Checkout**
- **Billing Agreement Signup**: Allow the customer to save the billing details for the next purchase through a billing agreement
- **Skip Order Review Step**: Skip the order review step when using**PayPal Express Checkout**

PCI compliance

PCI compliance ensures that your customers can securely use credit cards to purchase from your store. All credit card associations require merchants to implement PCI Compliance to protect their customers online.

Magento includes payment gateways that securely transmit credit card data through direct API post methods or hosted payment forms provided by the payment gateway.

The following are the requirements to meet the **Payment Card Industry Data Security Standard (PCI DSS)**:

1. Install and maintain a firewall configuration to protect cardholder data.
2. Do not use vendor-supplied defaults for system passwords and other security parameters.
3. Protect stored cardholder data.
4. Encrypt the transmission of cardholder data across open public networks.
5. Use and regularly update your antivirus software.
6. Develop and maintain secure systems and applications.
7. Restrict access to cardholder data to business need-to-know.
8. Assign a unique ID to each person with computer access.
9. Restrict physical access to cardholder data.
10. Track and monitor all access to network resources and cardholder data.
11. Regularly test security systems and processes.
12. Maintain a policy that addresses information security.

There are two methods to protect your customers and guarantee PCI compliance:

- **Direct post**: The information is sent directly to the payment gateway without data flowing through or being stored on Magento.
- **Hosted payment form**: The payment form is integrated in the Magento checkout, but it is hosted by the payment gateway rather than by the Magento application.

By keeping sensitive data outside the Magento instance, merchants can validate compliance through self-assessment at the SAQ A or SAQ A-EP level without having to go through the PCI compliance reassessment of the entire Magento platform.

Summary

In this chapter, we reviewed the list of default Magento payment methods, and we implemented **PayPal Express Checkout** for the store. In addition to that, we discussed PCI Compliance and SSL encryption.

In the next chapter, we will discuss the different shipping methods that are included in Magento 2, we will set up UPS as a shipping method, and we will cover the configuration of additional shipping methods for our Magento store.

16
Configuring Shipping

We will cover the following concepts in this chapter:

- An overview of the default Magento shipping methods
- How to set up shipping with UPS
- Other carriers

Overview of the default Magento shipping methods

In this chapter, we will go through the configuration for the Magento shipping methods. All sections for the configuration are located in the **STORES** | **Configuration** | **SALES** | **Shipping Methods** page.

On this page, you will see a list of all the shipping methods that are available by default in Magento 2:

As you can see in the preceding screenshot, the following shipping methods are included in a default Magento 2 installation:

- **Flat Rate**
- **Free Shipping**
- **Table Rates**
- **UPS**
- **USPS**
- **FedEx**
- **DHL**

Flat Rate

Let's start by reviewing **Flat Rate**. If you expand this section, you will see the following form:

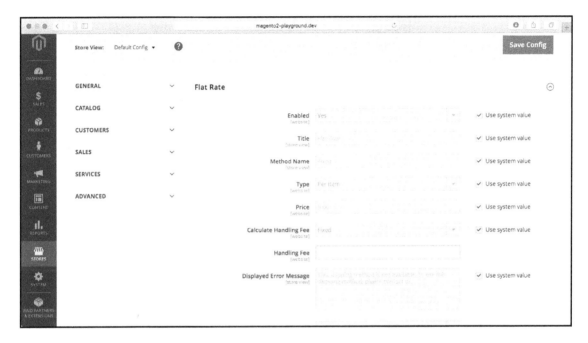

This is a predefined charge that will be applied to the orders in your store. The amount defined as the cost for shipping is fixed and depends on the configuration that you set from the admin panel.

In order to configure the method, you should update the following fields:

- **Enabled**: Specify whether **Flat Rate** should be available as a shipping method on the Storefront.
- **Title**: A descriptive title for the shipping method.
- **Method Name**: This is the label that is displayed next to the rate on the Storefront.

- **Type**: This is the calculation that is done by Magento to set the rate for the shipping method. The following types are available:
    - **None**: Flat Rate is available on the Storefront as a shipping method, but the rate will be zero (free shipping)
    - **Per Order**: The amount defined as the price for the **Flat Rate** shipping method will be charged to the order
    - **Per Item**: The amount defined as the price for the **Flat Rate** shipping method will be multiplied by the number of items in the cart to set the shipping rate for the order
- **Price**: This is the price that will be used to calculate the final shipping rate based on the option chosen in the previous field.
- **Calculate Handling Fee**: Set whether the handling fee is a fixed amount or a percentage, based on the price defined in the previous field.
- **Handling Fee**: This will be a fixed amount or a percentage to calculate the handling fee.
- **Displayed Error Message**: The error message to be displayed when the shipping method is not available.
- **Ship to Applicable Countries**: Specify whether the shipping method should be available for all countries or only specific countries. If you choose specific countries, the **Ship to Specific Countries** dropdown will be enabled to select the countries that will be available for this shipping method.
- **Sort Order**: Set the order to determine the position of **Flat Rate** in the list of available shipping methods on the Storefront. The lower the number, the higher it will appear on the list.

Free Shipping

The next available shipping method is **Free Shipping**. If you expand that section, you will see the following form:

The **Free Shipping** method, as its name suggests, is the ability to configure a specific shipping method exclusively for free shipping. This is one of the most frequent promotions in online stores and you can specify the rules to set free shipping as available in specific scenarios, from a minimum order amount to shipping cart price rules that should be met to allow **Free Shipping** for the order.

The following fields are available to configure the shipping method:

- **Enabled**: Specify whether **Free Shipping** should be available as a shipping method in the Storefront.
- **Title**: A descriptive title for the shipping method.
- **Method Name**: This is the label that is displayed next to the rate on the Storefront.
- **Minimum Order Amount**: Set the minimum amount for the order to qualify for free shipping.

- **Displayed Error Message**: The error message to be displayed when the shipping method is not available.

- **Ship to Applicable Countries**: Specify whether the shipping method should be available for all countries or only specific countries. If you choose specific countries, the **Ship to Specific Countries** dropdown will be enabled to select the countries that will be available for this shipping method.

- **Sort Order**: Set the order to determine the position of **Free Shipping** in the list of available shipping methods on the Storefront. The lower the number, the higher it will appear on the list.

Table Rates

Next, we will find **Table Rates** available to configure as a shipping method. If you expand the **Table Rates** section, you will see the following form:

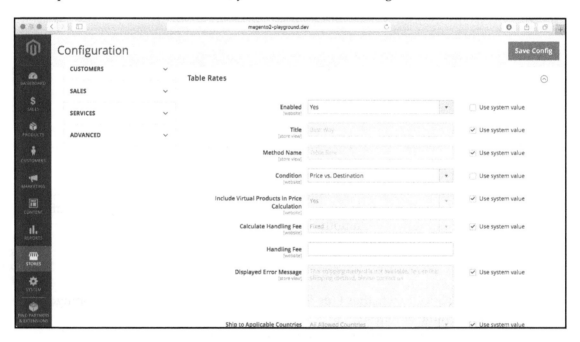

This shipping method allows you to define a CSV file to calculate the shipping rate. The format for the CSV file depends on the condition for the shipping calculation. You can choose any of the following conditions:

- **Weight Vs. Destination**
- **Price Vs. Destination**
- **# of items Vs. Destination**

The following fields are available in the **Table Rates** shipping method configuration:

- **Enabled**: Specify whether **Table Rates** should be available as a shipping method on the Storefront.
- **Title**: A descriptive title for the shipping method.
- **Method Name**: This is the label that is displayed next to the rate on the Storefront.
- **Condition**: This is the condition to calculate the rate based on the table that you upload. The available conditions are:
    - **Weight Vs. Destination**
    - **Price versus Destination**
    - **# of items Vs. Destination**
- **Include Virtual Products in Price Calculation**: Define whether virtual products should be included in the rate calculation. Since the table rates shipping is used to calculate the price based on the customer address (distance), most of the times, this option is set to **No** since virtual products are delivered through e-mail.
- **Calculate Handling Fee**: Set whether the handling fee is a fixed amount or a percentage based on the price defined in the previous field.
- **Handling Fee**: This will be a fixed amount or a percentage to calculate the handling fee.
- **Displayed Error Message**: The error message to be displayed when the shipping method is not available.
- **Ship to Applicable Countries**: Specify whether the shipping method should be available for all countries or only specific countries. If you choose specific countries, the **Ship to Specific Countries** dropdown will be enabled to select the countries that will be available for this shipping method.
- **Sort Order**: Set the order to determine the position of *Flat Rate* in the list of available shipping methods on the Storefront. The lower the number, the higher it will appear on the list.

Now, in order to upload the CSV file for the **Table Rates** method, you should filter by website using the dropdown in the top-left corner of the screen. After that, two new fields will appear in the **Table Rates** form: **Export** and **Import**. You can see the dropdown to filter by website and the new fields in the following screenshot:

You can export the current CSV for the **Table Rates** shipping method by using the **Export CSV** button in the **Export** field. If you haevn't uploaded a CSV yet, you will be able to download the CSV that is included in Magento by default. It is especially important to have a template to use to create your own CSV file for your store.

This is the CSV that is included in Magento by default:

	A	B	C	D	E
1	Country	Region/State	Zip/Postal Code	Order Subtotal (and above)	Shipping Price
2	USA	*	*	0	15
3	USA	*	*	50	10
4	USA	*	*	100	5
5	USA	AK	*	0	20
6	USA	AK	*	50	15
7	USA	AK	*	100	10
8	USA	HI	*	0	20
9	USA	HI	*	50	15
10	USA	HI	*	100	10

You can edit that CSV to have new information for your custom **Table Rates** shipping method, and then upload the CSV file using the **Choose File** button next to the **Import** field.

UPS/USPS/FedEx/DHL

Magento supports several carriers by default, allowing your customers to get shipping rates for their orders from those carriers on the Storefront.

These methods are also known as **online rates** since the rate for shipping is calculated on the fly based on the customer address.

To enable any of the carriers in Magento, you just have to set up the general information for the shipping method, such us **Enabled for Checkout**, **Title**, **Handling Fee**, which is the same information as the other methods that we reviewed, and specific information for the carrier, such us **Gateway URL**, **Account ID**, and so on.

In the next section, we will set up UPS to get shipping rates from that carrier on your Storefront and enable that shipping method in your Magento store.

How to set up shipping with UPS

United Parcel Service (**UPS**) is one of the most popular shipping carriers available by default in Magento, supporting more than 220 countries.

We will configure UPS as a shipping method in Magento to allow customers to choose that carrier on the Storefront for their orders.

If you go to the **SALES** | **Shipping Methods** | **UPS** section in the **STORES** | **Configuration** page, you will see the following form on the screen:

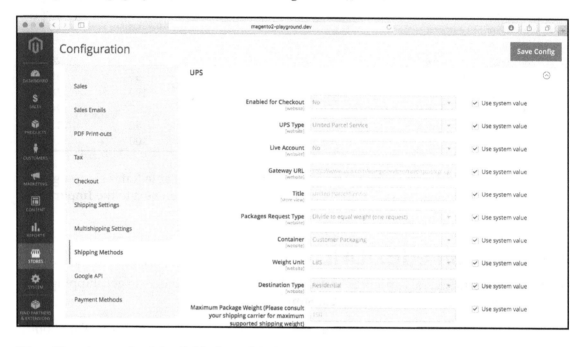

We will review each of the fields from this form:

- **General configuration**:
    - **Enabled for Checkout**: Specify whether UPS should be available as a shipping method on the Storefront.
    - **UPS Type**: You can choose between **United Parcel Service** or **United Parcel Service XML**. With **United Parcel Service**, you can get real-time shipping rates, and with **United Parcel Service XML**, you can get real-time rates and print labels for UPS.
- **UPS-specific configuration depending on UPS type**: The following fields depend on the **UPS Type** that you choose in the previous field that we reviewed. If you choose **United Parcel Service** as a **UPS Type**, the following fields will be available:
    - **Live Account**: Choose **Yes** to activate UPS in production. If you choose **No**, you will activate UPS as a shipping method in the test mode.
    - **Gateway URL**: The default gateway URL is included in Magento. If you need to change the gateway URL, you can do it from this field.

- **Title**: A descriptive title for the shipping method.
- **Packages Request Type**: You can choose **Divide to equal weight (one request)** or **Use origin weight (few requests)**.

And if you choose **United Parcel Service XML** as a UPS type, the following fields will be available:

- **Live Account**: Choose **Yes** to activate UPS in production. If you choose **No**, you will activate UPS as a shipping method in the test mode.
- **Access License Number**: Your UPS access key.
- **Gateway XML URL**: The default gateway XML URL is included in Magento. If you need to change the gateway XML URL, you can do that from this field.
- **Mode**: As you can see in the comment for the field, this setting enables or disables SSL verification of the Magento server by UPS.
- **User ID**: Your UPS User ID.
- **Origin of the Shipment**: Select one of the options from the dropdown to specify the origin of the shipment.
- **Password**: Your UPS account password.
- **Title**: A descriptive title for the shipping method.
- **Enable Negotiated Rates**: Enable negotiated shipping rates with UPS.
- **Packages Request Type**: You can choose **Divide to equal weight (one request)** or **Use origin weight (several requests)**.
- **Shipper Number**: This is a six-character UPS code, which is required for negotiated rates.
- **Tracking XML URL**: The default tracking XML URL is included in Magento. If you need to change the tracking XML URL, you can do that from this field.

Other configuration: The following fields are available for both **United Parcel Service** and **United Parcel Service XML** UPS types:

- **Container**: Set the container for the shipment.
- **Weight Unit**: Set the weight unit for the shipping method.
- **Destination Type**: Select whether the destination type is residential or commercial.
- **Maximum Package Weight**: Set the number for the maximum package weight in the carrier.
- **Pickup Method**: Set the pickup to any of the following methods:
    - **Regular Daily Pickup**
    - **On Call Air**

- **One Time Pickup**
- **Letter Center**
- **Customer Counter**

- **Minimum Package Weight**: Set the number for the minimum package weight in the carrier.
- **Calculate Handling Fee**: Set whether the handling fee is a fixed amount or a percentage, based on the price defined in the previous field.
- **Handling Fee**: This will be a fixed amount or a percentage to calculate the handling fee.
- **Allowed Methods**: Select the UPS methods that will be available for selection on the Storefront.
- **Free Methods**: Select the UPS method that should be available for selection as free shipping.
- **Free Shipping Amount Threshold**: When the total order amount is above this number, the UPS method that was selected in the previous field will be available for selection as free shipping.
- **Displayed Error Message**: The error message to be displayed when the shipping method is not available.
- **Ship to Applicable Countries**: Specify whether the shipping method should be available for all countries or only specific countries. If you choose specific countries, the **Ship to Specific Countries** dropdown will be enabled to select the countries that will be available for this shipping method.
- **Show Method if Not Applicable**: Specify whether or not the shipping method should be visible on the Storefront when the method is not available.
- **Debug**: Enable debug mode to log useful information for debugging during development.
- **Sort Order**: Set the order to determine the position of **UPS** in the list of available shipping methods on the Storefront. The lower the number, the higher it will appear on the list.

Once you set up the shipping method, customers will be able to get rates from UPS to select the shipping method for their orders.

Other carriers

It's well known that one of the most important factors for customers who buy online is shipping. That is why adding new carriers is something that you should consider if your customers are looking for a shipping method that is not included in Magento.

Fortunately, you can find many additional carriers and new features for shipping in the Magento marketplace.

You can search in the extension marketplace using the search bar at `https://marketplace.magento.com`:

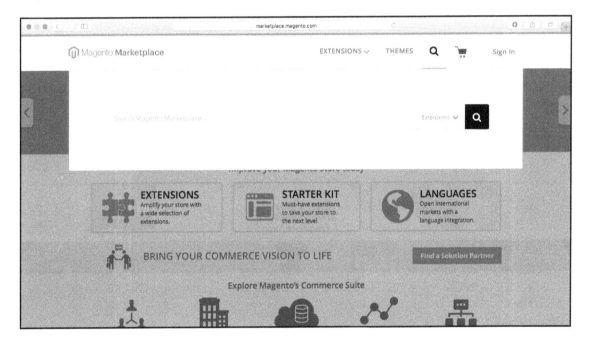

You can find all the extensions related to shipping at `https://marketplace.magento.com/extensions/shipping-fulfillment.html`.

There, you will see that you can filter by Magento edition, version, extension ratings, price, and type of extension developer:

Summary

In this chapter, we reviewed the shipping methods that are included in Magento by default. In the next chapter, we will review the process of fulfilling an order, including an overview of the life cycle of an order in Magento.

17
Fulfilling Orders

In this chapter, we will go through the following concepts:

- Order management
- State and status
- Invoices, shipping, and credit memos

Order management

Magento offers a powerful yet simple way to manage the orders that are placed in your store. You can even place orders from the admin panel if a customer calls by phone and wants to buy products from your store.

You can see and manage your orders from the **SALES** | **Orders** page in the admin panel:

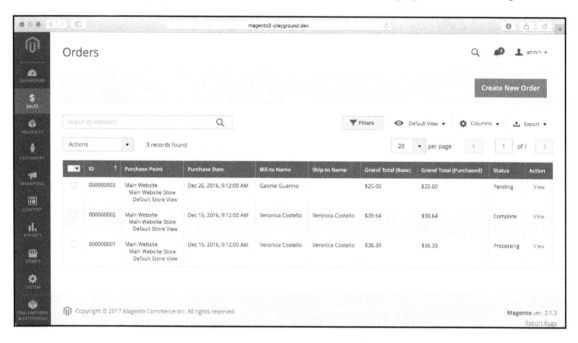

A very important aspect of this page is that you can select really useful mass actions to manage your orders:

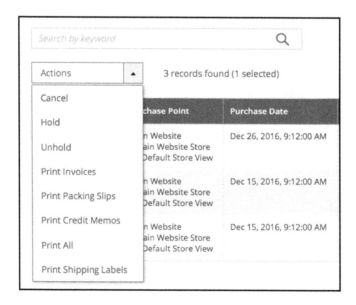

As you can see, you can put several orders on hold at the same time, print invoices for several orders, and so on. Besides this, the **Orders** grid allows you to continue using all the utilities from the Magento 2 admin panel grids, such as the following ones:

- Filters
- Selectable columns
- Export to CSV and XML
- Search by keyword

If you click on any order from the grid, you will be redirected to the order page:

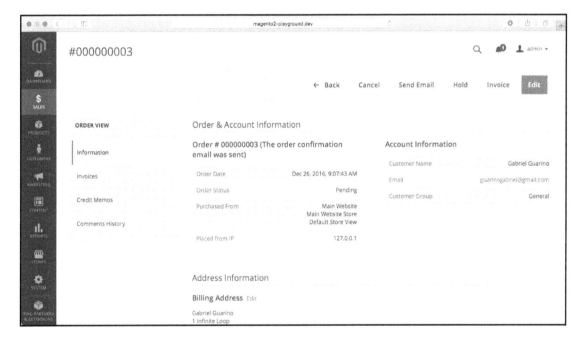

The first thing you will notice is that you have several actions for this order on the top-right corner of the screen:

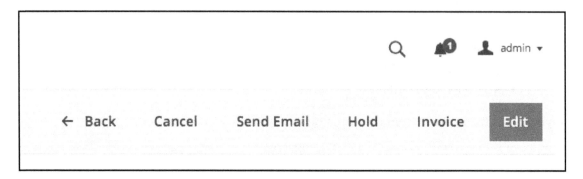

You can click on these buttons to quickly perform an action for these orders–from sending the order e-mail to the customer to putting the order on hold, creating an invoice, or even editing the order.

- **Information tab**

Let's take a look at each of the sections from the **Information** tab:

Order & Account Information

Order # 000000003 (The order confirmation email was sent)

Order Date	Dec 26, 2016, 9:07:43 AM
Order Status	Pending
Purchased From	Main Website Main Website Store Default Store View
Placed from IP	127.0.0.1

Account Information

Customer Name	Gabriel Guarino
Email	guarinogabriel@gmail.com
Customer Group	General

Here, you can see the basic information from the order. It's essential to know the store for this order (in the case of a multistore Magento website), the customer name, e-mail, and even the IP address in case of a suspicious order.

The next two sections are **Address Information** and **Payment & Shipping Method**:

Address Information

Billing Address Edit

Gabriel Guarino
1 Infinite Loop
Cupertino, California, 95014
United States
T: 123-123-1234

Payment & Shipping Method

Payment Information

Check / Money order

The order was placed using USD.

As you can see in the first section, you can edit the customer address (both shipping and billing) in case of any typo or mistake from the customer when the order was placed.

Finally, we have the **Items Ordered** and the **Order Total** sections:

In the **Items Ordered** section, you will find the list of items and the configuration chosen by the customer for each one of them (in the case of configurable products or products with custom options).

In the **Order Total** section, you will see the **Notes for this Order** and the **Order Totals**. A very important feature for order management in Magento is the ability to add comments to the orders to keep track of the history–from the moment the order was placed to the moment the order is delivered.

You can add as many comments as you need, and you can make those comments visible to the customer in the Customer Account page on the Storefront as well as notify the customer by e-mail. It's good to mention that Magento automatically adds comments in the order as well; for example, when the credit card payment is processed, you will be able to see the transaction amount as well as the transaction ID of the credit card.

Finally, in the **Order Totals** section, you can keep track of the **Grand Total**, the total amount paid, the total amount refunded, and the total amount due.

- **Invoices tab**

If you go to the **Invoices** tab, you will see a grid containing all the invoices that have been generated for this order. In the preceding example, you can see the grid with no invoices (we will generate an invoice later in this chapter):

The only mass action available for this grid is **PDF Invoices**, which downloads a copy of each of the selected invoices in the PDF format.

- **Credit memos tab**

In this section, you can see the full list of credit memos that have been generated for this order:

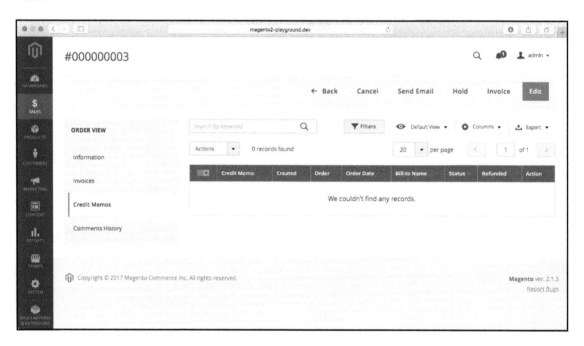

Just like the **Invoices** tab, there is one mass action available on this grid to download the PDF for all the selected credit memos.

- **Shipments tab**

In this section, you can see the full list of shipments that have been generated for this order. One thing to note is that the tab wasn't available in the previous images. This is because the shipments tab is only available in physical orders, and the order that we have been reviewing so far was an order that contains just 1 downloadable product.

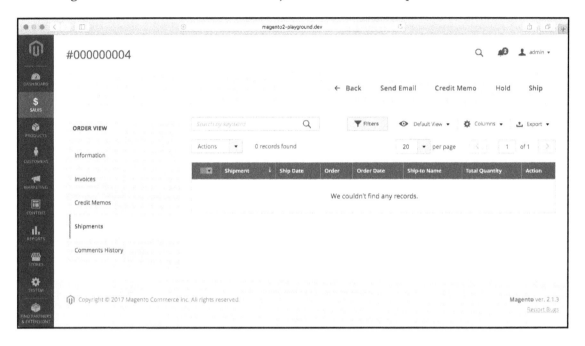

- **Comments history tab**

In addition to the **Notes for this Order** section in the **Information** tab, you can review the full list of comments on the order from the **Comments History** tab:

If you need to edit the customer order, you can do that by clicking on the **Edit** button in the top-right corner of the screen. However, if you click on that button, you will see the following message:

Even though the name of that action is **Edit**, the reality is that the current order will be canceled and you will be redirected to a form with the same information as that of the current order, but with the ability to edit that information before creating the order.

Editing the order would be necessary in case you needed to edit the items that the customer purchased, but it's not necessary to change the address information. If you click on the **Edit** button next to the **Billing Address** or **Shipping Address**, you will be redirected to the following form to edit those details:

As you can see in the message in the preceding screenshot, changing the shipping address is not going to alter the order total since the shipping, tax, and order amount are not recalculated.

This means that editing the address is useful when there is a typo in the street name, for example, but in the case of a completely different address, you should cancel the order and create a new one (basically, by pressing the **Edit** button) to get the updated shipping and tax rates.

Now, let's go back to the **Orders** grid. There you will see a button in the top-right corner of the screen to create a new order:

If you click on that button, you will be redirected to the following screen:

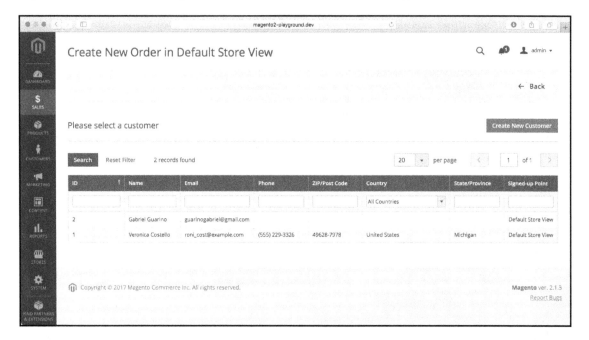

The first step in the process of creating a new order is selecting the customer. You can either select a customer from the list or create a new customer using the button that is in the top-right corner of the screen.

Once you have the customer, the next step is to add all the information related to the order on the following page:

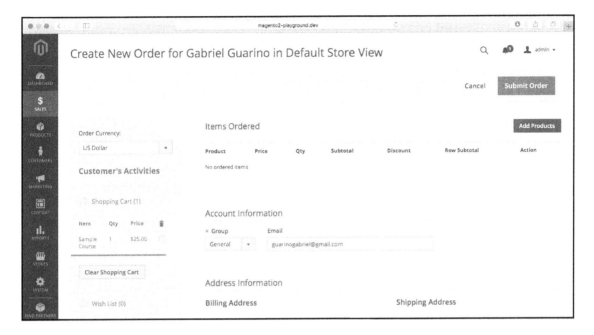

This is a very long form with a lot of options to configure the order.

The first thing to note is the sidebar on the left. You can select the currency for the order, and also, you can update the order based on the customer activity.

You will be able to see all the items that the customer has in the shopping cart on the Storefront, the list of items in the wishlist, the last ordered items, the products in the comparison list, the recently compared products, and the recently viewed products. This is a quick way of selecting the products for order, and it's based on the history of the customer's actions on the Storefront.

Now, let's start with the first section, **Items Ordered**.

If you click on the **Add Products** button on the right side of this section, the following grid will be displayed:

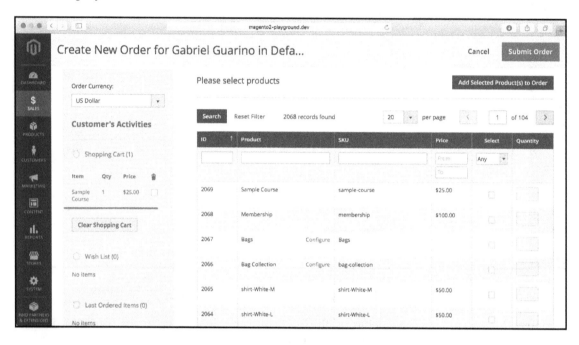

As you can see in the **Product** column, there is a **Configure** link available for bundle, grouped, and configurable products. If you click on that button, you will be able to configure those products for the customer in the following window:

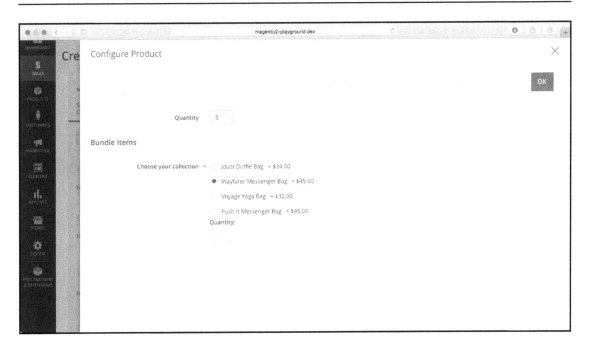

Once you've selected all the products for the order, you can click on the **Add Selected Product(s) to the Order** button to update the **Items Ordered** grid:

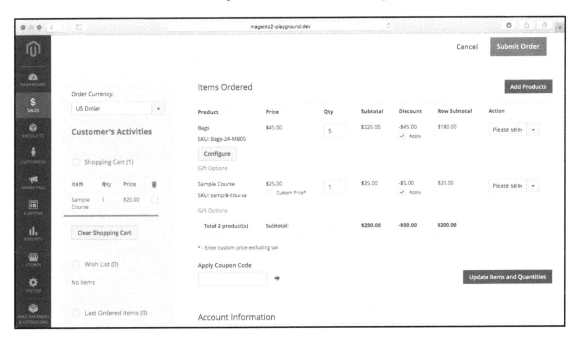

Finally, in the **Items Ordered** section, you can see the **Apply Coupon Code** field. Let's say, we received a call from the customer and we are placing the order from the admin panel; if the customer has a coupon code for a promotion in the store, you can add the coupon code in that field and the promotion will be applied.

Next, we have the **Account Information** and **Address Information** sections:

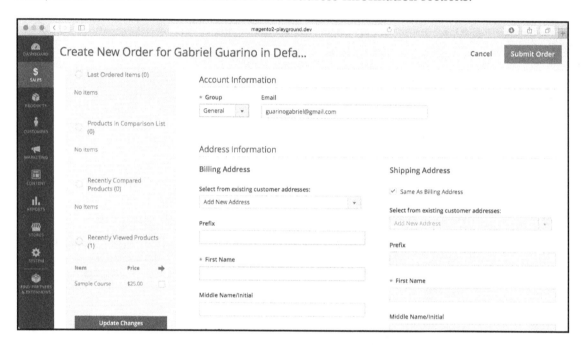

In the first section, you can change the customer group and the customer e-mail for the order. In the second section, you can select an existing address from the customer account, or add a new address in case you do not have any address available for the customer or you need a different address for the order. In addition to that, you can select **Same As Billing Address** to use the shipping address as the billing address (this option is marked by default in new orders).

Finally, we can see the **Payment & Shipping Information** and the **Order Total** sections:

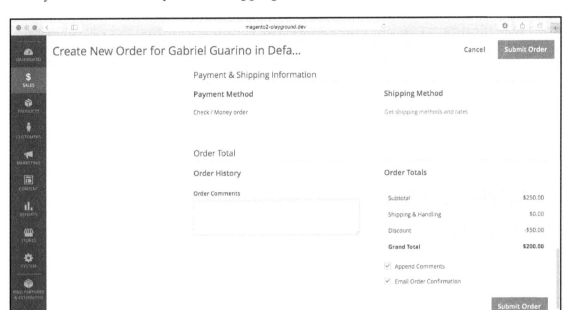

In the **Payment & Shipping Information** section, you can select the payment and shipping method for the order with the shipping rates calculated using the address that you'd specified in the previous section.

If you click on the **Get shipping methods and rates** link, the shipping rates will be calculated on the fly using the shipping address for the order, and you will be able to select the shipping method that the customer prefers.

Finally, in the **Order Total** section, you can add comments to the order as we saw earlier, review the order totals, and select whether you want to append the comments and send the order confirmation through e-mail to the customer.

State and status

Right from the moment the order is created in Magento, it is processed and goes through different states and statuses.

Magento uses the order states internally to identify the current phase of the order. These states are not customizable and not visible in the backend; they are only visible in the codebase and the database of Magento.

Order statuses are used by the store administrator to set up a flow for the order, from the beginning of the purchase to the moment the order is invoiced and the products are delivered. These statuses are customizable by the store administrator in the Magento admin panel.

You can see the list of all the internal order states in the `sales_order_status_state` database table:

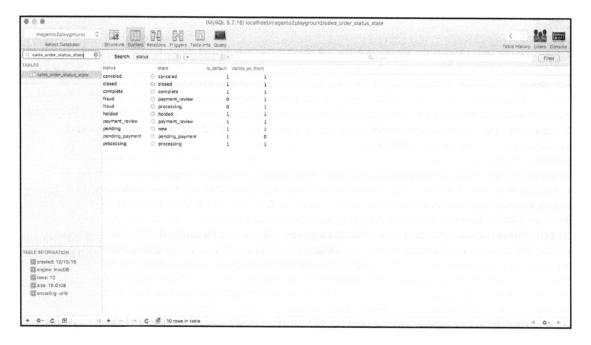

You can manage the order statuses from the following section in the admin panel:

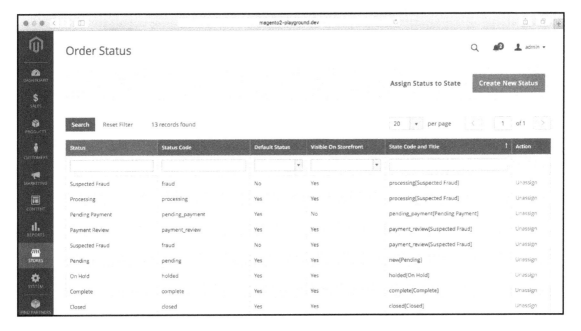

There are 13 statuses available by default in Magento 2:

- **Suspect Fraud**
- **Processing**
- **Pending Payment**
- **Payment Review**
- **Pending**
- **On Hold**
- **Complete**
- **Closed**
- **Canceled**
- **PayPal Canceled Reversal**
- **Pending PayPal**
- **PayPal Reversed**

You can create a new status by clicking on the **Create New Status** button in the top-right corner of the screen. The following form will be displayed on the screen:

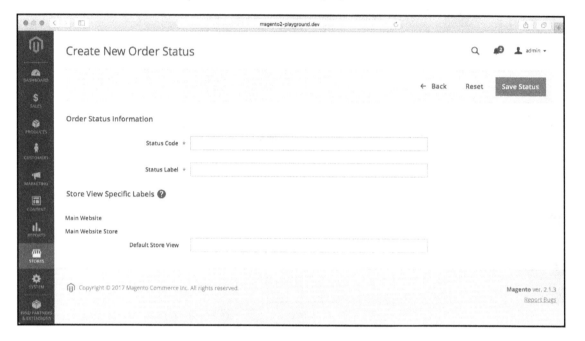

If you go back to the grid, you will see a second button next to the **Create New Status** button: **Assign Status to State**.

If you click on that button, you will be able to assign a specific status to an internal Magento state:

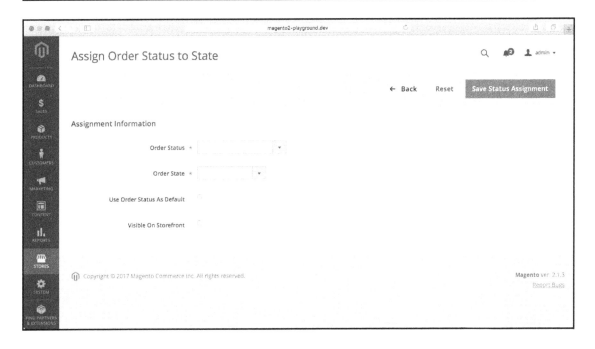

Invoices, shipping, and credit memos

The process of generating and managing invoices, shipping, and credit memos is very simple, and the process is the same for all of them.

If you go to the order page, you will see the tabs that we reviewed before, including the following ones:

- **Invoices**
- **Credit Memos**
- **Shipments**

From those two sections, as we saw before, we can see the list of invoices and credit memos for that order.

You can create an invoice for the order by clicking on the **Invoices** button next to the **Edit** button in the top-right corner of the screen:

When you click on the button, you will see a preview of all the information that will be included in the invoice, and you will be able to append comments and e-mail a copy of the invoice through e-mail:

When you click on **Submit Invoice**, the invoice is generated and the order status is updated. Next, you can create a shipment for the order.

If you go to the **Shipments** tab, you will see the list of shipments that have been created for the current order:

In order to create a shipment, you should click on **Ship** in the top-right corner of the screen. You will be redirected to the following page:

On that page, you can edit the shipping and billing address, add the tracking number for the shipped product, specify which items will be shipped, add comments, and send a copy of the shipment through e-mail. Once you click on **Submit Shipment**, the shipment is created, the order status is updated, and the information for the shipment can be reviewed from the shipments tab:

When the order is invoiced, you can create credit memos by clicking on the **Credit Memo** button in the top-right corner of the screen. You will be redirected to the following page:

There, you can mark the items to be returned to stock, set the quantity to refund, refund a specific amount for shipping, and adjust the refund and fee. In addition to that, as we saw for invoices and shipments, you can add comments and send a copy through e-mail:

If you click on **Refund Offline** , the credit memo will be generated and the following message will be displayed on the screen:

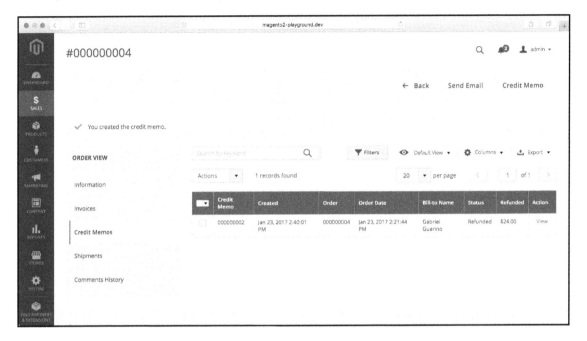

Summary

In this chapter, we went through the life cycle of an order in Magento. In the next chapter, we will review how to modify transactional e-mails in Magento and manage the store newsletter.

18
Transactional E-mails and Newsletter

In this chapter, we will cover the following topics:

- Modifying transactional e-mail templates
- Modifying newsletter templates
- Handling newsletters and their subscribers

Modifying transactional e-mail templates

Magento provides all the transactional e-mail templates that you need to launch your e-commerce store. A transactional e-mail is an e-mail that is automatically sent to the customer by Magento when a specific action occurs in your store, for example, when a user creates a customer account or when a new order is placed.

You can modify the default transactional e-mails that are included in Magento 2 from the **MARKETING** | **Communications** | **Email Templates** page in the admin panel.

If you open the page for the first time, you will see that the grid is empty:

Only the transactional e-mails that have been modified by the administrator will be displayed on the **Email Templates** grid. You can modify or add a transactional e-mail template by clicking on the **Add New Templat**e button.

The **New Template** page will be displayed:

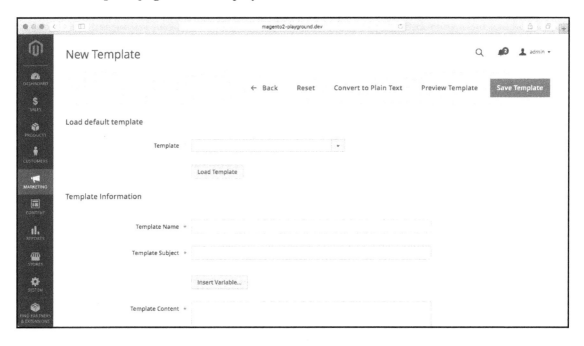

As you can see in the **Template** dropdown, this is the list of transactional e-mails that are included in Magento 2:

- **Customer Account:**
  - New Account
  - New Account Confirmation Key
  - New Account Confirmed
  - New Account Without Password
  - Forgot Password
  - Remind Password
  - Reset Password
  - Change Email
  - Change Email and Password
- **Customer Activity:**
  - Contact Form
  - Send Product Link to Friend
  - Wishlist Sharing

- **Newsletters:**
    - Subscription Confirmation
    - Subscription Success
    - Unsubscription Success
- **Product Alert:**
    - Cron Error Warning
    - Price Alert
    - Stock Alert
- **Promotions:**
    - Promotion Notification / Reminder
    - Admin Activity
    - Forgot Admin Password
    - Reset Password
- **Email Templates:**
    - Email – Header
    - Export Failed
    - Import Failed
- **Product Alert:**
    - Product Alerts Cron Error
    - Product Price Alert
    - Product Stock Alert
- **Order:**
    - New Order
    - New Order for Guest
    - Order Update
    - Order Update for Guest
    - Payment Failed
- **Invoice:**
    - New Invoice
    - New Invoice for Guest
    - Invoice Update
    - Invoice Update for Guest

- **Shipment:**
  - New Shipment
  - New Shipment for Guest
  - Shipment Update
  - Shipment Update for Guest
- **Credit Memo:**
  - Credit Memo Update
  - Credit Memo Update for Guest
  - New Credit Memo
  - New Credit Memo for Guest
- **System Notifications:**
  - Sitemap Generate Warnings
  - Currency Update Warnings

If you select the template and click on the **Load Template** button, the template content will be loaded in the form, as can be seen in the following screenshot:

In that form, you can set a descriptive name for the template, set the subject and the content, and add custom styles to render the layout for the template.

In addition to that, you can remove all the HTML tags from the template by clicking on the **Convert to Plain Text** button on top of the screen.

Next to that button, you will find the **Preview Template**, which allows you to see exactly how the template will be displayed to the customer.

As you can see in the following screenshot, the template is loaded in the Magento admin panel:

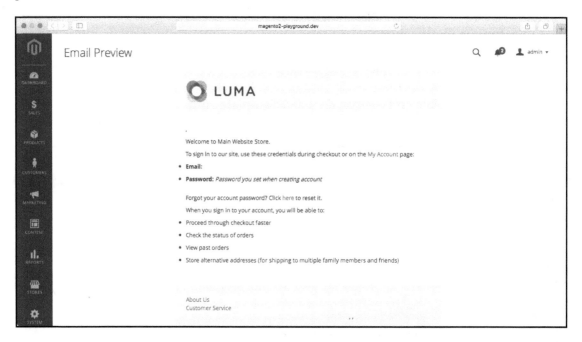

The logo for the e-mail is configured in the following section in the admin panel:

CONTENT | **Design** | **Configuration**

We will cover this section in `Chapter 20`, *Customizing your Magento Store*.

After adding the details and previewing the e-mail template, you can save the new template by clicking on the **Save Template** button.

You will be redirected to the **Email Templates** grid, and you will see a confirmation message:

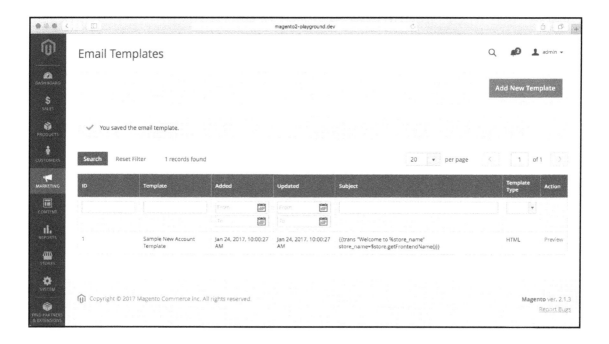

Modifying newsletter templates

You can see a list of the existing newsletter templates in the **MARKETING** | **Communications** | **Newsletter Templates** page in the admin panel.

As you can see in the following screenshot, the grid is empty in a default Magento 2 installation:

You can add a newsletter template by clicking on the **Add New Template** button in the top-right corner of the screen. The form is really similar to the new transactional e-mail template form and includes the same actions at the top:

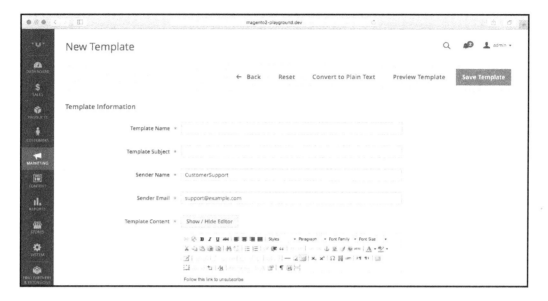

Since the form is really similar, and the actions are the same as the form that we reviewed before, we will go ahead and save a new template.

The new template has been saved and a confirmation message is displayed on the screen:

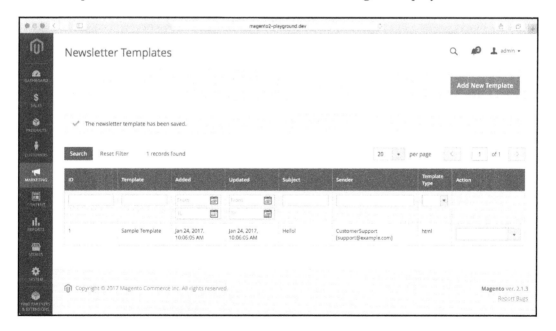

Handling newsletters and their subscribers

You can see a list of e-mail subscribers for your Magento store in the **MARKETING** | **Communications** | **Newsletter Subscribers** page in the admin panel.

As you can see in the following screenshot, the grid is empty when you first install Magento 2:

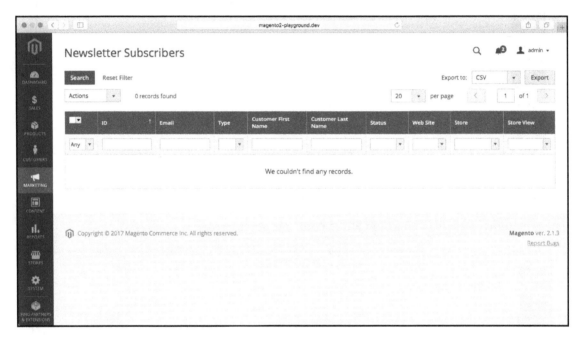

If we go to the Storefront, we will find the Subscribe box in the footer:

If you click on **Subscribe**, the following confirmation message will be displayed on screen:

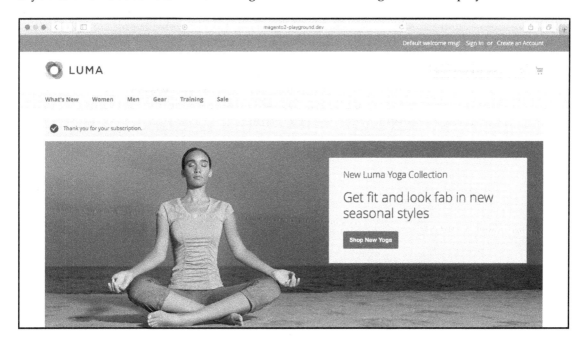

Now, if we go back to the **Newsletter Subscribers** page, we will see the new subscriber in the grid:

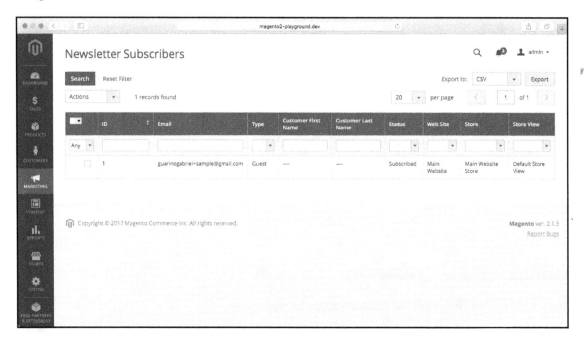

From that grid, you can unsubscribe or delete e-mail accounts using grid mass actions; you can export all the subscribers, filter them, and sort subscribers by column.

Now, if you go back to the **Newsletter Templates** page (**MARKETING | Communications | Newsletter Templates**), you will be able to add the newsletter template to the queue by using the dropdown in the last column:

You will be redirected to the **Edit Queue** page from which you can set the **Queue Date Start** to specify when the newsletter e-mail should be sent and edit the newsletter details:

After saving the template to include it in the queue, you will find that the template is pending, waiting to be sent to the **Newsletter Queue** page (**MARKETING** | **Communications** | **Newsletter Queue**):

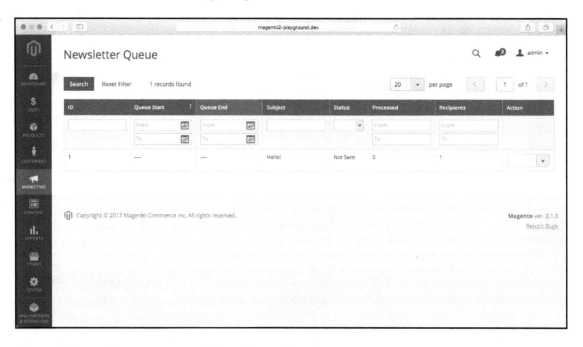

If you click on that row, you will be redirected to the same page as before, where you can set the **Queue Date Start** to specify when the newsletter should be sent and to modify the newsletter information.

Summary

In this chapter, we covered the process of modifying transactional e-mails and newsletters, and we scheduled a newsletter template to be sent to newsletter subscribers.
In the next chapter, we will create reports to track store sales, customer activity, and statistics related to the store catalog.

19
Reports

We will cover the following concepts in this chapter:

- Marketing reports
- Sales reports
- Customer reports
- Product reports

Magento reports

As a store owner and administrator, one of your key activities is tracking the activity and conversion rates of your Magento store. Magento includes several reports that you can review on a regular basis to always have the ability to take a look at the statistics of the store.

All reports can be accessed from the same menu item in the Magento admin panel: **Reports**

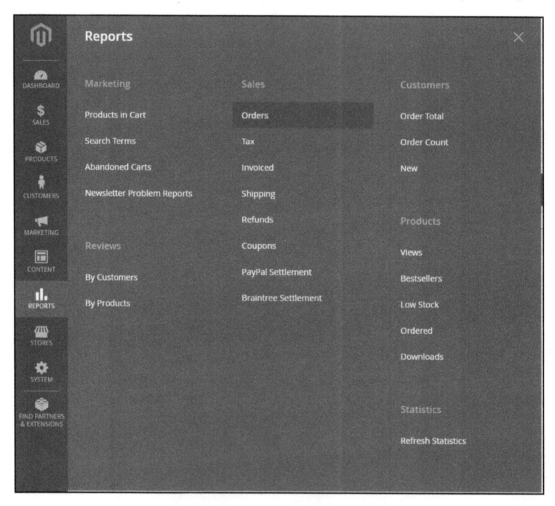

As you can see in the preceding image, Magento includes 22 reports divided into 5 groups, as follows:

- **Marketing**:
  - **Products in Cart**
  - **Search Terms**
  - **Abandoned Carts**
  - **Newsletter Problem Reports**

- Reviews:
    - By Customers
    - By Products
- Sales:
    - Orders
    - Tax
    - Invoiced
    - Shipping
    - Refunds
    - Coupons
    - PayPal Settlement
    - Braintree Settlement
- Customers:
    - Order Total
    - Order Count
    - New
- Products:
    - Views
    - Bestsellers
    - Low Stock
    - Ordered
    - Downloads

In addition to that, you will see an additional menu item at the end of the list: **Refresh Statistics**.

To optimize performance, Magento calculates and stores the information for each of the reports instead of calculating everything on the fly. In order to see the most recent information in your reports, you should refresh the statistics from that page in the Magento admin panel.

If you click on the **Refresh Statistics** menu item, you will be redirected to the following page:

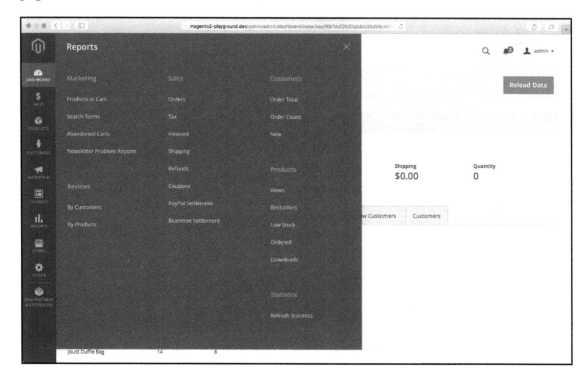

As you can see in the following image, there are two mass actions you can select to update the selected reports by refreshing lifetime statistics or just for the last day:

If **Refresh Lifetime Statistics** is selected, the confirmation message clarifies that the update may slow down the performance of your store:

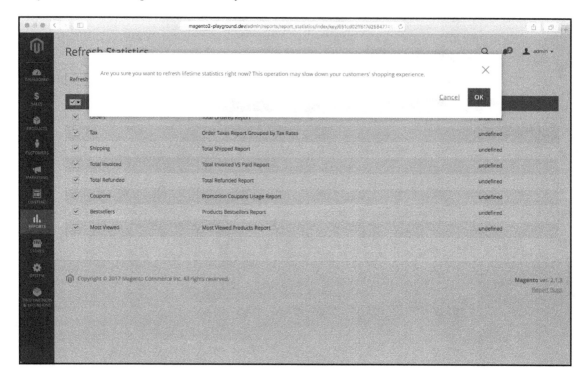

If you confirm the update, the data for your report will be up to date and the **Updated** date in the grid will show the time that the reports were updated at:

Let's review each of the reports:

- **Marketing | Products in Carts**: The first report in the marketing group is the **Products in Carts** report. As the name suggests, you can see the products that are currently in customers' shopping carts on the storefront or in pending orders in the admin panel.
- **Marketing | Search Terms**: The second report in the marketing group is the **Search Terms** report, which allows you to see the most popular search queries in your Magento store.
- **Marketing | Abandoned Carts**: The next report allows you to see the abandoned carts from your customers, which is really important in order to contact those customers again to motivate them to complete their order.

- **Marketing | Newsletter Problems Report**: If there are errors in the newsletter delivery, you will be able to see and review those errors from this report, and all the details about the errors will be located in the log file in the `var/log` folder.
- **Reviews | By Customers / By Products**: With these reports, you will be able to take a closer look at the statistics of the reviews in your store, grouping the statistics for those reviews by customers or by products.
- **Sales | Orders / Tax / Invoiced / Shipping / Refunds / Coupons**: See all the statistics related to orders, tax rates, invoices, shipping, credit memos, and coupons in your store. For all reports, there is a filter to see the report by period of time, date range, and order status.
- **Sales | PayPal Settlements / Braintree Settlements**: See the information for every transaction that affects the settlement of funds for PayPal and Braintree.
- **Customers | Orders Total**: See the total amount for the orders of each customer for a given period of time, including the average amount of orders by customer.
- **Customers | Order Count**: See the total number of orders by each customer for a given period of time, including the average number of orders by customer.
- **Customers | New**: Number of new customers by interval of a specific period of time.
- **Products | Views**: See the number of views for each of the products in the store in a specific period of time.
- **Products | Bestsellers**: Review the list of bestsellers for a given period of time.
- **Products | Low Stock**: Review the list of products that currently have a low stock quantity.
- **Products | Ordered**: See a list of ordered products and the quantity sold for the selected period of time.
- **Products | Downloads**: See the statistics related to downloadable products, including purchases and downloads.

Summary

In this chapter, we reviewed the existing reports in Magento 2, and we reviewed how to refresh the statistics to get up-to-date information from each one of them. In the next chapter, you will learn about managing Magento themes, inline translations, the Magento Marketplace, and more, to be able to customize your Magento store.

20
Customizing Your Magento Store

In this chapter, we will cover the following topics:

- How to manage Magento themes
- How Inline Translation works
- Magento marketplace

How to manage Magento themes

A theme in Magento defines the look and feel of the Storefront for your customers. By default, Magento includes the following themes:

- Magento Blank
- Magento Luma

You can review a list of the available themes in your Magento store in the **CONTENT** | **Design** | **Configuration** admin panel section:

By convention, the files for themes are located in the `app/design/frontend/<vendor>/` folder. The default themes that are included in Magento are located in the `vendor/magento/theme-frontend-<theme-code>` folder, as you can see in the following screenshot:

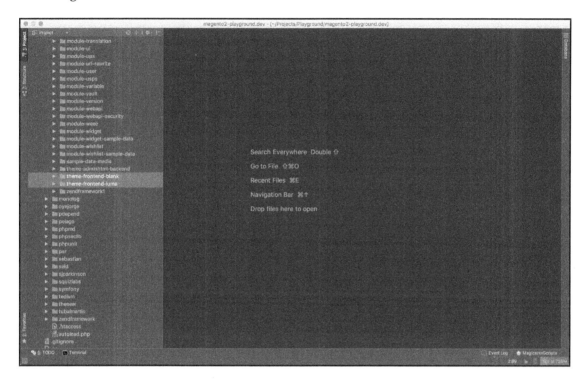

If you click on a theme in the grid on the **CONTENT** | **Design** | **Themes** page, you will see the information for that theme and a preview image:

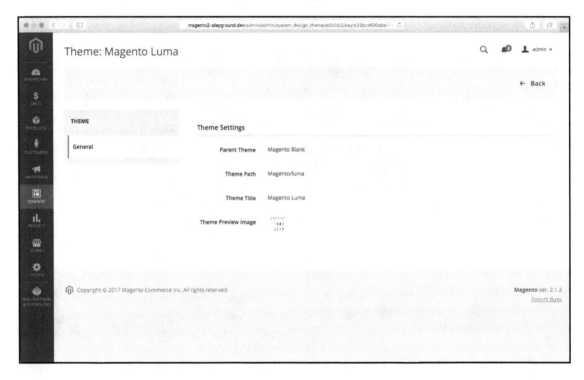

You can see and change the theme that is assigned to each website, store, and store view from the **CONTENT** | **Design** | **Configuration** admin panel page:

If you click on the **Edit** link in the last column, you will be redirected to the following form:

From there, you can change the theme using the **Applied Theme** dropdown, set user agent rules, and configure the following settings:

- **HTML Head**:
    - **Favicon icon**: Change the favicon icon. The following formats are supported:
        - ICO
        - PNG
        - GIF
        - JPG
        - JPEG
        - APNG
        - SVG
    - **Default title**: Set the default title for the pages.
    - **Title prefix**: Add a string before the default title.
    - **Title suffix**: Add a string after the default title.

- **Default description**: Set the default description metatag.
- **Default keywords**: Set the default keywords metatag.
- **Scripts and stylesheets**: Include a custom script and stylesheets in the HTML head tag.
- **Display demo store notice**: If the website is currently under development or testing, you can display a demo store notice on top of all the pages on the Storefront:

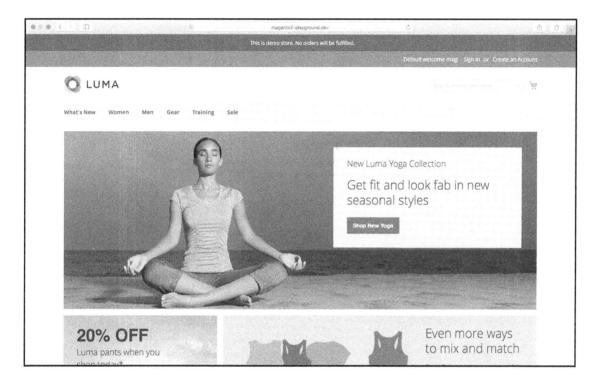

The demo notice will be displayed in the admin panel as well:

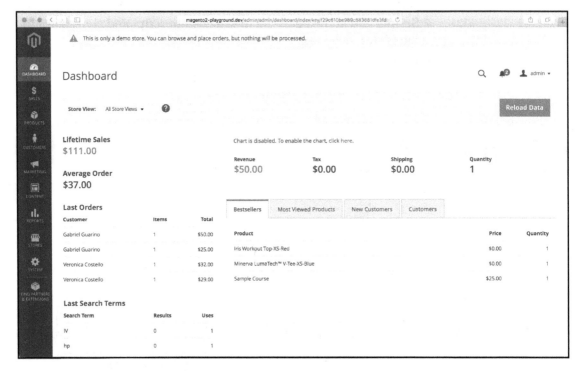

- Header:
    - **Logo image**: Set the logo image for the header. The allowed file types are:
        - PNG
        - GIF
        - JPG
        - JPEG
        - SVG
    - **Logo image width**: Set the logo image width in pixels.
    - **Logo image height**: Set the logo image height in pixels.
    - **Welcome text**: Set text to be displayed in the header. The actual look and feel and location for the welcome text depends on the theme. Here is how the welcome text looks in the Luma theme (**This is the welcome text message!** next to **Sign In** at the top of the page):

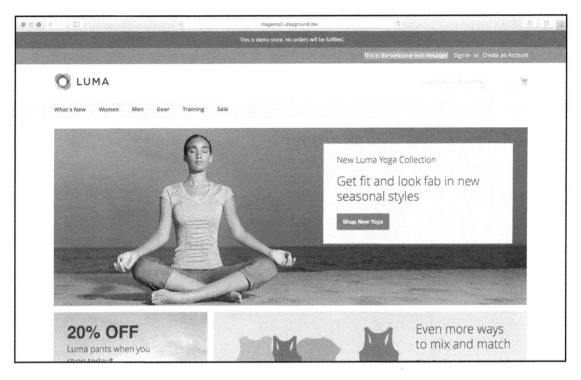

- **Logo image alt**: Text to be used as an alt tag in the logo image.
- Footer:
    - **Miscellaneous HTML**: The HTML that you add on this checkbox will be displayed before the closing body tag in all the pages
    - **Copyright**: Copyright text to display in the footer

- Pagination:
  - **Pagination frame**: The number of links to be displayed in the pagination control on the storefront. In the following example, the pagination frame has been set to 4:

- **Pagination Frame Skip**: Set the number of links that are skipped before showing the next set of pagination links. In the following example, the pagination frame skip has been set to 2:

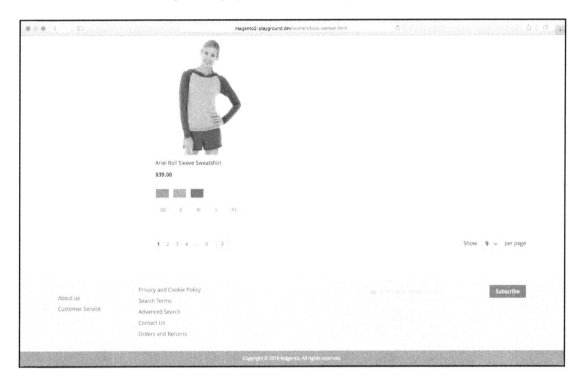

- **Anchor text for previous/anchor text for next**: If you set an anchor text for the next and previous links, the arrow image is replaced with the anchor text that you set. In the following example, the anchor text for previous has been set to **Previous** and the anchor text for next has been set to **Next**:

- **Product image watermarks**: In this section, you can upload the watermark image for the base, small, thumbnail, and swatch images, and you can set properties, such as the image opacity, size, and position.

- **Transactional Emails**:
    - **Logo image**: Upload the image to be used as the logo in transactional e-mails. The allowed file types are:
        - JPG
        - JPEG
        - GIF
        - PNG
    - **Logo image alt**: Alt text to be used for the logo image.
    - **Logo width**: Set the width for the logo image. The number in pixels should be entered without appending px at the end.
    - **Logo height**: Set the height for the logo image. The number in pixels should be entered without appending px in the end.
    - **Header template/footer template**: Select the template to be used as header and footer in the transactional e-mail.

How inline translation works

The right way of translating the Storefront in Magento is by using the translation dictionaries (.csv files) and language packages in the Magento codebase.

That being said, Magento also offers a quick way for store administrators to update and translate text on the Storefront: inline translation.

Inline translations are stored in the database and are theme-specific, which means that they don't apply if another theme is selected for the Magento store after the inline translation is done. As a result, the inline translation should be done again by the store administrator if the theme is changed.

In order to enable the inline translation tool, you should go to the **Stores** | **Configuration** page in the admin panel.

Once you are there, you should go to the **Advanced | Developer** section, and you will see the drop-down menus to enable inline translation on the storefront and the admin panel:

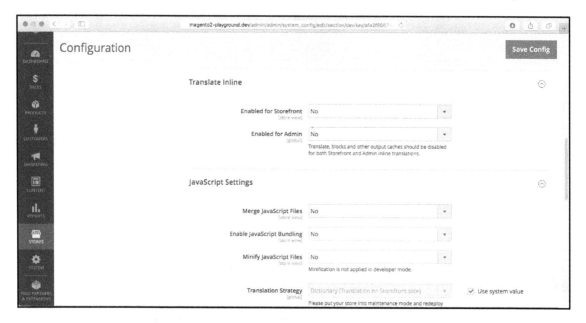

If you set the **Enable for Storefront** to **Yes**, and you save the new settings, then the inline translation tool will be enabled on the Storefront. If you have cache enabled, then you should clear the cache before reviewing the storefront.

As you can see in the following screen, the inline translation tool is now enabled and each string that can be translated is marked with a red box:

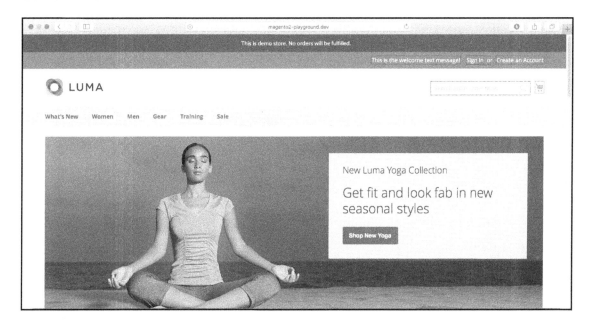

If you hover over the red box, you will see the *book icon* that is also visible in the preceding screenshot. If you click on the icon, the following window will be displayed:

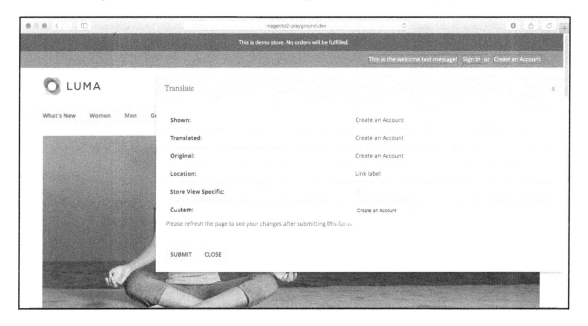

From there, you can specify whether the translation will be specific to the current store view, and then you can set the custom text. In the example below, we replaced `Create an Account` with **Register**:

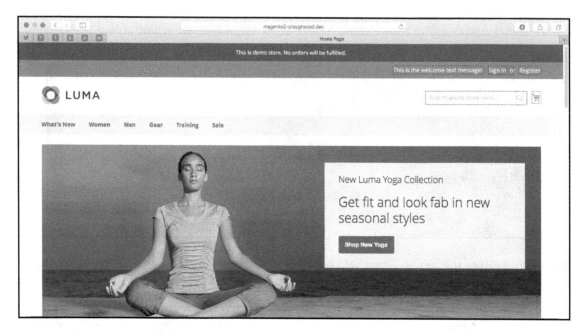

Now, consider that the inline translation tool has been enabled without restrictions. This means that anybody who has access to the website can see the tool, and they can change the text in your Magento store. This is dangerous and should be avoided.

In order to prevent that, Magento allows you to restrict the inline translation tool just for your computer. You can do this by specifying your IP address in the **ADVANCED | Developer | Allowed IPs (comma-separated)** section of the store's **Configuration** page (**Stores | Configuration**):

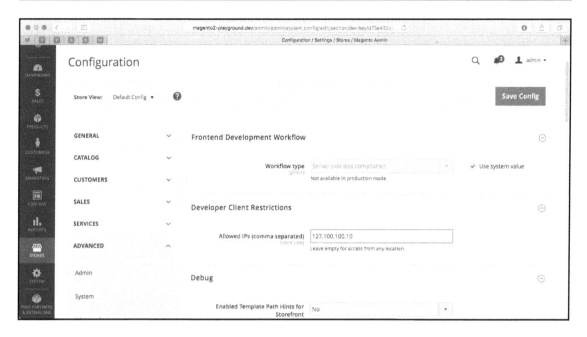

You can add more than one IP to a list of allowed IPs, and just those IPs will have access to the **ADVANCED** | **Developer** tools.

Magento Marketplace

One of the advantages of choosing Magento as a platform is the number of extensions that are available in the marketplace to add new features to your Magento store.

You can see a list of available extensions in the Magento Marketplace at `https://marketpl ace.magento.com`:

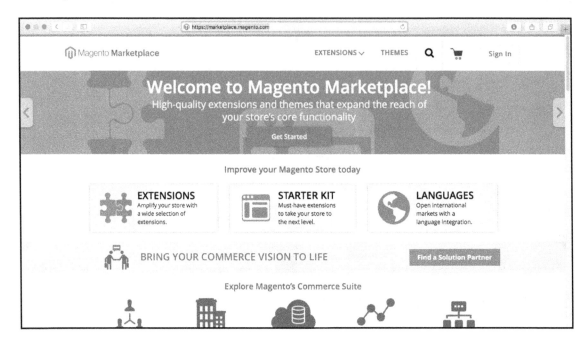

When you select an extension, you will see all the information that you need from the extension listing page, including:

- Available editions for the extension
- Available support by the vendor
- Installation service
- Pricing
- Description
- Current version
- Updated date
- Category

- Compatible Magento 2 versions
- Reviews
- Release notes
- Support

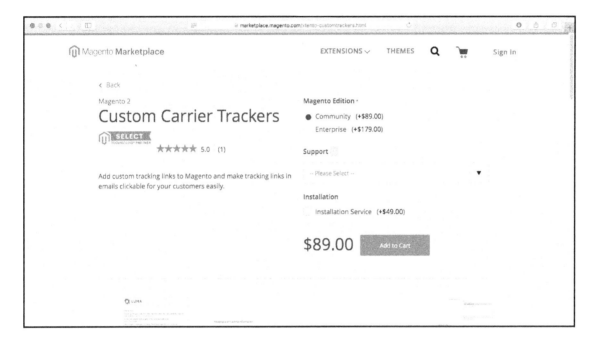

I recommend you to think of Magento Marketplace as a place where you can find three different types of customization for your store:

- **Extensions**: `https://marketplace.magento.com/extensions`
- **Themes**: `https://marketplace.magento.com/themes.html`
- **Language Packs**: `https://marketplace.magento.com/extensions/content-customizations/translations-localization.html`

Besides these, the Marketplace is really intuitive and provides a really easy way to find the extensions that you need and review all the information for those extensions, including information about the vendor.

These extensions can be installed by a vendor, or by an experienced Magento developer who will review its code to integrate the extension in your Magento store.

Summary

In this chapter, we reviewed the process of managing Magento themes, translating strings using the inline translation tool, and the Magento Marketplace to download themes, extensions, and language packs.

In the next chapter, we will review how to back up, restore, and manage your Magento database, improve the performance of your Magento instance, optimize the SEO for your website, manage the cache and indexes, and upgrade Magento to the latest version.

21
Store Maintenance

In this chapter, we will cover the following topics:

- Backup, restore, and database management
- Performance tuning
- Search engine optimization
- Cache and index management
- Upgrading Magento to a new version

Backup, restore, and database management

Creating a backup is essential to ensure we have a way to restore our Magento store in case something unexpected happens. Magento allows us to create a code base and database backup through the admin panel and the Magento 2 command-line tool.

In order to create a backup from the admin panel, you should go to the following section: **SYSTEM** | **Tools** | **Backups**

In that section, you will see a list of all the backups that you have created. In addition to that, you will be able to create three types of backup:

- **System Backup**: Creates a code base and database backup with the ability to include or exclude the media folder
- **Database and Media Backup**: Creates a database and media folder backup
- **Database Backup**: Creates a database backup

For all these backup types, you have the ability to put the Magento store in maintenance mode, since the process takes a lot of server resources.

If you click on **System Backup**, the following window will be displayed:

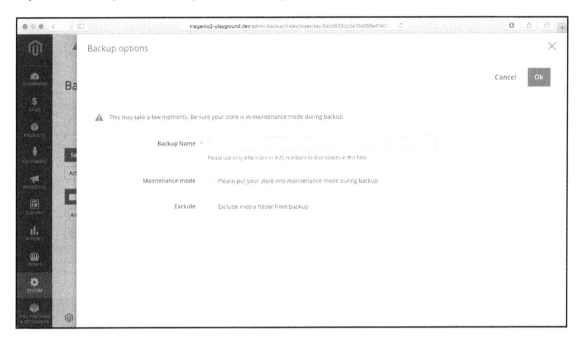

When you proceed with the backup, a spin loader image is displayed and the backup will be created by the system. Since this backup includes the code base and database, the process takes time to get completed.

Once the backup is created, you will see a confirmation message on the screen and the backup will be listed on the grid:

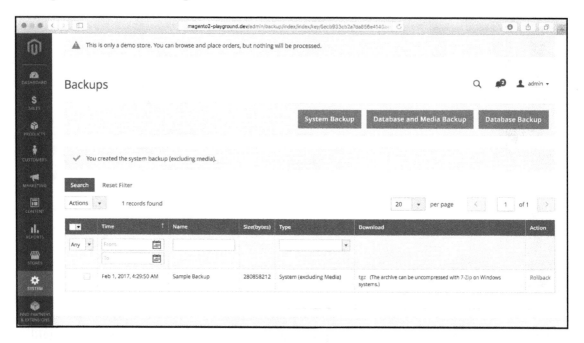

In addition to that, the backup file will be located in the `var/backups` folder in the code base.

As you can see in the grid, you have the ability to download the backup in the `.tgz` format or restore it using the **Rollback** action in the last column.

The process is the same for the **Database and Media Backup** and **Database Backup**. Now, we should really consider automating this process so that we always have a backup for our Magento store.

Magento allows you to schedule the backup to be automatically created on a regular basis by the system. In order to do so, you should go to the store configuration page (**STORES** | **Configuration**), and click on **ADVANCED** | **System**.

On this page, you will see the **Scheduled Backup Settings** section:

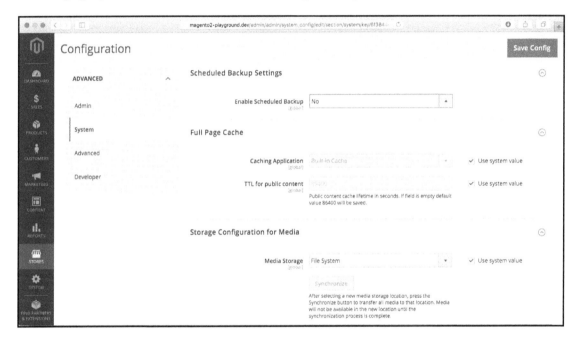

If you select**Yes** in the **Enable Scheduled Backup** field, the following form will be displayed:

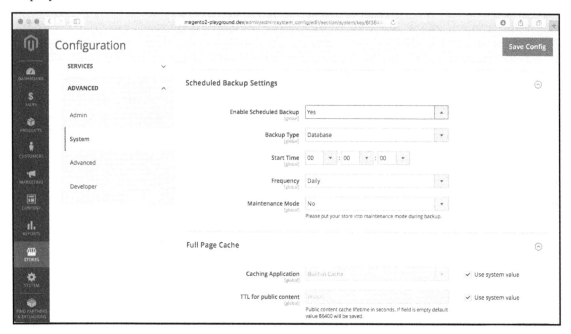

From there, you can choose the backup type for the scheduled backup, the start time, and the frequency and also define whether the website should be put into maintenance mode during backup. It's recommended to schedule the backup to be done on a daily basis at night when the store has less traffic, for example, every day at 2 AM.

In addition to the admin panel backup, you can create a backup using the Magento 2 command-line tool.

In order to do that, you should go to the Terminal and change the current directory to the document root for your Magento 2 instance.

If you run php `bin/magento`, you will see the `setup:backup` command to create the backup, which backs up the Magento application code base, media, and database.

In addition to that, the `setup:rollback` command is available to restore a backup, which rolls back Magento Application code base, media, and database.

In order to create the backup, you should pass the type of backup to be created as a parameter. The available arguments are:

- `--code`
- `--media`
- `--db`

As you can tell by the name of each parameter, you will be able to specify whether the code base, media, and database should be included in the backup.

For example, to create a code base and database backup, you should run the following command:

```
php bin/magento setup:backup --code --db
```

As you can see in the following screenshot, you can keep track of the progress from the command-line output:

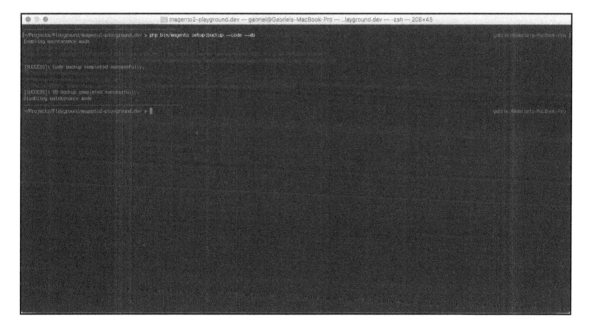

You can see a list of available backups by running the `magento info:backups:list` command:

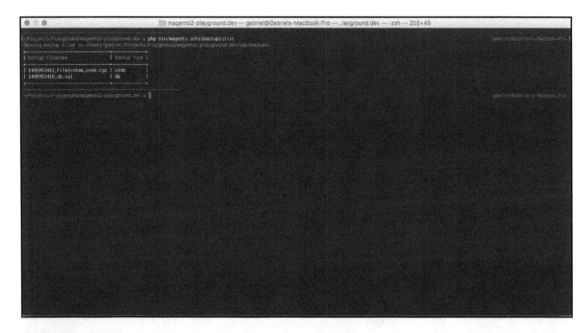

This is essential to know since the `setup:rollback` command requires you to specify the name of the file to restore each of the parameters:

```
magento setup:rollback [-c|--code-file="<name>"] [-m|--media-file="<name>"]
[-d|--db-file="<name>"]
```

Performance tuning

When it comes to the conversion of your Magento store, performance is the key to have a high conversion rate. Nobody likes waiting for the pages to be loaded, and you want your customers to place their order as soon as possible when they decide what products they want to buy.

In this section, we will review how to optimize Magento to have the fastest performance possible, including Magento configuration, server optimizations, and more.

To compare the performance between the previous version and the new version of the platform, we will include in the book the performance statistics shared by Magento. Take into account that these statistics have been created using Magento Enterprise Edition 2.0, but they are a good reference to review:

- **Orders per Hour**: Magento Enterprise Edition 2.0 can process 597 orders per hour, which is an additional 130 orders per hour in comparison with Magento Enterprise Edition 1.14.2:

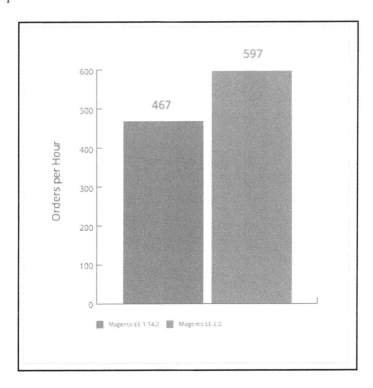

- **Catalog Browsing**: The response time for catalog browsing is almost immediate in Magento Enterprise Edition 2.0 with Varnish:

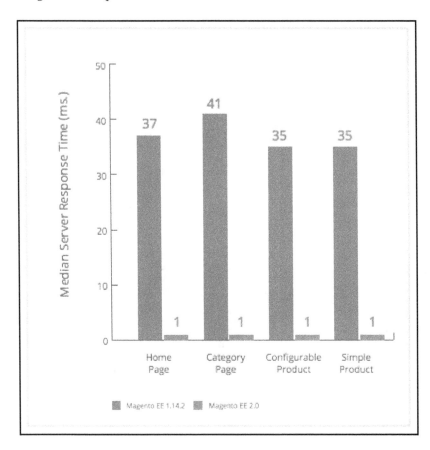

- **Add to Cart**: The Add to Cart action is 66% faster in Magento Enterprise Edition 2 in comparison with Magento Enterprise Edition 1.14.2:

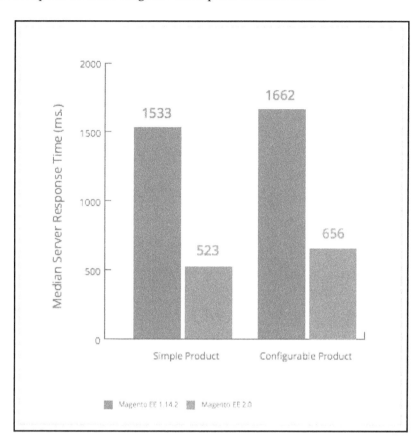

- **Checkout Process**: The checkout process (all the steps combined) is 48% faster for guest checkout and 36% faster for customer checkout in Magento Enterprise Edition 2 as compared with Magento Enterprise Edition 1.14.2:

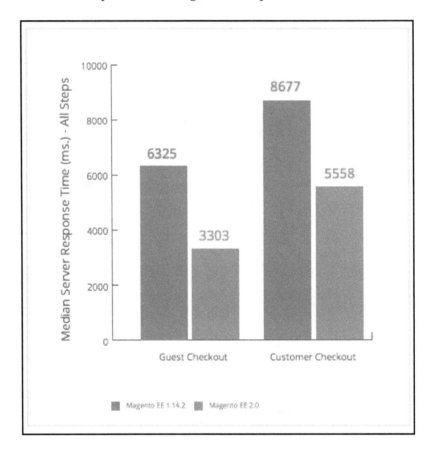

Now let's see how we can increase the performance of the Magento store:

- **Server Configuration**: Even though Magento 2 is compatible with PHP 5.6, it's recommended to use PHP 7 with Varnish to achieve the best performance results.

- **Magento Configuration - Varnish**: We have mentioned Varnish previously; in order to enable it, you should deploy and configure Varnish first. After that, you will be able to enable it from the Stores Configuration page (**STORES | Configuration**) in the admin panel and open the **ADVANCED | System** page. From there, you will be able to select Varnish as a caching application and set the configuration:

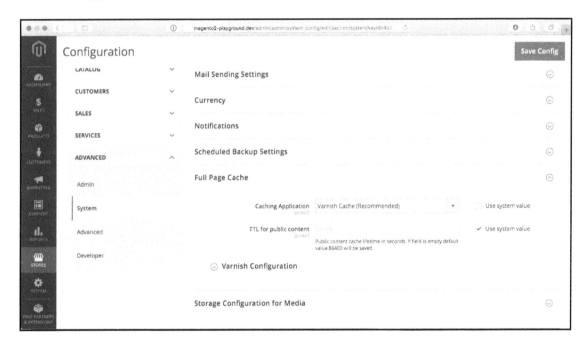

- **Magento Configuration - Redis**: Redis can be used instead of `Zend_Cache_Backend_File` for backend caches, and it's also used for PHP session storage.

- **Magento Configuration - Developer Settings**: The following developer settings are recommended to increase the performance of your Magento store; you can set these configurations from **STORES** | **Configuration** | **ADVANCED** | **Developer**. You will see the following sections in that page:

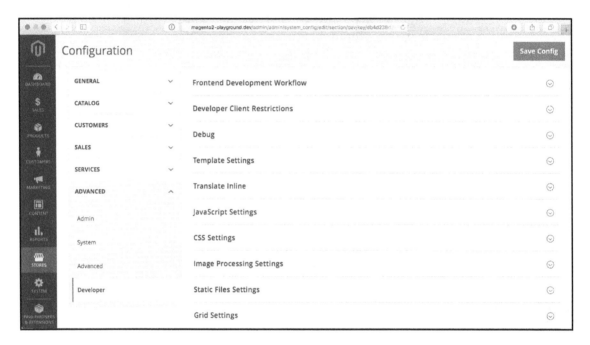

Set the following configurations:

- **Grid Settings** | **Asynchronous indexing**: Enable
- **CSS Settings** | **Minify CSS Files**: Yes
- **JavaScript Settings** | **Minify JS Files**: Yes
- **JavaScript Settings** | **Merge JavaScript Files**: No
- **Template Settings** | **Minify HTML**: Yes
- **JavaScript Settings** | **Enable JavaScript Bundling**: Yes

- **Magento Configuration - Content Delivery Network (CDN)**: CDN is a system of distributed servers that allows you to serve content based on the geographical location of the user, the origin of the website, and the CDN server. You can set the URL for static view and media files for CDN from the **General** | **Web** | **Base URLs (Secure)** store configuration section:

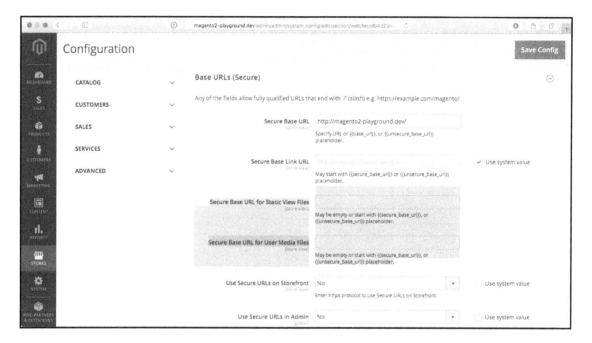

- **Magento Configuration**: **Email**: You can set the e-mails to be generated asynchronously from the **STORES** | **Configuration** | **Sales** | **Sales Emails** section. As you can see in the following screenshot, you can mark **Asynchronous** sending as enabled:

- **Magento Configuration - Flat Catalog**: We described the Flat Catalog feature for categories and products in `Chapter 10`, *System Configuration*. As we mentioned in that chapter, this setting improves the performance of the store by combining all the category and product information in a flat table to fetch data in a single query. You can enable the Flat Catalog from the **CATALOG | Catalog** store configuration page; these settings are under Storefront as **Use Flat Catalog Category** and **Use Flat Catalog Product**, as you can see in the following screenshot:

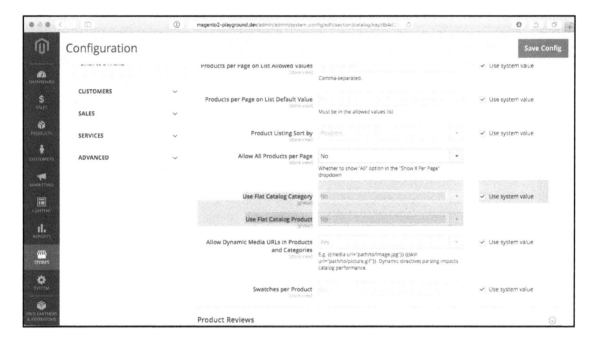

- **Magento Configuration - Index**: Instead of the indexes being updated at the moment when you make a change in the catalog through the admin panel, you can set the reindex process to be done by schedule according to the cron job configuration. You can make that change in the **SYSTEM | Index Management** admin panel page. From there, you will see that you can set the indexes to be updated by schedule using the mass action:

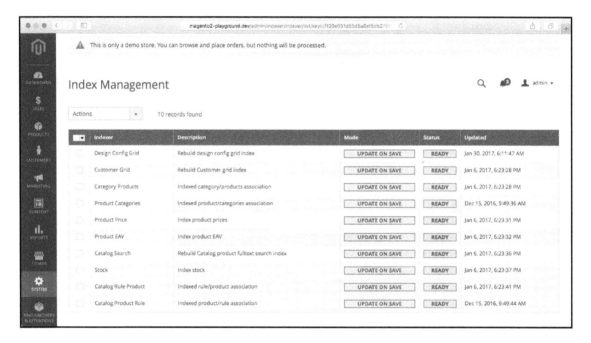

- **Magento Configuration - Production Mode**: When the server and Magento have been configured, you should set Magento to run in **Production Mode**. In the production mode, static view files are served from the cache instead of going through the fallback mechanism from Magento. In addition to that, errors are logged by Magento in the `var` folder and they are not displayed to the user on the storefront. You can enable the production mode by running the following command in the Magento 2 command-line tool:

```
php bin/magento deploy:mode:set production
```

You will see output similar to the following screenshot:

Search engine optimization

In addition to off-site SEO factors, such as backlinks, onsite SEO factors are under your control, and you can optimize the SEO of your Magento store from the Magento admin panel. In this section, we will cover all the Magento 2 settings that are available out-of-the-box for SEO.

One feature from Magento 2 that is really convenient is metatag autogeneration for products. You can set up the feature from the following admin panel section (**STORES** | **Configuration** | **CATALOG** | **Catalog** | **Product Fields Auto-Generation**):

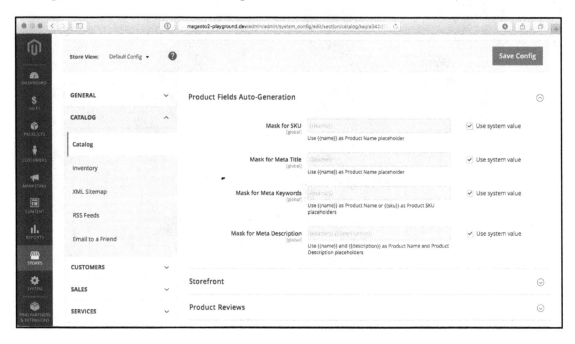

From there, you can use placeholders and custom text to autogenerate the metatags for SEO for all the products in your catalog.

It's important to clarify that you can't set up this feature for each store view since these fields are global for your Magento instance, and new changes for the autogeneration configuration won't be applied to existing products.

In addition to that, you can override the autogenerated value from Search engine optimization in the product settings at any given time.

In the following screenshot, you can also see that you can specify an SEO-friendly **URL key** for the product as well. You can configure the **ALT Text** for all the product images from the same page by updating **ALT Text** from the **Image Detail** window in the **Images and Videos** section:

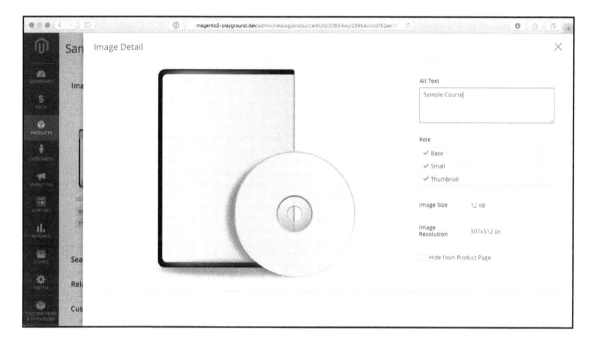

If you go to **PRODUCTS** | **Categories**, you will be able set the **URL key**, **Meta Title**, **Meta Keywords**, and **Meta Description** for each of the categories as well:

Finally, two very important aspects of SEO are the XML sitemap and the `Robots.xml` files for your website. You can set up the XML sitemap for your store from the **STORES** | **Configuration** | **Catalog** | **XML Sitemap** section:

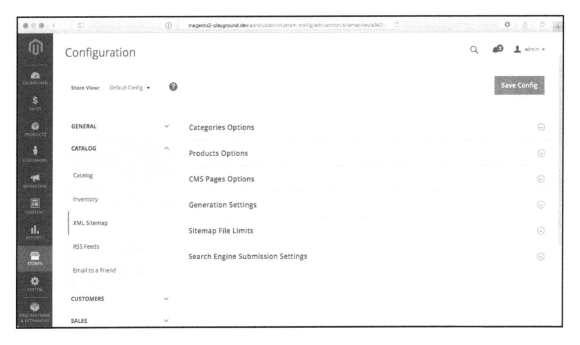

From this page, you can set the following settings:

- **Categories / Products / CMS Pages Options**: Set the frequency and priority for the sitemap. In the case of products, you can add images to the sitemap as well.
- **Generation Settings:** Enable sitemap generation and set the frequency, error e-mail recipient, error e-mail sender, and error e-mail template.
- **Sitemap File Limits**: Set the maximum size and number of URLs per file.
- **Search Engine Submission Settings**: You can add the XML sitemap to the Robots.txt file directly without having to manually modify the file.

The `Robots.txt` settings can be found in the **STORES** | **Configuration** | **General** | **Design** | **Search Engine Robots** section:

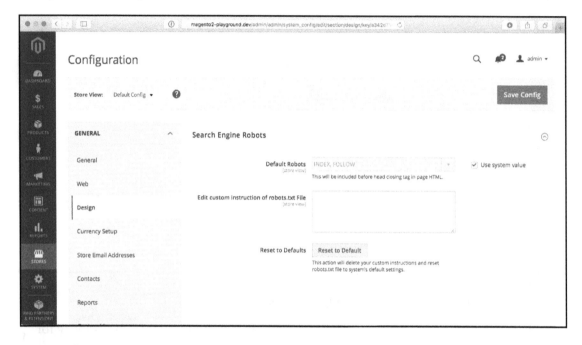

In this page, you can set:

- **Default robots**: Choose the default robots rules:
  - **INDEX, FOLLOW**
  - **NOINDEX, FOLLOW**
  - **INDEX, NOFOLLOW**
  - **NOINDEX, NOFOLLOW**
- **Edit the custom instruction of robots.txt file**: Enter the custom instructions for the `Robots.txt` file if required
- **Reset to Defaults**: Delete custom instructions and reset the Robots.txt configuration to default

Cache and Index Management

Two aspects to consider when managing a Magento store are cache and index.

Every time you make a change to the storefront, such as adding a new banner or changing a title, if the cache is enabled, you have to clear it to allow your customers to see updates on the storefront.

Similarly, every time you make a change to the catalog, you have to reindex it to display the updated information for your customers.

If you open the **SYSTEM** tab in the Magento admin panel, you will see that both sections are available under the **Tools** sub-menu:

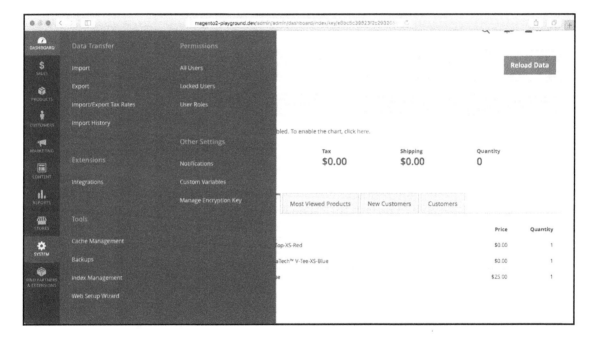

That said, let's open the **Cache Management** page. When the page is loaded, you will see the following grid on the screen:

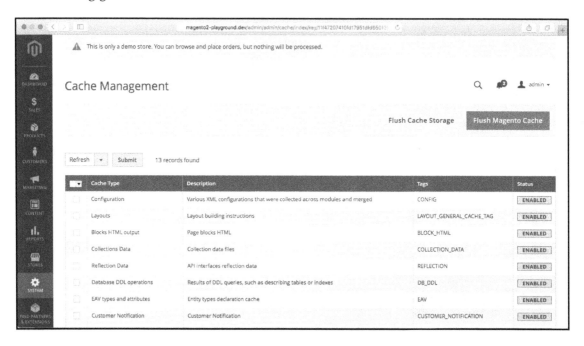

From this grid, you can enable, disable, and refresh each cache type. It's recommended to turn on all cache types in production to improve the performance of your Magento store. From here, you will be able to refresh the cache types if necessary. If a change is made from the admin panel and refreshing the cache is required, then a notification in the admin panel will be displayed, as we saw before. If you modify a frontend file in the code base, then you should manually refresh the cache types through this page.

Now, if you go to **SYSTEM** | **Tools** | **Index Management**, you will see the following grid on the screen:

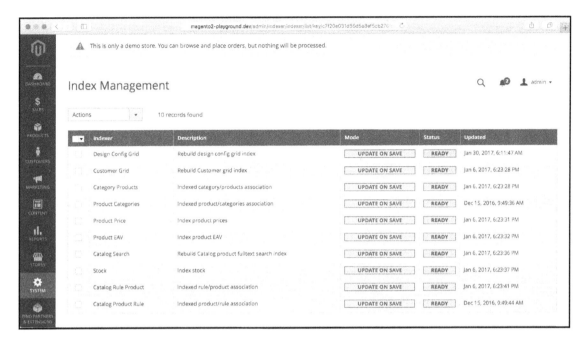

There are two modes for indexers:

- **Update on Save**: The indexed data is updated when a change is made to the catalog through the admin panel
- **Update on Schedule**: The reindex process is made by the cron job, based on its configuration

Upgrading Magento to a new version

In this section, we will review how to upgrade Magento 2 to the latest version. As an example, we will upgrade the website that we have been reviewing in the book from Magento 2.1.3 to 2.1.4.

Before proceeding with the upgrade, you can see in the footer that the Magento version we are using is the one that we have previously mentioned:

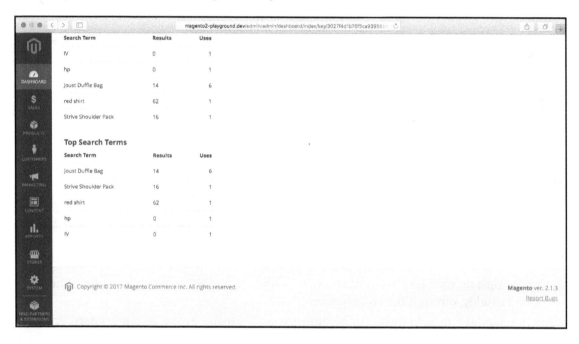

To run a system upgrade, you should go to the following section in the admin panel:

SYSTEM | Tools | Web Setup Wizard

The following page will be displayed on screen:

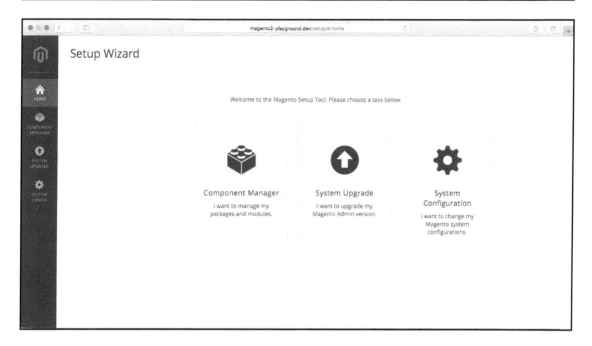

Click on the **System Upgrade** button on that page. Your Magento access keys will be required in the next page:

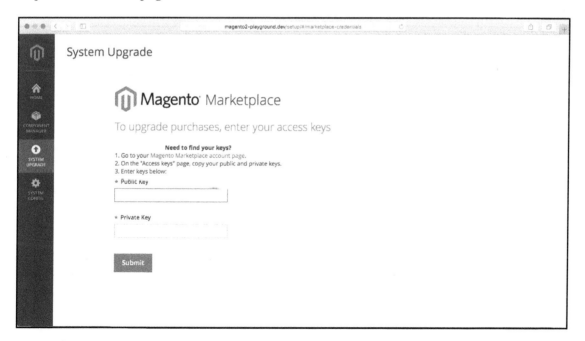

Use the access key that we generated for your Magento store in `Chapter 3`, *Migration*, and click on **Submit**.

After this, Magento will check whether a new version is available:

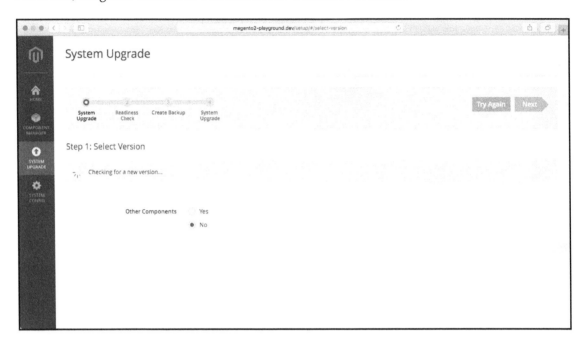

If there are new versions of Magento available for your store, then you will see them listed in the dropdown, as follows:

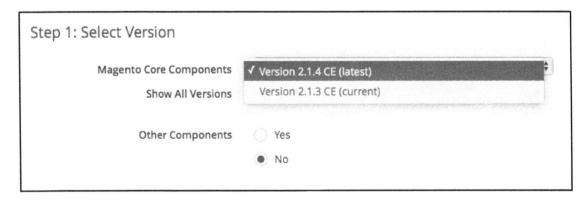

After selecting the Magento version for the upgrade, you can click on **Next** to go to the next step, **Readiness Check**:

Similar to the first step in the Magento installation, which we reviewed in `Chapter 2`, *Installation*, the system will check whether your Magento instance is ready to proceed with the wizard.

The difference between the**Readiness Check** in the installation and the one in the upgrade is that the cron jobs should be configured for the upgrade.

If there are errors with the cron job, PHP version, settings, or extensions, then you should consider reviewing the status and the configuration of your cron.

If the **Readiness Check** is successful, you should see all the items marked with a checkmark:

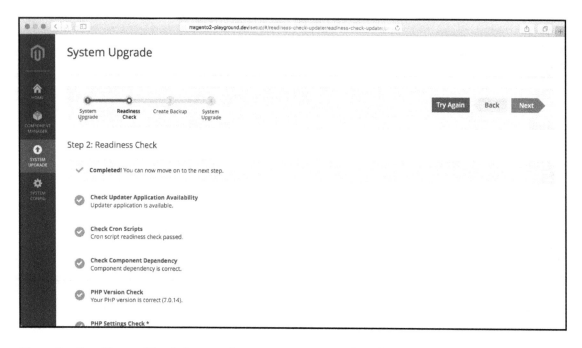

Once the **Readiness Check** is complete, you can proceed to the next step, which allows you to create a code base, media, and database backup:

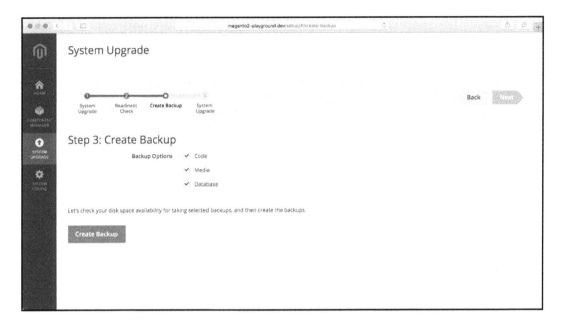

When the backup is complete, you will see the following message on the screen:

The last step notifies you that the website will be temporarily offline and that maintenance mode in your store will be enabled:

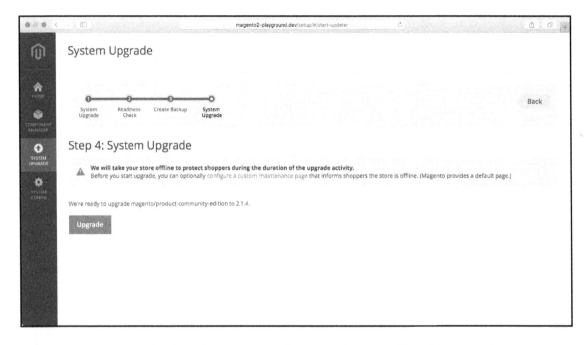

If you click on **Upgrade**, then the process will start and you will be able to track its progress from the browser:

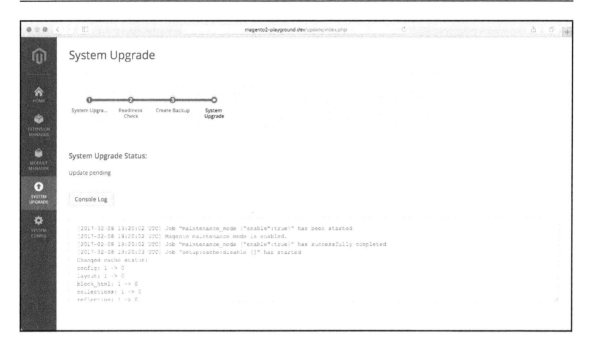

Once the upgrade is complete, you will see the following page on the screen:

The maintenance mode will be disabled and your Magento store will be running the selected Magento version, as you will see in the Magento admin panel footer:

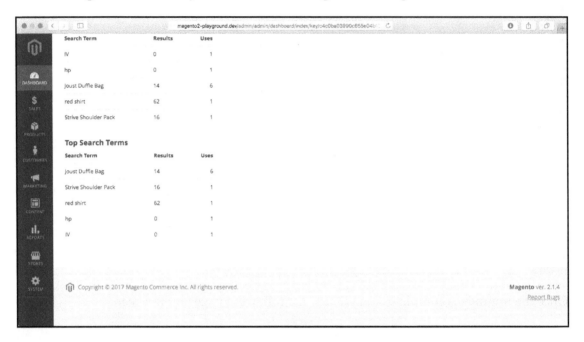

Summary

In this chapter, you learned how to back up and restore your Magento store, how to improve its performance, how to update your store configuration for SEO, how to manage the Magento cache and indexes, and how to upgrade your website to the latest version.

This is the end of the book, but the beginning of your journey managing your Magento store. We were able to cover all the activities of a Magento store owner and administrator, and you are ready to succeed using the knowledge that you have now. Keep the book really close, as it can be useful for you to quickly take a look at the pages when you are working with the Magento platform. Good luck!

Index

A

admin users
  managing 249, 250, 252
Amazon AWS
  URL 36
Amazon EC2
  Amazon AWS account, setting up 35
  instance, creating 38, 40, 41, 42, 44
  instance, preparing for Magento 2 44, 45, 47, 48
  Magento, installing 35
  URL 35, 38
attribute 99
attribute sets
  about 110
  associating, with product 116, 117, 118, 119, 120, 122, 123
  creating 111, 112, 113, 114, 115

B

backup
  creating 387, 388, 389, 390, 391, 392, 393, 394
BigCommerce
  about 11
  pros and cons 11
Bundle Product
  about 149
  creating 150, 152, 153, 154, 155, 157

C

cache
  managing 411, 412, 413
catalog price rules
  setting up 269, 270, 271, 272, 273, 274, 276
CATALOG, system configuration
  Catalog 224, 225, 226

Email to a Friend 227
  Inventory 226
categories
  about 169
  enabling, in top navigation 185, 186, 187
  hierarchy, setting 181, 182, 183, 184
  managing 170, 172, 174, 176
CMS Pages
  managing 189, 190, 191, 192, 193, 194, 195
code audit, Magento 1.x store
  about 52
  business logic, in templates 52
  custom extensions, implementing 53
  custom JavaScript 54
  migration requirements, reviewing 54
  modified Magento core 52
  third-party extensions, reviewing 53
  unused extensions, reviewing 54
command-line installation
  of Magento 30, 32, 33
Composer
  URL 30
configurable products
  about 130
  creating 131, 133, 134, 135, 136, 137, 138, 139
credit memos
  generating 337, 338, 339, 340, 341, 343
CUSTOMERS, system configuration
  about 227
  Customer Configuration 228
  Persistent Shopping Cart 229
customers
  accounts, managing 239, 240, 241, 242, 243, 244, 245
  adding 246, 247, 248

D

Data Migration Tool
  access code, URL 55
  compatible versions 56
  migration process 56, 57, 58, 59, 60, 61, 63,
    64, 66, 67, 68, 69, 70, 71, 72, 73, 74
  URL 60
  using 55
database management
  handling 387, 388, 389, 390, 391, 392, 393,
    394
default/global scope
  selecting 214, 215
DigitalOcean
  URL 35
Downloadable Product
  about 160
  creating 160, 161, 162, 163, 164

E

e-commerce solutions
  about 8
  hosted e-commerce solution 10
  self-hosted e-commerce solution 8

G

GENERAL, system configuration
  Contact Management 224
  Contacts 224
  Currency Setup 223
  General 220, 221
  Store Email Addresses 224
  Web 222, 223
Grouped Product
  about 142
  creating 143, 144, 145, 146, 147, 148, 149

H

hierarchy
  setting, for categories 181, 182, 183, 184
hosted e-commerce solution
  about 10
  BigCommerce 11
  Shopify 11

hosting provider
  managed servers 34
  selecting 34
  self-managed servers 35

I

images
  assigning 88, 89
  configuration, updating 90
index
  managing 411, 412, 413
inline translation
  enabling 379, 380, 382, 383
invoice
  generating 337, 338, 339, 340, 341, 343

L

Linode
  URL 35

M

MageMojo
  URL 34
Magento 1.x store
  code, auditing 52
  migration plan, preparing 51
  reviewing 51
Magento 2, technologies
  Composer 12
  Elasticsearch 12
  Full Page Caching 12
  jQuery 12
  Knockout.js 12
  LESS 12
  Magento UI Library 12
  RequireJS 12
  Varnish 4 12
Magento 2
  admin panel upgrades 13
  Amazon instance, preparing 44, 45, 47, 48
  features 12
  frontend upgrades 14
  installing 19
  system requisites 17
  tools 13

upgrading, to latest version 414, 415, 417, 418, 420

Magento Enterprise Edition 2.0
  performance statistics 395, 396, 397, 398, 399

Magento Marketplace
  about 383
  Extensions, URL 385
  Language Packs, URL 385
  selecting 384, 385
  Themes, URL 385
  URL 384

Magento Tech Resources
  URL 52

Magento, scopes
  about 207
  default/global scope 214, 215
  multistore configuration, example 208, 209
  store views 210, 211, 212, 213, 214
  stores/store groups 210
  websites 209

Magento
  about 7
  codebase, obtaining 20, 21
  command-line installation 30, 31, 32, 33
  installing, in Amazon EC2 35
  resources 14
  Setup Wizard installation 22, 26, 28, 29
  URL, for downloading 20

Mail Transfer Agent (MTA) 19

managed servers 34

Manufacturer's Suggested Retail Price (MSRP) 93

marketplace extension
  URL 313

Model-View-ViewModel (MVVM) 12

N

newsletter
  handling 354, 358
  subscribers, handling 354, 358
  templates, modifying 351, 352, 353

Nexcess
  URL 34

O

online rates 309

OpenCart
  about 10
  pros and cons 10

orders
  managing 315, 316, 317, 318, 320, 321, 322, 323, 324, 325, 326, 327, 328, 330, 331, 333
  state, viewing 334, 335, 336
  status, managing 334, 335, 336

P

Payment Card Industry Data Security Standard (PCI DSS) 299

payment methods
  default payment methods 287, 288, 289

PayPal
  setting up 289, 290, 291, 292, 293, 294, 295, 296, 297, 298

PCI compliance
  about 298
  direct post 299
  hosted payment form 299
  implementing 298

performance
  tuning 394, 395, 399, 400, 401, 402, 403, 404

PrestaShop
  about 9
  pros and cons 9

pricing
  fields, reviewing 92, 94, 96, 97
  setting 90

product attributes
  about 99
  creating 102, 103, 106, 108, 109, 110
  managing 100, 101

product, types
  about 125, 126, 127
  Bundle Product 149, 150, 152, 153, 154, 155, 157
  configurable products 130, 131, 133, 134, 135, 137, 138, 139
  Downloadable Product 160, 161, 162, 163, 164
  Grouped Product 142, 143, 144, 145, 146, 147,

148, 149
simple products 127, 128, 129, 130
Virtual Product 158, 159, 160
product
  adding 77, 78, 79
  attribute sets, associating with 116, 118, 119,
    120, 122, 123
  creating 85, 86, 87
  information, adding 79, 80, 81, 82, 83, 84

R

Rackspace
  URL 34
reports
  about 359
  customer reports 366
  marketing reports 365
  products report 366
  reviewing 359, 361, 362, 363, 364, 366
  reviews report 366
  sales report 366
restore
  performing 387, 388, 389, 390, 391, 392, 393
roles
  managing 252, 254, 255, 256

S

SALES, system configuration
  about 230
  Checkout 231
  Google API 232
  Multishipping Settings 232
  Payment Methods 232
  Shipping Methods 232
  Shipping Settings 231
  Tax 230
Search Engine Optimization (SEO)
  about 405
  setting up 406, 407, 408, 410
self-hosted e-commerce solution
  about 8
  OpenCart 10
  PrestaShop 9
  WooCommerce 8
self-managed servers 35

Setup Wizard
  for Magento installation 22, 26, 28, 29
shipping extensions
  URL 313
shipping methods
  default shipping methods 301, 302
  Flat Rate 303, 304
  Free Shipping 305, 306
  other carriers 313, 314
  setting up, with United Parcel Service (UPS)
    309, 310
  Table Rates 306, 307, 308
  UPS/USPS/FedEx/DHL 309
shippments
  creating 337, 338, 339, 340, 341, 343
Shopify
  about 11
  pros and cons 11
shopping cart
  price rules, setting up 276, 278, 282, 285
simple products 127, 128, 129, 130
static blocks
  about 196
  accessing 196, 197, 198, 199
store views 210, 211, 212, 213, 214
stores/store groups 210
system configuration
  Advanced 233, 234
  CATALOG 224, 225, 226
  CUSTOMERS 227, 228
  GENERAL 220, 221
  SALES 230
  sections 217, 218, 219

T

tax zones and rates
  about 266
  rules, managing 266
  tax rate, adding 267, 268
tax
  setting up 259
  tax classes, assigning 260
  tax rules, reviewing 260, 261, 262, 263, 264,
    265
themes

managing 367, 368, 369, 370, 371, 372
modifying 372, 374, 376, 377, 378, 379
tools, Magento 2
  Code Migration Toolkit 13
  Data Migration Tool 13
  Magento 2 Command Line Tool 13
  Magento 2 Developer Documentation 13
  Magento Performance Toolkit 13
top navigation
  categories, enabling 185, 186, 187
transactional e-mail templates
  modifying 345, 347, 348, 349, 350, 351
Transport Layer Security (TLS) 19

U

United Parcel Service (UPS)

about 309
shipping methods, setting up 309, 310

V

Virtual Product
  about 158
  creating 158, 159

W

websites 209
widgets
  about 199
  managing 200, 201, 203, 204, 205
WooCommerce
  about 8
  pros and cons 9